The Fastnet Disaster
AND AFTER

By the same author

CATAMARAN RACING (Cassells) with Reg White
THE LONGEST RACE (Stamford Maritime) with Peter Cook
CREWING IN RACING DINGHIES AND KEELBOATS
(Stamford Maritime)
SMALL BOAT RACING WITH THE CHAMPIONS (Barrie & Jenkins)
BETTER SAILING (Octopus Books)

The Fastnet Disaster
AND AFTER

BOB FISHER

PELHAM BOOKS
London

First published in Great Britain by
PELHAM BOOKS LTD
44 Bedford Square
London
WC1B 3DU
1980

ISBN 0 7207 1253 X

Set in Great Britain by
Cambrian Typesetters, Farnborough, Hants
Printed and bound by
Billing and Sons Ltd, Guildford

Line Drawings
Figures 1 and 2 are based on
Crown Copyright Admiralty Charts
Figures 3, 4, 5, 6 and 7 are reproduced
by courtesy of *Yachting World*, copyright
Alan Watts.

To ocean racing sailors . . .
that they may continue

CONTENTS

PREFACE

There are more than two and a half thousand stories of the 1979 Fastnet Race; those of each of the competitors and the rescue services. I began by writing the day-to-day story of the race and was forced to change when the storm turned the race into a disaster that the world wanted to read about. Since those days in Plymouth I have learned much about the happenings on board many of the boats in the race and of the actions of the rescuers who went out to those in distress. I have overcome, quite easily, the temptation to write a condemnation of those who raced and those who organised the race for they have no blame to answer. Ocean racing is understood by those involved in it as being a sport where danger is an acceptable factor but one which they take all reasonable precautions to avoid. I have been unable to include everyone's story in this book but I have chosen those which I consider to be significant and those which destroy many of the lies that were prevalent at the time of the race. I have also tried to include those facts which, when aired, may help to make ocean racing safer for more of the people who wish to take part; for it is a sport which I enjoy.

Bob Fisher
London
March 1980

ACKNOWLEDGEMENTS

In the preparation of this book I have found enormous co-operation from officials and competitors alike. All seem concerned that the facts which they supplied should be totally accurate; for that particularly I am indebted to them all.

My thanks are due to my research assistant Jeanne Frazer, whose diligence has unearthed leads to some of the finer points which would otherwise have been missed. Jeanne was assistant to the Champagne Mumm Press Officer, Roger Ware, during the Fastnet Race and knew much of what lay ahead before she agreed to tackle the job. Even then she agreed to do it and her special relationship with the armed forces opened otherwise closed doors.

The rescue operation material was provided by Second Officer Judy Sherwood WRNS; Surgeon Commander Clive Millar RN; the Operations Section and the Coastguard Liaison Officer at RNAS Culdrose; Lieutenant David Roué RN and Squadron Leader J. Winchurch at RAF St Mawgan; Commander Jake Backus RN, Commanding Officer HMS *Scylla*; Captain Tony Norman RN, Commanding Officer HMS *Broadsword;* Lieutenant Commander David Poole RN, Commanding Officer HMS *Anglesey;* Kapitein-Luitenant P. Smit, Commanding Officer HNLMS *Overijssel;* Tim Hunt, the Staff Public Relations Officer, Mount Wise, Devonport; and the Secretary, Department of Defence, Dublin, for the armed services.

The RNLI provided concise details of its efforts and for these I thank Joan Davies, Editor of *The Lifeboat;* Lieutenant Colonel Brian Clark, National Organiser for Ireland; and Ray Kipling, the Public Relations Officer in London. So too did HM Coastguard and my thanks there go

9

particularly to Mr P. Cardale, Regional Controller, Brixham; and Mr S. Roberts, District Controller, Gwennap Head.

For assistance with meteorological detail I owe special thanks to Alan Watts, who also supplied the weather maps, and to Peter Baylis of the Department of Electrical and Electronic Engineering at the University of Dundee for his help with weather satellite details and for providing the satellite pictures. Lawrence Draper of the Institute of Oceanographic Sciences gave me interesting facts about waves.

The Flag Officers and staff of the Royal Ocean Racing Club have been more than helpful to me in my preparation of this book and to them I am particularly grateful for their permission to reproduce parts of the Fastnet Race Inquiry Report. It might be wrong to single out any one of them but mention must be made of the speed at which Janet Grosvenor, the Deputy Secretary, has provided answers to my questions. My own admiration for the work done by Alan Green, the Secretary, at Plymouth where he held the fort for the Club when the storm was at its height and afterwards, remains undiminished. If there were to be a man of the event it would certainly be Alan Green whose patience in dealing with the hostile questioning that he received at press conferences was an object lesson to us all.

Rodney Hill who skippered the junior radio relay escort vessel, *Morningtown,* let me use his log and his radio log which provided a considerable amount of the information about this side of the rescue operation. For that and for the delightful breakfast at which we discussed these matters. I add my thanks to those who used his services during the race.

Photographs were provided by Ambrose Greenway, Jonathan Eastland, Beken of Cowes, RNAS Culdrose and Peter Webster; for delving into their files I thank them very much.

Most of all I thank those competitors who took time to write to me or talk to me, thus providing much of my material. Principally among them were Alan Bartlett, *Trophy;* Peter Bateman, *Morning Cloud;* Peter Blake, *Condor of Bermuda;* Peter Bowker, *Tenacious;* Alain Catherineau, *Lorelei;* Martyn Chase, *Endeavour;* Dr John Coldrey, *Charioteer;* Mike Flowers, *Gunslinger;* Neil Graham, *Griffin;* Jeremy Heal, *Charioteer;* Matthew Hunt, *Ariadne;* John B. Kilroy, *Kialoa;* David Lewis, *Hestrul II;* Bob Lloyd, *Gunslinger;* Jim Mant, *Flashlight;* Larry Marks, *Morning Cloud;* Rod Newbolt-Young, *Charioteer;* Ron Packer, *Police Car;* John Pennington, *Flashlight;* Chris Purchase, *Prairie Oyster;* Nick Ward, *Grimalkin;* Ted Watts, *Quixote* and Gordon Williams, *Assent.* For all the other Fastnet competitors with whom I talked I am grateful of your indulgence and ask your forgiveness for not mentioning you by name.

Perhaps for me one of the most worthwhile experiences resulting from writing this book has been in meeting and gaining experience from Joe Cross and his staff at the Robert Gordon's Institute Offshore Survival Centre, Aberdeen. Their work should be more familiar to yachtsmen.

Without my agent Gill Coleridge this book would never have been. She suggested that I write it and has continued to encourage me and to protect me from the outside influences that no author needs. Without the skill of Lesley Gowers who edited it for Pelham, it would doubtless have lacked polish, and no one worked to tighter deadlines than Lesley.

Finally my personal thanks are due to Stuart and Carrie Westaway who invited me to use their home as a quiet place of refuge in which to write the book once most of the research was done. They read the early chapters and made the right sort of noises of encouragement and criticism which made me want to go on. Bless you both.

ABBREVIATIONS USED IN THE TEXT

IOR	International Offshore Rule
ORC	Offshore Racing Council
RDF	Radio Direction Finder
RORC	Royal Ocean Racing Club
SORC	Southern Ocean Racing Conference

Chapter 1

THE STORM STRIKES

'They that go down to the sea in ships . . . and occupy their business in great waters'

Psalm 107, v. 23

'There will be a press conference in fifteen minutes.' The words were those of Roger Ware, press officer for the Admiral's Cup. 'Alan Green, Secretary of the Royal Ocean Racing Club, and John Clothier, one of the Rear Commodores, will be here and I hope that we will be able to give you an up-to-date state of the play.'

It was mid-morning on Thursday 16th August. The suite at one end of the first floor of the Duke of Cornwall Hotel, Plymouth was noisily crammed with journalists from all over the world. It was just fifty hours since the awful truth had first dawned on those ashore that the Fastnet Race had gone wrong, terribly wrong. What had once been an adequate press office for the Fastnet Race had now become a hopelessly inadequate press centre for a major disaster. Yet somehow Roger Ware was managing to keep it under control.

'The figures are still not yet complete, but we do have track of most of the boats.' Roger again, previewing the press conference. The handful of yachting journalists that had been there from the start were with him all of the way but those that had arrived later, and perhaps didn't understand the nuances of the sport of ocean racing, were some way behind Roger in the detective inquiries that were necessary to put together the tragic story of the 1979 Fastnet Race.

In Plymouth the morning of Tuesday 14th August was a grey one, more reminiscent of autumn than August. I looked out of my bedroom window in the Mayflower Post Hotel at the waters of the Sound. There were a few white caps and I breathed a sigh of relief. I had listened to

13

the 0015 shipping forecast on 1500 metres which had promised gales in the Plymouth area and worse for the sea areas Lundy, Fastnet and Irish Sea. I felt that once again the forecasters had got it wrong.

I dressed quickly, left the hotel and drove to the Race Control centre in Millbay Dock. It was 0645 and I had but half an hour to my first deadline of the day — a report for the London *Evening Standard* on the fortunes of the British Admiral's Cup team in the Fastnet Race. Things had not been going well for them in their defence of the Cup. Ernest Juer's *Blizzard* had gone the wrong way when leading one of the inshore races and Ted Heath's *Morning Cloud* had broken her carbon-fibre rudder in the double-points counting Channel Race and had been forced to retire. *Blizzard* and *Morning Cloud* were lying thirty-second and thirty-seventh after four races and although *Eclipse* was second best individual points scorer at this stage, the British team were only lying seventh going into the Fastnet, 132 points down on the leaders, Ireland. It needed a miracle to retain the Cup, but everybody is aware that in ocean racing there is always an outside chance that the impossible can happen. No one, however, would have hazarded a guess at the unusual turn events would take in this Fastnet Race.

The Race Control duty officers are from the Royal Western Yacht Club, which issues a rota to those of its members who volunteer for the task. They man the office twenty-four hours a day from the Sunday morning after the Fastnet starts at Cowes until all the boats have finished or are accounted for. It is a routine, necessary and generally thankless task which needs a deliberate thoroughness. It is the sort of operation which members of the Royal Western Yacht Club have vast experience of, dealing as they do with not only the biennial Fastnet but also the four-yearly Singlehanded Transatlantic and Two-handed Round-Britain Races.

I walked into the stone building in the corner of the dock, glanced left into the RORC office and turned into the right-hand doorway where the duty officers were changing shifts. 'Nothing of importance for you,' I was told. I tend to take that sort of remark with a pinch of salt and went to look at the Log. It was being used so I sorted through the rough notes that the duty officers make before they enter each piece of information in the Log. There were no position reports from the Admiral's Cup fleet of fifty-seven and that is why, I suppose, I was told there was nothing of importance for me.

That statement couldn't have been further off the mark. One or two items caught my eye and I began to make notes in my book. Then I noticed something which stopped me in my tracks: 'Four men in a life-raft reported by RAF Nimrod – Sea King helicopter called out.'

Alone that would have been enough to begin a news story but there was more among the notes that made me realise that something had gone very wrong and that I had found only the tip of the iceberg. Normally race communications stop overnight and begin again at dawn. On this day there was so much incoming material from the first hour that it was patently obvious that there was much more to come, and there were other pointers to that as well.

The Log was finally freed for a few minutes and I began to feel that I was the only one in that room who realised just what the various single items in it added up to. Individually they didn't have the impact of the 0405Z (0505 BST) report from the RAF Nimrod but collectively they provided me with a pattern on which I could reliably forecast a picture.

There was a weather report from the Scillies where the wind was west-south-west force 10 and the sea state was 'rough'. The St Ives and Sennan Cove lifeboats had been called out but no details of why and when were then available. The Irish Admiral's Cup yacht *Regardless* was being towed into Baltimore, and no reason was given for that. The Dutch team member *Schuttevaer* was reported as rigging a jury rudder. *Accanito*, ninth in the Admiral's Cup listings after four races and the top French yacht, was making for Cork with rudder problems as was *Scaldis*, a Dutch yacht in Class I.

All the boats that had reported that they were in trouble were relatively large ones, from Classes I and II, and if the weather conditions had been sufficiently bad to damage them, I reasoned that the smaller yachts would suffer far greater damage. Since it was not a race requirement for each yacht to carry a radio transmitter, there would have been less likelihood of hearing from the smaller yachts that were in trouble at this stage. Very few would have been carrying single-sideband MF or HF transmitters and would have relied on VHF transmission through a nearby competitor or the yacht *Morningtown* which was following the fleet as an observation boat for the RORC and was there for the purpose of relaying radio messages and positional reports of the Admiral's Cup fleet. There was no report in from *Morningtown* by 0700 that morning.

Gathering my notes, I left the Race Control and made my way out of the dock to the nearby Duke of Cornwall Hotel. Roger Ware was just opening the press office as I got there and I told him the facts and my opinion as to the state of the race and the likelihood of an increase in the population of the office.

I filed my first story for the *Evening Standard*, warning the News Desk that there would be irregular updates but that there would be many of them throughout the day. As a freelance I turned my mind to my other possible employers. The *Guardian* News Desk would not come to life before 11 a.m. but the BBC should be informed and so I rang the 'Today' programme at Broadcasting House in London. The reaction there was that it was worth a report direct so I took myself off to the unmanned studio in Plymouth, first calling back to the Race Control for the latest update. Only a few minor items had been entered in the Log and so my first piece for radio was of a necessarily speculative nature. It was enough, however, for the producer to send a reporter down from London to cover the story.

As more information became available it was obvious that there was a full-scale disaster to report and journalists were augmented by reporters from radio and television together with all the necessary paraphernalia of their trade. The small suite which formed the press office became horribly overcrowded. The four pay-phones were too few, the three incoming lines were overloaded and the telex facility was stretched beyond its limit. The press had outgrown its home because the very nature of the exercise had changed.

On the first day the inquiries were mostly those of the media but towards the end of the day, the press office staff were receiving calls from friends and relatives of crew members of competing boats, anxious for news. There was no way that these could be filtered off. The GPO telephone manager in Plymouth set up a special switchboard at the exchange to deal with as many public inquiries as possible. The press officer's staff were re-rota'ed to cover twenty-four-hour working, whilst Roger Ware went into non-stop operation, liaising with Alan Green and the rescue services. For the next four days there would be no respite.

By early evening of the first day we were aware that there were people dead; just how many was a matter of conjecture. Here the responsibility of some journalists appears to have been sadly lacking. Highly distorted stories began to appear the next day all over the world. Those eager to sell stories found ready outlets and the following day they reaped the harvest of their foolishness. By-lines attached to some of the more bizarre reports were quite fictional, and it was depressing to be part of the reporting staff engaged in the disaster. Most of the highly sensational reports were saved for foreign newspapers, particularly those in the United States, Hong Kong and some in Australia. These brought anguish to relatives and friends of those competing and a fresh wave of overseas journalists to Plymouth. Some foreign newspapers ran obituaries of people who were not dead; one, at least, was for someone who had not even gone on the race.

I listened to one American filing his copy over the telephone and had to ask him afterwards if he and I were reporting the same disaster. His report bore little relation to the facts that I had before me and I couldn't believe that all the extra bleak information he was sending back to the United States was real.

Those of us who were used to reporting ocean racing, those of us who are ocean racing sailors, and those of us who had any feeling for the sport were distressed to find that so much misrepresentation of the facts was indeed taking place. In such time as we had at our disposal we talked together and became more determined than ever to help put things right, not only in our reports but in trying to correct the misapprehensions of others. We counselled those who would be counselled, and they were in the majority, and cold-shouldered those who blatantly refused to be helped. One particular radio reporter, who constantly took a highly aggressive line of questioning, was finally reported to his employers for his attitude.

It is often believed that journalists spend much of their time hiding facts from their fellows in order to pull off a scoop. That is not true, especially on occasions like this one. We had to cooperate, and those who had finished their work for the day pitched in to help the rest, answering inquiries or ferreting out background information. Peter Smith of the *Portsmouth Evening News* filed his late story and set off in his car for Culdrose where survivors of the helicopter rescues were being landed. With no paper until the next day Peter was happy to file his information at Culdrose to the daily paper writers at Plymouth. We all, and our readers, benefited by his action.

By Wednesday evening the density of population of the press office was at its greatest. The transatlantic contingent had arrived, disbelieving much of what they had read in their newspapers. Most were yachting magazine men who understood the sport but who were hardly prepared for what they found in Plymouth. They had imagined that the sensationalism was that of the headline writers, and in a way they were right, but by the time they arrived the picture was plain enough for all to see and only the final figures had to be filled in. We were aware that more than a dozen had died, that the rescue figures were going to exceed a hundred and that there were many boats abandoned and some sunk. It was a grim awareness, all too easily communicated to the new arrivals.

Even at this stage reporting was far from easy. We hadn't seen survivors or anyone from boats that had retired to find out how bad the winds and seas had been at the height of the storm. The framework of our reports was there but not the cladding. We were expected to produce objectivity from pure surmise and this perhaps is one of the reasons why the sensationalists went as far as they did. There was nothing to contradict them at the time.

Not until Wednesday afternoon when the first boats began to finish did the lies begin to be laid. Even so, the crews of *Condor* and *Kialoa* had not been in the very worst of the storm. The biggest boats had been well on their way back from the Fastnet to the Bishop Rock when the winds had increased to force 10 and more, and they had been away from the area where the seas had been at their most destructive. But at least those sailors were able to provide some guidelines for us all.

Now we felt we could write with greater authority but it wasn't until we had talked to some of the survivors that we had any idea of the enormity of the problems of those who encountered the storm at its height. One knew that some of them had got it wrong, even though they believed that they were doing it right. There was desperation in many of their faces and it became our problem to interpret their stories; stories which even with the passing of time have not been mellowed by those who told them then. They were all in mild shock and when that had passed, their own awareness of the gravity of the situations that they had survived did nothing to dilute their recall or decorate it with extension.

Chapter 2

THE EARLY FASTNET RACES

'That Age is best, which is the first,
When Youth and Blood are warmer;
But being spent, the worse, and worst
Times, still succeed the former.'

Robert Herrick
To the Virgins to make much of Time

The race which started on Saturday, 11th August 1979 was the twenty-eighth Fastnet Race; its origins and history holding more bearing on ocean racing than any other event. The race is responsible for the RORC, and that organisation in turn is responsible for much of the development of the sport for the past half century. The importance of the Fastnet is not totally in the private 'Everest' that it provides for the competitors but in its history and traditions. Much of the administration of today's ocean racing is based on the experience of the RORC in running the Fastnet Race, and many of the regulations have been formulated as a direct result of occurrences in this 605-mile classic.

The Fastnet was not the first ocean race; the Americans pre-empted the British in 1906 with the Bermuda Race and before that there had been two Transatlantic Races from west to east, in 1870 and 1887. Nevertheless the Fastnet created its own charisma in short order, possibly because of the varied and tough weather conditions which the early races imposed on those who took part. None of its magic has diminished and that is why in 1979 there were 303 starters involving close to 2,500 sailors representing twenty-one countries.

Early in 1925 some notices appeared in the press announcing what was described as the Ocean Race. The race was to start from Ryde, Isle of Wight, on August 15th of that year and was to be open to any fully

19

decked yacht measuring between 30 and 50 feet on the waterline. The course was to be from Ryde, leaving the Isle of Wight to starboard, to the Fastnet Rock and back to Plymouth.

The Ocean Race was the brainchild of Lt Commander E. George Martin, the owner of *Jolie Brise*, a converted Le Havre pilot cutter 48 feet on the waterline. Together with Malden Heckstall-Smith, the editor of *Yachting Monthly*, and Weston Martyr, who had taken part in three Bermuda Races while living in the United States, Martin forged the plans that received the blessing of the Yacht Racing Association (now the Royal Yachting Association) to organise the race. The Royal Victoria Yacht Club agreed to manage the start and the Royal Western Yacht Club the finish. In addition Martin persuaded Commander Humphreys, the King's Harbour Master of Plymouth, to join the Committee and he in turn asked the naval authorities to grant him permission to make any special arrangements necessary for the finish of the race. The spirit of George Martin, and his foresight, hangs over the Fastnet Race today. Such little details as honorary temporary membership of the Royal Western Yacht Club to competitors on arrival at Plymouth continue to the present time.

Support for the race was enthusiastic by many of those who had cruised their yachts for extensive distances. It would be incorrect, however, to say that this support was universal. The ethics of ocean racing raised doubts in many minds and drew considerable correspondence in the newspapers of the day. One of the most experienced cruising yachtsmen of the time, Claud Worth, was moved sufficiently to write in *The Field*, while the race was under discussion, that he doubted whether the latitudes were suitable for a public ocean race. He felt that while two owners, experienced in ocean cruising, might arrange a match involving several hundred miles of deep water, it was a private affair and they knew exactly what they were doing. He went on to make a statement whose prophesy must still be the worry of the RORC's Committee every time a Fastnet Race is planned: 'a public race might very well include some owners whose keenness is greater than their experience.'

That article of 1925 in *The Field* went on to provide so much sound sense that it possibly provoked a feeling of resentment towards those who were planning the Ocean Race. But it was the sound sense of a cruising yachtsman who had little conception of how ocean racing was to develop. Yet Worth's fears for the keen-but-inexperienced were borne out fifty-four years later:

If the weather should be bad, so long as there is a head wind they would probably come to no harm, for a good boat and sound gear will generally stand as much driving as the crew can put up with. But when running before anything approaching a gale of wind and a big sea in open water, conditions are very deceptive. A vessel of good shape and a reasonably long keel may run so easily and steadily that even an old hand, under cruising conditions, is apt to keep her running longer than is prudent.

Of course, one does not suggest that it is always necessary to heave-to when one gets a strong wind and a biggish sea. It requires much judgment to know whether a following sea has reached the dangerous stage. I have been more than once compelled very reluctantly to heave-to and watch a fair wind running to waste, and have soon after had reason to be very thankful that I was safely hove-to in good time.

Then comes what is perhaps the most pertinent paragraph of the entire article:

But if one had been racing one would probably have been tempted to carry on, knowing that some other competitor might take the risk. These conditions might not occur once in a dozen ocean races, but the magnitude of possible disaster should be taken into account.

Ten years later, just before his death, Worth was asked whether a well-balanced, modern, fine-lined yacht might not, given sea room, run before a gale rather than heave-to. The experience of those early years of ocean racing had altered Worth's ideas and he considered that such yachts might be kept running far longer than those of the past, because their fine lines prevented their disturbing and upsetting the stability of following seas.

It might have been considered that Worth's criticism could bring the proposed Ocean Race into prior disrepute but its proposers had plenty of support in equally respected places. The Committee of organisers added little to their original proposals for the race, except to add the following safety regulations:

It has been decided in the interests of safety that each yacht must carry a serviceable boat such as she normally uses when cruising. In case of doubt an owner should consult the Committee as to the suitability of the boat which he proposes to carry.

One lifebuoy, lifebelt, or lifesaving cushion for each person must be carried on board during the race.

Board of Trade regulations as to lights and fog signals must be complied with.

Thus derived the basis of today's RORC Safety Regulations. Those of 1925 may seem hopelessly inadequate by present standards; standards that have come under severe criticism from outsiders and from certain areas of yachting establishment alike; nevertheless these same standards are adopted by most of the world's ocean racing organisers with very little adaptation.

Fourteen yachts were entered for the first ever Fastnet Race, including one from America. Seven of these, including the American yawl, failed to make the starting line on 15th August 1925 but those that did enjoyed a race which gave as varied a set of weather conditions as one is ever likely to encounter in the race. Of the seven who did race, five finished and two retired, one within half a mile of the finishing line having met a foul tide and a light head wind and realising she was out of contention for a prize in the race.

The race was won by George Martin with *Jolie Brise* in a time just short of six days three hours, with the last boat home arriving in Plymouth thirty-six hours later. *Jolie Brise* had carried light winds almost all the way to the Fastnet, and *Gull* and *Saladin* were only forty and seventy-five minutes astern of her when she rounded the Fastnet Rock early in the evening of 19th August. The barometric pressure had begun to fall and a freshening wind from the west backed into the south-west and gave the leaders a fast reach back to Plymouth. It took *Jolie Brise* just one day and nineteen hours for the leg home. In 1979 it took the 78-foot *Condor* of Bermuda (owned by Bob Bell) a minute and a half under twenty-four hours to complete the same leg, with the added distance of rounding the Bishop Rock and the Scilly Islands, when she broke the Fastnet Race record.

On 23rd August 1925, as *Banba IV*, the last boat home, was approaching the finishing line, in the dining room of the Royal Western Yacht Club, the Ocean Racing Club was being founded. Martin and his fellow competitors believed after the race that their ideals were worth promoting further and while this meeting was held in a natural spirit of euphoria, it was to become one of the major milestones of the sport. Martin was elected Commodore and the future of ocean racing in Britain appeared to be on a firm footing, particularly when seven weeks later a Committee meeting of the Ocean Racing Club was called to frame the rules and to fix a date for the Ocean Race of 1926.

In that year the Ocean Racing Club applied for and was granted official recognition by the Yacht Racing Association. It was also in that year that the start was moved from Ryde to Cowes in order to give the fleet a more comfortable place to lie before setting off. Of the eleven entries for the second Fastnet Race, nine came to the Royal Yacht Squadron line in light airs, including the first overseas entry, *Primrose IV*, an Alden-designed schooner from America.

Qualification for the Ocean Racing Club was achieved by completing a Fastnet Race but this restriction had been waived for Herbert L. Stone, editor of the American magazine *Yachting*. He was one of the thirty-four founding members and was elected to the original Committee as the American Representative. Stone had done much to resurrect the Bermuda Race after the First World War and did much valuable work for the Ocean Racing Club in its early days in the United States.

The second race contained a mixture of weather that varied from periods of flat calm to gale-force winds. The outright handicap winner, *Ilex*, set a sometimes forgotten pattern in the light airs and calms of the early stages by staying well offshore as she went down Channel and benefited from her strategy. The 50-foot waterline Fife-designed *Hallowe'en* was first to round the Rock after two and a half days. She was the first boat designed to the Ocean Racing Club's rule and had a much criticised Bermudian mainsail in her cutter rig. On her way home from the Rock some of the hanks and slides on the mainsail tore away in strong winds with the result that the sail was jammed aloft at night and *Hallowe'en* was forced to carry more sail than her owner would have liked.

The wind did moderate and *Hallowe'en* flew back to Plymouth in a time of three days, nineteen hours and five minutes, a record that was to stand until 1967. *Ilex* and *Primrose IV* were, however, able to save their time on handicap and thus beat *Hallowe'en*. But there was one point that did emerge from the race that was to have a profound effect on the organisers of all future ocean races. Mrs Aitken Dick's *Altair* retired into Baltimore after the storm off the Fastnet and failed to report her action. It led to considerable anxiety for her safety in England and the despatch of a destroyer in search of her. In the 1979 Sailing Instructions the requirement for information of retirement was either to the RORC office in Millbay Dock or the HM Coastguard at Shoreham-by-Sea.

The Fastnet Race of 1927 came up against some pretty heavy weather. Of the fifteen starters only two boats completed the course, one an American schooner, of which two were entered. The start was delayed overnight because of a bad forecast and immediately after the yachts were underway the forecast winds materialised. Three and a half days later all but two boats were back in one port or another, retired with some damage and there was some anxiety for the boats still at sea. One of them, the schooner *La Goleta*, was launched only a few days earlier and was known to be leaking 'like a sieve'.

There was no need for concern. *La Goleta* and the cutter *Tally Ho* were having one of the greatest duels in the history of the Fastnet Race. The British cutter, having weathered one storm on the way to the Fastnet, rounded the Rock in light airs just a quarter of a mile ahead of the American schooner. The pair of them were then in the eye of the depression and there was more in the way of strong winds to come. On the way home they had north-easterlies that veered into the north-west. Lord Stalbridge, the owner of *Tally Ho*, described it later: 'We had to drive her along for all we were worth, not only to beat *La Goleta*, but to get sea room. And drive her we did, more under water than over I fear, but by 4 a.m. (just two and a half hours after rounding the Rock) it had got too bad and we had to heave-to and reef again.'

The determination of a racing crew had once again overcome the cruising man's reticence to run before strong winds.

La Goleta finished fifty minutes ahead of *Tally Ho* but the cutter took the race by four hours on corrected time. The crews of the two finishers no doubt reported to the Ocean Racing Club which was to begin its further development at the next annual general meeting. The Club considered that, in the case of prolonged bad weather, the smaller yachts would have little chance of success in a 600-mile race, and proposed that a race for smaller yachts should start on the Wednesday preceding Cowes Week, over a 250-mile course. This event was called the Channel Race and was established for yachts of between 27 and 35 feet on the waterline. It is now the shorter of the two offshore races which, with the Fastnet and three inshore races, biennially form the Admiral's Cup series.

The 1928 Fastnet was remarkable only for the subsequent wranglings that were caused by the performance of the American schooner *Niña*. This boat caused considerable controversy by being first home, first on handicap but, more importantly, built with an ocean racing rule in mind. This latter fact seemed to incense the writers of the time, particularly those with no knowledge of ocean racing (how like today). Some went as far as to express the opinion that the participation of American yachts in the Fastnet Race was becoming undesirable. It brought a retort from her skipper Sherman Hoyt which must have surprised *Nina's* critics by its moderation. When it was placed before the Committee of the Ocean Racing Club the critics were firmly put in their place. The Honorary Secretary was instructed to write to Sherman Hoyt in the following terms:

> I have been asked by my Flag Officers to inform you that you have been unanimously elected Rear Commodore of the Ocean Racing Club at the recent General Meeting held on the 17th December.

The Ocean Racing Club showed then the stroke of genius that has marked its progress through the years.

The next two races, in 1929 and 1930, were both won by *Jolie Brise*. They were in conditions which favoured the leading boat and the former Le Havre pilot cutter led the fleet home both times.

It was a time of mixed fortunes for the Ocean Racing Club. It was under fire from some members of the yachting establishment, notably Brooke Heckstall-Smith, the brother of Malden Heckstall-Smith, one of the founders of the Fastnet Race. Brooke, however, had an ingrained objection to ocean racing and described the Ocean Racing Club's fleet as 'dullest company even in a second-rate cruisers' match'. He maintained the doctrine that ocean racing had to be inferior because it was necessary that 'at night a yacht should shorten sail'. He appears to have been totally out of touch even though he was then Secretary of the Yacht Racing Association, but he still continued to bombard the press with letters deprecating the sport of ocean racing. Meantime plans were going forward to make the Ocean Racing Club the Royal Ocean Racing Club. At first these plans were refused but on 5th November 1931 they came to fruition with the command of the King.

That same year the Fastnet Race was a notable one on many counts. There were seventeen starters of which six were American and two French. It was won by the American *Dorade*, designed by Olin Stephens and skippered by his brother Rod, marking the start of many years' domination of the prize lists of ocean racing all over the world by boats from the famous firm of Sparkman & Stephens of Madison Avenue, New York.

The race was sadly marred by the loss overboard from *Maitenes II* of one of her owners, Colonel C. H. Hudson. *Maitenes II* had been hove-to under bare poles for a day in a gale before starting to run home before the wind. It was at this time that Colonel Hudson was washed overboard when going aft to read the patent log. (It must be remembered that at this time ocean racing yachts did not have guard rails around them.)

The Fastnet Race then became biennial and there were other changes that didn't appear to be all for the good. The starting date was altered to 22nd July and the course increased to one of 720 miles finishing at the Spithead Forts. The fleet was reduced to six — ocean racing was under considerable criticism at the time — and it was light airs all the way round. *Dorade* won for a second time in that race of 1933.

It appeared for some time that this race might be the last Fastnet. It was becoming unpopular. The RORC was short of members and particularly short of boats. By 1935, however, the Fastnet was the most successful ever with seventeen starters. There were new boats and eleven had Bermudian rig. The old order was changing. Once again the Stephens brothers emerged on top. *Stormy Weather* was long and beamier (*sic*) than *Dorade* and won in even greater style providing the Stephens with a unique treble.

Races other than the Fastnet were now beginning to fill the ocean racing calendar, providing breeding grounds for sailors who wanted to enter the 'Ocean Race'. Their value was inestimable for by 1937 the entry for the Fastnet had increased to twenty-eight. Of these, eighteen were British, seven German and there was one entry each from France, Holland and America. Victory again eluded the home fleet with Connie Bruynzeel's *Zeearend* from Holland winning on handicap; but it was another win for the Stephens brothers who designed the yacht.

The last of the pre-war Fastnets was a fast race with a popular winner in the Nicholson-designed *Bloodhound*, later to become a royal yacht. In the highly charged international climate, it was surprising that the race was held at all and perhaps more surprising that there were German and Dutch entries.

The RORC decided not to run a Fastnet until 1947; the first post-war races had been held amid Channel minefields. It was taking some time for yachts to re-commission after being laid up for six years and the Committee felt that a Fastnet too soon would have been wrong.

It gave at least one owner the opportunity to design a boat to the Club's rule of measurement without compromise. It was the first time that anyone had gone so far but John Illingworth was very determined to win the Fastnet Race. In her appearance *Myth of Malham* was a shock to the traditionalists, and even more of a shock to her fellow competitors. She was of moderately light displacement (for the time) and

John Illingworth had spared nothing in his attempts to save weight aboard. He even had the winch handles drilled out for lightness.

Illingworth's attention to detail was rewarded. The 1947 Fastnet was the slowest on record. The leading boat, *Latifa*, took six days, ten and a half hours to complete the course, and the last boat arrived in Plymouth three days later. Fourth home of the twenty-seven starters was *Myth of Malham*, winner on corrected time. *Myth* was to point the way for the future. Illingworth had exploited the rule and at the same time had produced a seaworthy and weatherly boat. This was proved in the Fastnet of 1949 when, during a gale, *Myth of Malham*, going down Channel, was the only boat which did not heave-to or retire, working her way to windward in huge seas. It gave her another success, in a race which saw only a third of the fleet complete the course and the slowest taking eleven days!

By 1951 there had been more boats designed with the rule in mind and certainly the attention of some designers was towards light displacement. Connie Bruynzeel had commissioned van der Stadt to design him a 35-foot waterline boat which displaced less than five tons. Bruynzeel's *Zeevalk* came close to winning the Fastnet that year with only Owen Aisher's *Yeoman* able to beat this extremely light displacement boat. Class I was taken by *Jocasta*, a yacht which had used composite construction to save weight while retaining strength. A pattern of new design concepts was beginning to emerge, a pattern created to produce boats to win the Fastnet Race.

Pressure on the Club brought a major rule change for the Fastnet of 1953 and subsequent years. The minimum size requirement was reduced to 24-foot waterline, thereby allowing Class III yachts to take part. And as if to hammer home the wisdom of that decision, Sir Michael Newton's 24-foot waterline yawl *Favona* was the overall winner of a race which was described by a contemporary reporter as 'one of dry decks and sunshine'.

The popularity of ocean racing was growing and nowhere is this reflected more than in the entry for the Fastnet Race. It is a barometer of the sport and it reached an all-time high two years later when the fleet had swollen to forty-seven of which forty-four finished in winds that gave close reaching for most of the race. By contrast the 1957 race, the first year of the Admiral's Cup series — then only Britain and America were competitors — was one which tested men and boats to the full. Of the forty-one who left Cowes only twelve reached Plymouth but they did include another of Illingworth's creations, the light displacement *Mouse of Malham*, winner of Class III. The overall winner was the American *Carina*, a centreboarder, which cracked a number of frames up forward in the early stages of the race, forcing her crew to pump for most of the race and eliciting the famous remark from her owner Dick Nye, as she crossed the finishing line: 'OK boys, we're over now; let the damn boat sink.'

It was a race which marked the end of an era of Fastnets. The Admiral's Cup had begun and it was to have an enormous effect on the Fastnet Race and on yacht design. The race and design development had gone hand in hand since 1925 and while the sport of ocean racing was spreading all over the world, it was to the Fastnet that the top ocean racing sailors looked; and designers and owners alike most wanted to notch this one on their belts.

Chapter 3

THE SAILORS' EVEREST

'The Cormorants to drie land did addresse,
And cried away, all soules that us'd the seas.'

George Chapman
Presage of Storme

As *Eclipse* made her way back from the Fastnet Rock, steering the 39-footer was not easy in the huge waves generated by storm-force winds. The forty- to fifty-foot waves were closer together than any her crew had previously experienced and their direction was uncertain because of the shift of the wind. To tackle such waves the helmsman needed the help of a crew member to warn him as to how the waves astern were building. There was not time for him to look, for the steering of the boat into the waves in front took all his concentration if he was to stop her from burying her bow and pitchpoling, but still he needed to know which way the stern was likely to go. The tops of the waves were being blown off and the sea was in a ferment. In anything but a race he would have tried to ease the motion of the boat, but this was the 1979 Fastnet Race and *Eclipse* was a member of the British team that was defending the trophy. Lying seventh before this race began, the British team needed to score a near maximum with each of the teams in front having a boat retire. The force 11 storm provided the possibility of the latter and aboard *Eclipse* they were going flat out to achieve the former. The extreme pressure of the Admiral's Cup was dictating the way the crew of *Eclipse* handled their boat. A few hours earlier a former British Admiral's Cup team captain, Robin Aisher, had retired from the race just five miles short of the Fastnet Rock because, on this occasion, those pressures were not there.

29

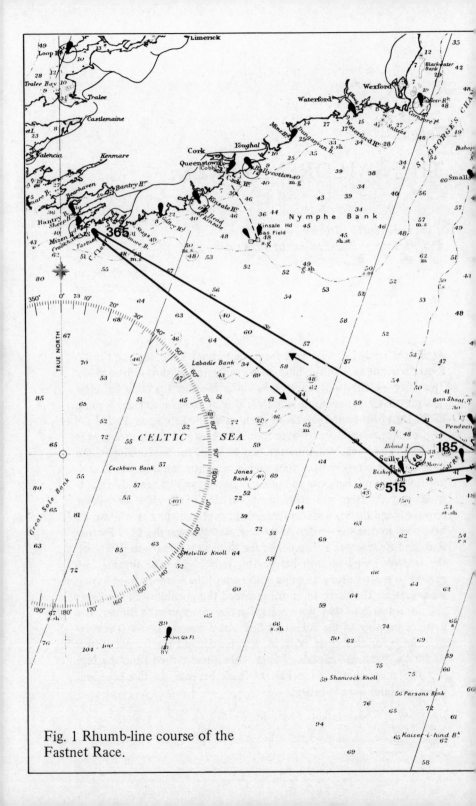

Fig. 1 Rhumb-line course of the
Fastnet Race.

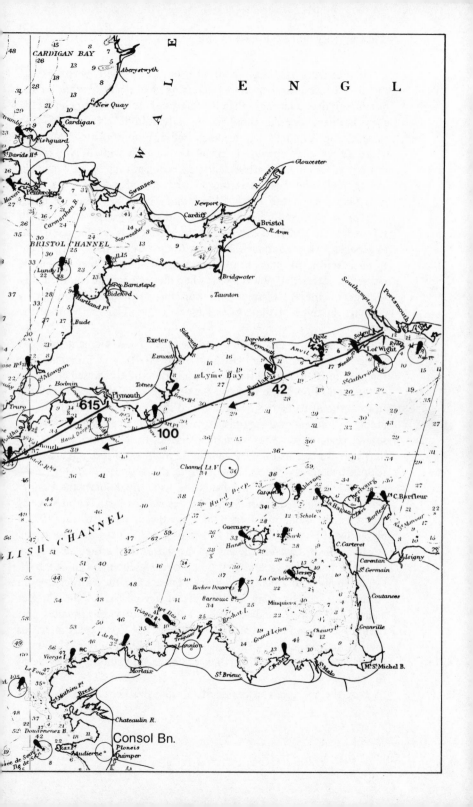

The Fastnet is all things to all men. In 1979 for Jeremy Rogers and the crew of *Eclipse* it meant rather more than it did to many of the others, certainly a lot more than it meant to those who competed in the early Fastnets, even to those in the early Admiral's Cup series. The value of the Admiral's Cup has increased disproportionately. Much of ocean racing development is timed to coincide with it, yet it was formulated simply to attract overseas competitors to take part in Cowes Week and Fastnet racing. On the other hand there are those who take part in the Fastnet Race who would not dream of doing another ocean race during the year. These are the people Claud Worth referred to in 1925, the type 'whose keenness is greater than their experience'. They consider their entry to the Fastnet their right, a right to an adventure. In their hearts they must realise that they have little chance of success. 1979 was a year when they might have had their way — four of the six classes were won by restricted division yachts although in three of these cases these were not their first wins of the year.

The late fifties and sixties were a time of development in yacht design. The International Offshore Rule (IOR) was formulated to replace the RORC's own handicap rating rule and those used elsewhere in the world in order to level out the differences of ocean racing yachts from different parts of the world so that they might race together more evenly in international regattas. It needed many amendments and took several years to settle into a workable state. It needed both short and long races to test its efficacy and the Fastnet was a focus of attention for rule makers as well as designers during this period.

Those years had their highlights and with triple points the Fastnet was always where the Admiral's Cup was won or lost. The number of teams in the Admiral's Cup built from the original two in 1957 to eleven by 1969 and during that time the United States won it twice and Australia once. Towards the end of the sixties the Fastnet was won by two very innovative yachts. In 1967 the French schooner *Pen Duick III*, skippered by Eric Tabarly, took line honours and the Fastnet Cup on corrected time, breaking the old course record as she did so. Her elapsed time was three days, fifteen hours and fifty-four minutes, just over three hours faster than *Hallowe'en* in 1926. Two years after this the Fastnet Cup went to the American yacht *Red Rooster*. This was a lifting-keel boat designed by Dick Carter, again exploiting the rule of the day.

That the sport gained popularity during this period can be gauged by the increase in the number of starters in the Fastnet Race. The 59 who started in 1959 seem few compared to the record number of starters, 209, in 1967; but it must be said that the average size of the yachts was getting smaller. World economics were also a telling factor in ocean racing.

In 1971 the race record was smashed again, this time by a boat designed and built for a much different purpose. *American Eagle* was originally conceived as a 12-metre for the defence trials for the America's Cup, an event as far removed from ocean racing as it is possible to imagine. She was converted for ocean racing by Ted Turner and with her he went on to win the World Championship series and among his race wins was a line honours and handicap win in the Sydney to Hobart 630-miler. The overall winner that year was Syd Fischer's *Ragamuffin*, an Australian Admiral's Cup yacht which sailed home from the Rock under full sail in fresh winds, risking her spinnaker throughout while others went for less forcing rigs.

There followed three Fastnets in increasingly light winds. The entries swelled to 286 yachts and there was no doubt that the race had lost some of the mystique that had previously surrounded it. It had been associated in the past with gales and was universally acknowledged to be an adventurous challenge. 1973, 1975 and 1977 had Augusts where calms were more prevalent than winds and strong winds were non-existent. These three races must have lulled the keen-but-inexperienced into believing that the Fastnet Race was well within their capabilities. The number of entries had swelled to exceed 320, although only 303 came to the starting line at Cowes for the 1979 race.

This does nothing to diminish the importance of the Fastnet Race internationally. Entries from twenty-one countries prove that it is the most highly rated race in the world. As more people go ocean racing there are greater numbers seeking entry in the more charismatic races, and since there are more ocean racing sailors around European shores than elsewhere, it follows that entries for the Fastnet will exceed any other race of this type. It is a necessary milestone in any ocean racer's life.

The Admiral's Cup fleet has grown, too, over the years so that by 1979 there were teams of three boats from nineteen nations taking part from all the continents. Upwards of £20 million was estimated to have been spent in the challenges, and defence of the Cup. It was big yachting business, and the Fastnet was still the deciding race of the series. With triple the points for each boat compared to the points of any one of the three inshore races or the double points of the Channel

Race, the results in the Fastnet could radically alter any team's position.

That is not to say that the teams would take any of the other races less seriously, but there were many who would pin their hopes, and faith, on doing well in the Classic. It has all so often proved right, not only in the Admiral's Cup but also in the other two events which have grown up because of it — the Southern Cross Cup and the Onion Patch. The latter two have similar points-scoring systems which give triple points loading to the Sydney-Hobart and the Bermuda Races respectively.

The trend of yacht design is influenced greatly by the Admiral's Cup series. It is necessary to do well in all five races, so that speed around the inshore courses is almost as important as the seaworthiness of a boat for an ocean race. On the other hand no designer would possibly put his reputation at risk with a boat which would be likely to win all of the three inshore races only to break up in the sea conditions that are found offshore. Boats have to be designed to win in the Solent and cope with the heavier seas of ocean races. Offshore there are different skills required of the crew members, but the type of boat that wins is still the same as that which wins races inshore.

Fingers have been pointed at designers suggesting that their interpretation of the IOR has been irresponsible, and that they have aimed for speed at the expense of seaworthiness. In 1979 their concepts of what made a fast ocean racer were dictated, to a large extent, by the IOR but their development has been along a well-defined progression which has eschewed the deep draught, heavy-displacement yachts of yesteryear, gradually but remorselessly. The designers are not the only arbiters of taste. They are answerable to the owners who demand faster and faster yachts but nevertheless yachts in which they can safely race at sea.

There has to be some compromise. The designer sees the stresses and strains that a race like the Fastnet can impose on a yacht, while at the same time realising that many of the races which his latest creation will be entered for will be round-the-buoys events similar to the inshore races of the Admiral's Cup. Designers search for new materials that will combine strength with a saving in weight. More and more they look towards the technology of the aerospace industry for spin-offs from that highly sophisticated source whose research and development budgets are almost limitless. No prospective owner of an ocean racer can afford such budgets and so the knowledge comes to him secondhand. Again it comes as a compromise.

Testing new ideas and new materials is a quantitative affair. Calculating the shock loads that can be imposed on a yacht, particularly on its rig, is difficult. In masts, for instance, there has been progressive development aimed at reducing the weight and the cross-section. Ultimately this led to a high failure rate. At this point a step back was needed, or more sophisticated rigging plans for the lighter smaller spars. Experienced sailors can use lighter gear more safely than the average offshore racer but at the top limits of wind and waves even the expert is hard pressed. Thus, designers face a further compromise.

In 1979 designers were experimenting with lightweight rudders for a gain in speed and handicap benifit. The advantage of a lighter rudder is twofold: it reduces the radius of gyration of the boat and it helps to lift the stern for improved measurement. As much as 100 lbs can be saved in the rudder of a 45-footer using carbon-fibre reinforcement instead of stainless steel, aluminium, wood and glassfibre, the more usual materials for this purpose. There was nothing new in the use of carbon fibre; *Moonshine,* Jeremy Rogers's 1977 Admiral's Cup yacht, had a rudder reinforced with this material. The innovation was in the way the carbon fibres were being laid in the resin to reinforce these new 'state-of-the-art' rudders.

There were warnings early on in the year that these lightweight rudders were not all the designers and manufacturers had hoped that they would be. *Imp*, the Fastnet winner of 1977, had one fail in the Southern Ocean Racing Conference (SORC) series in Florida early in 1979. So too did the Ron Holland designed *Aries*, and both were chosen as members of the United States Admiral's Cup team. In addition, both their rudders were built by Ron Holland's brother-in-law, Gary Carlin, at the Kiwi Yachts company. The failures, it must be stressed, showed no similarity. The indications, however, suggested that perhaps rudders were going the same way that masts had done two years previously.

A further warning came in the Channel Race, just one week before the Fastnet. The carbon-fibre rudder of *Morning Cloud* fractured in only moderate sea conditions. Edward Heath rushed to attend a press conference at Cowes to explain why he had been forced to pull *Morning Cloud* out of the race. As captain of the British team, he owed the world an explanation.

He arrived at the press conference clutching the broken stock of his yacht's rudder, which had been withdrawn when *Morning Cloud* was taken out of the water at Moody's yard at Bursledon. It showed quite clearly where the rudder had failed — just where the stock entered the blade — and how the stock had been fabricated of an aluminium alloy thin-walled tube wrapped with carbon-fibre laminates.

The lesson became more obvious on the Thursday of Cowes Week, just a couple of days before the Fastnet start. The Irish yacht *Moonduster*, a Swan 441, broke her carbon-fibre rudder in one of the most boisterous days that the regatta has known. It might be worth noting that this, like *Morning Cloud's*, was another Kiwi Yachts fabrication and that for a yacht of this size the cost was in the region of £2,000. Such is the price an ocean racing owner will pay in order to have the very best equipment with the greatest possible advantage over his rivals.

By this time there must have been many worried owners and crews. They could have taken consolation only in that their rudders had not failed during the Thursday gale. Otherwise all those with carbon-fibre reinforced rudders must have felt apprehensive about the weather for the Fastnet, including *Imp* and *Aries* which had had their failed carbon-fibre rudders replaced with new ones of a similar material.

The pressure that was building up for the Fastnet Race was heightened by the Admiral's Cup competition. In that there was no quarter given or asked, at the first attempt to make a start there was a multi-boat pile-up. One yacht, the Brazilian *Madrugada*, was holed so badly that she was lucky to remain afloat. Brazil's luck was not good; the reserve boat that was chartered, David May's *Winsome Gold*, buckled her mast in the next race and was withdrawn from the competition too.

On the whole, however, masts were staying in boats rather better than they had before although the winds were much stronger than had been experienced at this time of the year for many years. Certainly the boats were getting thorough testings. The antics of the Admiral's Cuppers in the second inshore race on Thursday 2nd August, not the Thursday of Cowes Week, should have given more cause for concern than they did. The winds were brisk, force 6 gusting 7 from the south-west, and the course twice up and down the West Solent.

On the downwind legs, with spinnakers and bloopers set, many of the fifty-seven boat fleet yawed wildly, often broaching out of control. Some of the broaches were so sudden that the boats almost pivoted on their axes and turned to face the way they had come.

It was gyrations of this nature that led to two crew members being taken to hospital. One, a Japanese crew member of *Togo VI*, was only slightly injured, but the other, Harvey Bagnall, helmsman of the Irish yacht *Inishanier*, a sistership of *Eclipse*, was badly hurt. He was hit over the head when the boat gybed involuntarily and sustained a fractured skull and deep wounds. He was taken off the yacht by a Royal Navy helicopter to the naval hospital at Haslar.

The ocean racing 'heavies' tend to dismiss the sort of boat behaviour exhibited in that race, referring to boats doing 'three-point turns' or 'a tip-truck'. However, one out-of-control situation had claimed the life of a crewman in the SORC that year. Tom Curtis was killed by a boom which swung across the boat as he was trimming the spinnaker. No preventer tackle had been rigged and the yacht, *Obsession*, had just done a round-up broach and was being brought back on to course when a new sea got under her stern and swung her faster than the helmsman might have expected. It was so fast that the involuntary gybe could not have been avoided. The boom swung across and Curtis's head was smashed by its force.

In that same series Tom Curnow, at the time unwell, was lost overboard one evening from the yacht *Pirana*. Two horseshoe lifebuoys and strobe lights were thrown to him immediately and the yacht brought round to the spot. *Pirana* passed within fifteen feet of him but Curnow was not able to grasp the line which was thrown. After two more passes and further searching for two hours the rescue proved fruitless.

Don Graul, writing of the incident in the American magazine *Yachting*, said: 'There should be some rethinking of priorities aboard racing boats. As several veteran offshore racing sailors have suggested, to win these days a boat must be sailed at and beyond the edge of safety and survival.' Graul is himself an ocean racing sailor and knows just how narrow the dividing line is; unfortunately others do not.

Chapter 4

THE STORM—
THE COMPETITORS' STORIES

'The sea is a mistress oft wanton and cruele'

Anon O.E.

PRAIRIE OYSTER

Prairie Oyster is a Carter threequarter tonner which gives Chris Purchase and his crew a great deal of enjoyment in round-the-buoys and offshore racing. For them the Fastnet is a must.

They were well prepared for the 1979 race; the boat had been thoroughly checked: the stores had been carefully selected (after all, Chris Purchase is a wine merchant); items of safety equipment had been specially bought or made; and there was an air of expectancy as they started with Class IV from the Royal Yacht Squadron line.

Purchase had built *Prairie Oyster* himself from a glass-fibre hull and deck unit and she was finished off to his requirements. He is a perfectionist and is therefore careful about all the yacht's safety gear. He took, on trial for this race, some new production prototype safety harnesses which had been designed by Peter Hankey for his company Britax Wingard. Purchase hoped he would not have to use them other than as routine, for like most skippers, he insists on crew members wearing them at night in a fresh breeze.

Purchase considered that he needed a new dan buoy to conform to Special Regulations and so, with some time to spare, he built one that he felt would be better than any on the market.

The early part of the race was uneventful for *Prairie Oyster* as it was for all the boats. Life on board had settled into racing routine. Fog had provided some hazard on the way down Channel and the hazard wasn't alleviated by the watch which came off at 1000 on Monday morning not keeping the log updated. That the log reading went from only

582.03 to 585.75 in four hours was hardly a major sin but the log book records 'Navigator's compliments to log keeping of last watch.' An hour and a half later more than six miles had been recorded and the Runnelstone was abeam. After a couple of sail changes, where the spinnaker came down and was replaced with the number one genoa and progress became faster, Round Island was abeam in three hours. After that the wind dropped before returning from the south.

It wasn't until 2230, still with a number one genoa set, that a reef went into the main. By then Round Island light was in the south-east quadrant and the apparent windspeed was up to 25 knots. Three hours later the wind was up to 35 knots and the boat had done more than twenty-two miles. The sail had been reduced to the working jib only, with the mainsail off and the boom lashed down to the deck. The decision was made to put up the storm jib and carry on racing toward the Rock.

By now *Prairie Oyster* was almost a quarter of the way from Land's End to the Fastnet and, to use the skipper's words, 'Flying along, perhaps too fast for comfort.' All appeared well with the world until 0300 when the wind had risen to force 9-10 and the sea was 'steep with breaking crests'.

Nick Matthews and Doug Harcourt were on watch. Both were clipped on to the toe-rail on the port side. The storm jib was set and the mainsail lashed down to the starboard side. The course was 350°magnetic and the boat was 'running nicely'. Ten minutes after that log entry, *Prairie Oyster* hit a crest and a gust at the same time.

By this time Nick Matthews had had a 'gut full' already. He had been on deck to take down the number two genoa soon after midnight and had nearly gone over the side when the inner forestay became unclipped while his life-line had been snapped on to it. He immediately re-clipped onto the toe-rail. Shortly after the crew saw a red flare off the starboard side but as there were two mast-head navigation lights nearer to the flare than they were, they presumed the distressed vessel had help standing by.

Nick had just finished a thirty-minute spell on the helm and Doug had taken over when the wave hit. Nick was on the floor of the cockpit and was thrown towards the guard rails as the boat rolled over to a horizontal knockdown. In his words: 'I can't remember how I was stopped, either by my hands or my harness.' For Doug, things were worse: 'I was pitched over, backwards, and grabbed the starboard pushpit rail as I went.'

39

He held on to the rail until he was forced underwater and, to save himself from drowning, let go. At this time *Prairie Oyster*, without a helmsman, righted herself. Doug found himself being towed along on the end of his harness, first on the starboard side and then on the port. His oilskin trousers were stripped off by the force of the water and he tried hard to kick off his boots, which were dragging and putting extra strain on his safety harness. His thoughts strayed to his vanity in buying tight-fitting sea boots. Normally he bought his boots three sizes larger than his normal shoes, but this pair were such a good fit that he couldn't ease them off. As a result it was almost impossible for him to haul himself back to the boat. Another thought which ran through his mind was that if he became detached from the boat there would be no dan buoy to mark his approximate position – he had successfully destroyed Chris's new dan buoy when he fell against it as the boat rolled. Chris, he felt, would be none too pleased after all the effort he had put into it.

The cry 'Man overboard!' from Nick brought Chris and Darryl Ackerman on deck. There was chaos down below. Chris and Darryl helped to get Doug on board and while Darryl took the helm, Nick went forward to douse the storm jib. He passed it to Hugh Bett through the fore hatch and later wondered whether the fore hatch had been properly clipped shut during the knockdown because he knew that earlier it hadn't.

A decision was made to run before the storm with bare poles and streaming warps. The crew settled down to a routine with the skipper and Darryl steering alternately and Mike, Hugh and Nick doing half-hour-on/one-hour-off watches in the cockpit. Doug was excused duties for a while to recover. Everything that could be used to stream behind the boat to slow it down, was brought into action. Kedge warps, mooring lines and spare sheets were all out, and still the boat surged on at 8 knots and more on occasion. But the general impression of the crew was that they were not going to be knocked over again although there was some apprehension when they were swamped by breaking waves.

The mast-head navigation light had been washed away in the knockdown and there was a mess below. Otherwise the boat was unharmed. One of the water tanks had ruptured and there were a couple of bottles of gin that were broken to add to the torrent of water that poured in through the fore hatch when the boat went over. The inner forestay, whose fitting was fractured, was secured with a lanyard and, once settled down, *Prairie Oyster* provided her crew with a sense of security.

Chris Purchase described the seas as being between forty and fifty feet, crest to trough, and the wind was off the end of the dial of the windspeed indicator (60 knots). For him it was a never to be forgotten experience:

> I felt that the sea in this state was one of the most magnificent sights that I have ever seen in my life. I would never seek that experience again, but there was no time to be afraid and in a strange way we were enormously grateful to have taken part in it.
>
> We had only a receiving radio set and we heard some awful messages over it. Our regret throughout the storm was that we were looking after ourselves but it was our families that were doing the worrying.

Two months later he admitted that had he been able to radio ashore to let relatives and friends know that *Prairie Oyster* was afloat and all were well on board, he would have felt easier.

This was Douglas Harcourt's tenth Fastnet Race and one which he is unlikely to forget. Nevertheless he says he will take part in another. So, too, will Chris Purchase, with the same crew. Soon after *Prairie Oyster* returned to Plymouth he confirmed: 'I have a lot of confidence in the boat and was lucky to have such a superb navigator and marvellous crew – I would certainly do it again, if they would come with me.'

Prairie Oyster ran before the wind for seventeen hours before her crew felt that the wind had moderated sufficiently for them to hoist some sail and head home. At eight o'clock on the Tuesday evening they had already decided to retire and they hoisted the storm jib with all the reefs in the mainsail and began to beat back, making their first landfall close to St Agnes Head on the north coast of Cornwall. Twenty-four hours after they had begun sailing again, the crew of *Prairie Oyster* were 'coasting' across Mounts Bay and by nine o'clock the next morning they were tied up in Millbay Dock, Plymouth.

There the log reverted to understatement: 'Very eventful trip.'

ASSENT

At twenty-three years old, Alan Ker was probably one of the youngest skippers in the 1979 Fastnet. He jointly owns *Assent*, a Contessa 32, with his father and had with him a young crew including two young women. *Assent* was entered in Class V and all those on board were aware that their principal effort would be directed towards winning a

Contessa 32 class prize from the other eleven that were to take part. The crew assembled at Cowes on the day before the Fastnet and devoted all their energies to the boat's preparation.

Their log records pleasant sailing for the first two days, hampered only by fog and light winds. Monday morning found them becalmed just short of the Lizard and, as the tide turned to flood against them, they were forced to drop anchor in 38 fathoms, making use of the generous kedge warp carried on board. Land's End was passed in the afternoon when the wind returned with the change of tide and the problem for *Assent*'s crew was to make good boat speed in the light airs and lumpy sea. The competition of another Contessa 32 nearby produced extra effort from the crew.

At 1755 they heard the shipping forecast which gave the first warning of the gale, although they had been aware that the unstable weather pattern made the chance of a strong blow a distinct possibility. They felt, however, that there was no cause for alarm since they had plenty of sea room between themselves and the Welsh coast to leeward and they comforted themselves with the knowledge that as offshore racing yachts are designed to sail through summer gales, they must expect to sail through them from time to time.

It was time, however, to take stock and Fiona Wylie prepared the type of supper which could see them through for several hours, a huge spaghetti bolognese. Gordon Williams worked to repair an eight-foot rip in the foot of the spinnaker where it had caught on the pulpit in the sloppy seas off Land's End while, on deck, Bill Barker-Wyatt and Alan Ker progressively reduced sail as the wind increased. They were down to storm jib and fully reefed mainsail when they heard the 0015 warning of force 10. By then stitching the spinnaker had become impossible.

This was more than a 'summer gale'. At 0100 Gordon and Fiona took over the watch on deck and in addition to wearing safety harnesses, they lashed themselves securely into the cockpit on the insistence of the skipper, as a further protection against getting washed overboard by the increasing seas which were beginning to break over the yacht. The wind and seas continued to increase but *Assent*, on port tack, seemed to take it in her stride and held a close-hauled course for the Fastnet Rock at 5½ knots.

After they had been on watch for an hour, Gordon and Fiona were made rather more aware of the dangers of the situation. *Assent* was picked up by a breaking wave and knocked down until the mast-head hit the water. It occurred so suddenly that Gordon records: 'We had no time to fear the consequences and as the boat righted quickly, with Fiona and I still tied to our places and only a modest amount of water in the cockpit, we shouted to Alan that all appeared to be well and remarked that we could now reckon a knockdown amongst our sailing experience.'

Down below, the entire contents of the port-side cabin lockers had flown straight across the saloon to hit the starboard lockers before cascading into Alan's bunk, the starboard-side saloon berth. Rosalind Gilbert had been securely held in the port saloon berth by some extra large non-standard cot sides while Bill was safe enough on the sail bags on the saloon floor. He had left the quarter berth earlier complaining that water was getting into the berth from the companionway. The only damage was the loss of the anchor locker hatch and the loo door coming adrift.

From the foredeck, however, a noise indicated that all was far from well. The head had pulled out of the storm jib and all the hanks had ripped off. The sail had slipped down the luff wire and was flogging furiously. It was a difficult sail to tame and take off, but it was a job that had to be done. Gordon got thoroughly soaked in the attempt. This time it was Alan's job to repair the sail for it would certainly be needed again, although at the time the crew thought the motion of the boat was easier without it hoisted. Gordon recalls the scene:

The sail that followed through the rest of the night after the knockdown was as fantastic and exhilarating as one could expect to encounter in a lifetime of sailing. A half moon had appeared in the clearing sky to light the wild seascape of foaming breakers. Phosphorescence in the spray was streaming over the sail and cabin top, and the wind was screaming through the rigging and life-lines like a pack of coyotes, while all the time *Assent* continued steadily on her course at 4 knots to windward with a much easier motion following the loss of the jib. After climbing up and up each successive sea, we could not help whooping with excitement, and not a little relief, as she crested each summit and slithered down into the next trough.

For *Assent* the wind appeared to reach its maximum around 0430 and continued to blow without any respite until after midday. Her crew could not determine the wind strength accurately as they did not have the electronics of their rivals and stated later that they were probably happier as a result. Even their log was out-moded by modern standards

— it was a Walker Patent, streamed astern; old-fashioned but reliable.

During the day *Assent*'s crew began to pick up the broadcast reports of the disaster and while they retained every confidence in the yacht and in their own ability to carry on, they were naturally apprehensive that these same radio reports would be causing some alarm among their friends and relatives, but there was no way that they could allay these fears as *Assent* did not have a radio transmitter. These worries were lessened as *Assent* was sighted several times by search and rescue aircraft and all on board felt they would then be reported safe and well.

It was the worries of the friends and relatives ashore that motivated much of my reporting on the first day of the disaster. I realised that there were many yachts which would have no means of making their safety known as they did not carry radio transmitters. As an ocean racing sailor, I knew how the crews of those yachts would be reacting; many would want to go on yet they felt that their first duty was to inform the people ashore. How much more sensible it would have been to have made radio reporting by each yacht in the race a mandatory requirement.

Ashore the 'popular press' was having a field day at the expense of the relatives and friends of the competitors. Remainder figures, those of boats not sighted, were used as those of boats 'missing' and the pressures placed on the organisers were unseemly. Incorrect deductions were being made about yacht design and thus it was left to the very few of us who participate in the sport as well as report it, to attempt to alleviate the unnecessary fears of those ashore and to moderate the reports by giving them all the information we could about ocean racing and the potential seaworthiness of the boats taking part. The horrific stories of the loss of life and boats would then stand on their own rather than be bolstered by dramatic misrepresentation.

As the wind began to moderate in the afternoon of August 14th, *Assent* sighted the Dutch yacht *Sandettie II*, a UFO 34, which had been dismasted. They came upon it suddenly, first sighting it when no more than three hundred yards away because the waves were so high. *Assent* stood by for twenty minutes in order to ascertain that the boat was not in distress and that there were no injuries among the crew, at whose suggestion *Assent* continued in the race. *Sandettie II* made it back to Plymouth under a jury rig.

With a moderating wind *Assent* was able to carry more sail and her crew are of the opinion that the yacht possibly suffered greater stress then than during the height of the storm. By now, an accurate navigational fix was becoming important and Alan busied himself with the radio direction finder and placed the boat not far off the rhumb line between Land's End and the Fastnet Rock. The lights along the Irish coast were sighted that night. Then the wind moderated to the point of light airs and *Assent* was back to slow progress until the Fastnet was rounded at 1005 on the Wednesday morning.

From there the reach home was everything that they could have asked for — good breeze and warm sunshine. It gave the crew time to dry out their wet clothes and bedding and to recharge the yacht's batteries after managing to start the petrol engine. But the forecast of a second gale they considered to be 'rather unsporting' after what they had already been through.

At 2300 a trawler came too close for comfort and a white hand flare was lit to show all was well. At this time there were several green flares dropped from aircraft to mark disabled yachts and *Assent*'s crew presumed that the trawler had altered course towards her because it believed that she was disabled.

Soon afterwards the wind began to increase and back and the spinnaker had to come off at 0200. *Assent* held a course to miss the Bishop Rock by ten miles or so because of the deteriorating conditions. It was not seamanlike to head for a lee shore in low visibility. On their course *Assent* was given a close inspection by the frigate, HMS *Scylla*, shortly before she altered course for Plymouth. During this final leg the wind rose to a full gale and there was driving rain and minimum visibility. In normal circumstances *Assent*'s crew might have felt some apprehension but following their earlier experiences in this race their conception of wind strengths and wave heights had become so distorted that they sailed as though they were in no more than a good breeze with a whole crew fully fit.

When the wind eased more sail was piled on; this crew had been at sea long enough and they wanted to get home to some shoreside comforts. The spinnaker went back up and lasted until it was blown out in a broach just five miles from the finish at Plymouth Breakwater. *Assent* thus suffered her most serious damage well after the storm that caused the disaster. She crossed the finishing line at 0145 on the Thursday morning and sailed to Millbay Dock where her crew was told that they had been reported retired and headed for Cork.

They were furious. Skipper Alan completed the declaration form and in high dudgeon the crew marched en masse to the Race Control Office to see the record corrected. It was then, and only then, that they found out that they were the only boat expected to finish out of fifty-eight in Class V. They also discovered they had won the Favona Cup and the Battler Beedle Quaich for Class V in addition to the Spangle Trophy, the Contessa 32 prize, that they had initially set out to win.

All were agreed that handling a boat like *Assent* in the storm conditions which they had experienced needed fit, rested people. For this reason, during and after the storm they had slipped into a six-hours-on/six-hours-off routine which gave a greater proportion of the off-watch period for sleeping after the struggle of getting in to and out of wet clothes, oilskins and safety harnesses. They sailed well as a team and were pleased to have completed the course. They said they enjoyed the sail and added, 'Perhaps we were all mad.'

Their seamanship in a small boat was outstanding. They went to sea in a boat they knew they could trust and they raced hard. They paced themselves excellently and no one was more deserving of success.

ENDEAVOUR (*Seltrust Endeavour*)

Seltrust Endeavour was perhaps the most unusual yacht in the Fastnet Race. She is a pencil-thin 50-foot schooner designed by her owner Michael Dunham to compete in the Parmelia Race from Plymouth to Perth, Western Australia, after the Fastnet was over. She bore no relationship to the modern breed of ocean racers being a mere 9 foot 6 inch beam on 50 foot overall. She had an hydraulically lifting keel and two short (40 foot) masts. She looked quite out of place at the start and, when other yachtsmen saw her heel to quite large angles in the slightest gusts of wind, all were worried about her safety. They felt certain that she would have no chance on handicap either — she rated 51.6 feet, longer than her overall length, and she had shown that she was a slouch in the Channel Race the previous weekend.

Endeavour, she had to drop the commercial *Seltrust* because of the International Yacht Racing Union's rule concerning advertising and sponsorship, was developed from a 100-footer called *Sundancer* which had three masts and had shown some turn of speed in short-handed races. Michael Dunham is a master mariner with his own ideas of yachting and had planned to do the Parmelia Race from the moment it was announced. He had a limited budget and wanted a boat which would not be certain to finish last because it was the smallest, and *Endeavour* was the answer to his problems. Unfortunately, he seems to have got it wrong because not only was *Seltrust Endeavour* last on handicap in the Fastnet, she was also last in the Parmelia Race and the Sydney to Hobart!

In the evening of Monday, *Endeavour* sighted *Assent* a mile astern when the wind had begun to rise. By the time it had reached 30 knots, the spinnaker had to come off *Endeavour*. By 0200 on Tuesday, *Endeavour* was down to a storm jib only with her eight-man crew working two normal watches. The angle of heel was horrifying — 45 degrees and more continuously. The waves were breaking clean over the boat dousing the crew on deck at regular intervals.

It was a hard shakedown for the Parmelia Race. Dunham planned to use the Fastnet to discover the shortcomings of his craft — and he was finding out the hard way. However, the long thin yacht moving along at a severe angle did, he believed, present much less resistance to the huge seas than a barely moving, upright, beamy IOR yacht's hull. In addition, *Endeavour* never felt she was near to being rolled over or even laid flat; she went to her extreme angle and stayed there. She continued to make between 5 and 6 knots throughout the storm.

There was no doubt that the yacht was ill prepared for the Fastnet Race. Water poured in down below through ineffective hatches. The compass repeatedly came out of the binnacle. The life-raft, which had been only temporarily secured before the start, came adrift in the early hours of Tuesday morning and it had to be re-fastened in place. This took two crew members some time and brought to light the fact that there were no jack stays fitted to attach life-lines as they worked forward.

More water came through the decks because many of the deck fittings fastening bolts were poorly sealed. Sleep was therefore difficult and it is remarkable that only two members of the crew suffered from sea-sickness and then only on one occasion.

More crucial to the safety of the boat was the hydraulically raising keel. The deck bolts which should have fixed it down had not been completed and there was a danger that if the yacht had suffered total inversion through a knockdown, the keel would have come through at the deck and the boat, without it, would never have righted herself.

In the rush to get to the start several items had been left behind and none more important than the spare batteries for the radio direction finding equipment. By the time the storm began to abate there were serious doubts as to *Endeavour*'s position. It wasn't until 1930 on Tuesday that the crew were able to sight the gas platforms off Cork and thereby establish their position.

From there on they had similar conditions to *Assent*, only in the case of *Endeavour* there was no RDF to help with a landfall. Dunham's skill with dead reckoning took the yacht up Channel to a perfect landfall with the Eddystone light. For the crew the consolation of the race came in the final hour, during which they averaged 10 knots.

TENACIOUS

Everyone wants to win a race but two people on board *Tenacious* had special reasons for wanting to win the 1979 Fastnet. Ted Turner, her ebullient, extrovert owner from Atlanta, Georgia, wanted to win not only because he believes that anything less is unbearable, but also because in an earlier boat, the converted 12-metre American *Eagle*, he had held the course record but had not won the race. For Peter Bowker, the boat's navigator, the desire to win was equally deep seated. He had navigated *American Eagle* to a Sydney-Hobart Race win in 1973 and six months after that was navigator on Chuck Kirsch's *Scaramouche* when she won the Bermuda Race. Winning the Fastnet Race would give him a unique triple crown that others would find hard to emulate.

To make perfectly certain of receiving the weather forecasts without interruption Peter Bowker tuned into the radio early and listened with a headset. By doing so he took the broadcast off the loudspeaker in the cabin. At 1800 on Monday he emerged from the navigator's cabin on *Tenacious* with a wry smile on his face. Ted Turner remembers it well: 'He came out with a silly grin and said, "Mmm . . . guess what I just heard on the radio – force 7 to 8, locally 9. Mmm." Of course, with that grin on his face, we all thought he was pulling our legs. The man's a comic, we were sure he was having us on.'

At the time, *Tenacious* was running square on port gybe just half an hour away from the Fastnet Rock. There was nothing like the forecast wind, just force 4 to 5 from slightly west of south. Peter was happy with his fix; navigation had not been difficult even with the restricted tools he was allowed to use. *Tenacious*, like most American ocean racers, had Loran and Omni, tools which the RORC ban and which Peter feels are necessary with an aluminium boat the size of *Tenacious* which distorts the beams of RDF beacons. He might not have been totally happy that *Tenacious* was running square; had the wind veered as he expected it to, the 61-foot *Tenacious* would have been travelling faster towards the Rock on a reach. So too would Ted.

Tenacious rounded the Fastnet Rock at 1830, setting a number two genoa before she dropped her spinnaker. She tacked as soon as she could clear the Rock and set off on starboard tack, close-hauled. She was 15° low of the rhumb-line course but no one on board was worried about that — the veer was expected and it would lift them up on course to the Bishop Rock.

The wind began to increase and with it came the veer. At first a reef was put in the mainsail, then the number two genoa was replaced by the number three, and then a second reef was tucked into the mainsail. But the wind was getting stronger all the time; maybe Peter hadn't been having them on about that forecast. The number four genoa was next up and a third reef was taken in the mainsail. Gary Jobson's watch made all these changes between 2000 and midnight.

When Jim Mattingley's watch came on at midnight the wind was close to 50 knots but it had freed *Tenacious* sufficiently that she was pointing at the Bishop Rock with a 60° apparent wind angle. By 0100 Jim reckoned that *Tenacious* was overpowered and his watch took down the mainsail and secured it to the boom. *Tenacious* was close-reaching under the number four genoa with a lot of white water flying around streaked with phosphorescence. The spray was stinging the eyes of those on deck.

Ted turned to Peter: 'There'll be a lot of boats in trouble in this wind. I wouldn't want to be in a small boat.'

The watch changed at 0400. Gary took the wheel; steering the yacht in the confused seas was difficult. He was harnessed to the boat but it bucked in the waves and keeping a firm footing was necessary to keep the boat on track. After a while it became apparent that the worst of the storm was over and the wind began to moderate; the scream of the wind in the rigging dropped a note or two.

Down below, Peter took the opportunity to get some sleep. He had laid a course to the Bishop Rock which he hoped was right but he had no idea of the exact amount of leeway *Tenacious* was making in the huge waves that battered her in two directions. The first seas set up by the southerly gale were still there and on top of them was a second wave pattern that the west-north-west wind had caused. He needed to let the boat sail for an hour or two to get a true idea of the leeway she was making. The navigator's berth was to leeward and he didn't fancy that so he lay down on the trysail in its bag and dozed off. He'd been there for a few hours when Gary decided that he needed more sail on *Tenacious* and the call came for the trysail.

Peter regretfully gave up his bed at 0500 so that the crew could set it and he sat down to clear up the mess underneath where the bagged sail had been. Somewhat to his surprise, as *Tenacious* is sailed as a 'dry' ship, he found that he had been sleeping over a couple of cases of beer. They wouldn't make a comfortable bed, but on the other hand . . . so he cracked a can and drank it. 'It seemed the right thing to do at the time!'

It was getting near problem time for Peter. Because of *Tenacious*' aluminium hull, he couldn't guarantee the accuracy of his RDF fixes. He was making scanty use of the French Ploneis Consol beacon because reception was bad and had to rely a great deal on the Round Island Radio beacon coming up every sixth minute.

Gary steered throughout the 0400 to 0800 watch and Jim's watch was back on when Peter came on deck to take another fix on Round Island at 1030. Visibility was bad in the driving rain and the wind was still blowing around 50 knots. Normally Peter would take his RDF bearings from the hatch, standing on the companion ladder. Now this wasn't possible because, with the trysail set, the boom had been lashed down to the deck on the leeward side. Instead he knew that he would have to go aft into the cockpit to get a 'view' of the beacon which wouldn't be distorted by the boom. He packed the Brookes and Gatehouse RDF set into a plastic bag and took it on deck with the handset and earphones. He sat up on the weather deck and took his first bearing on Round Island. He was waiting for its call sign again on the six-minute cycle when *Tenacious* was laid flat.

A combination of two waves picked up the boat and threw her on her side. Peter had not bothered to put a harness on and when he went flying through the air he thought that he had 'had it'. A breaking wave carried him across the boat and aft at the same time. In his flight he hit the steering wheel and bent it and then he hit the leeward life-lines. He was saved by Jim Mattingley falling on top of him. Jim was steering at the time and was quickly up behind the now bent wheel as the big boat came upright again. Peter now had one hand firmly around a stanchion; in the other was the Brookes and Gatehouse handset. The earphones were still on his head but their wires went nowhere. The plastic bag was still in the cockpit but the main part of the RDF set had gone over the side.

Throughout the hours of darkness the helmsmen of *Tenacious* had been worried about hitting other boats coming the other way. They were sailing back on a reciprocal course and saw a lot of lights activity. In the huge seas it was difficult to judge distance and waves tended to throw boats together. It had been easier to bear off to take avoiding action than to luff, and each time this action was taken it put another possible inaccuracy in the navigator's dead-reckoning plot.

By 1100 Peter put the Bishop Rock about four miles abeam to leeward and *Tenacious* was made ready for the run south of the Scillies to Plymouth. The mainsail was hoisted and the trysail taken in and two headsails were set on the forestay; the reaches to leeward and the number two genoa poled out to windward as *Tenacious* ran square on starboard gybe. They held this course and sail combination until due south of the Wolf Rock when the decision was made to hoist a spinnaker because the wind had begun to moderate. Before they did so, however, they gybed and *Tenacious* was then on course for Plymouth.

It was at this time that the crew of *Tenacious* became aware of the proportions of the disaster caused by the storm. Peter had listened to the 1355 shipping forecast and had left the radio on, through the loud-speakers, while the BBC news bulletin was read. Ted Turner's fears were founded.

The first spinnaker that was hoisted was the dacron flanker, a narrow-headed reaching sail which doubled as storm spinnaker. As the wind moderated further it gave way to a full sized 2.2 ounce nylon tri-radial and finally to the 1.5 ounce tri-radial. *Tenacious'* crew were driving the boat as hard as Ted was driving them. He knew that he must have a good chance of doing well in the race.

At 1755 *Tenacious* was south of the Lizard as Peter listened for the shipping forecast. It was preceded by a request for all Fastnet competitors to report their position, so immediately after noting the details of the forecast, Peter radioed the Lizard Coastguard.

The Fastnet race finishing line 'runs in a direction 314° true from the centre of the lighthouse situated at the western end of the Plymouth Breakwater'. *Tenacious* crossed it in daylight at 2222 and on board there was a fair amount of lighthearted horseplay. The boat and crew had done well but now they were going to have to wait for quite a while before they were certain that they had won.

I have seen Ted Turner in this situation before and the behaviour pattern in Plymouth was totally predictable. After a night's sleep ashore Ted was down at the Race Control Centre in the morning, eager for information. His jaws were clamped onto a fat cigar and his grey and white engine-driver's hat at a jaunty angle on his head. He strutted around, collecting a small crowd eager to hear his witticisms — some are totally unrepeatable.

Ted is a man steeped in the knowledge of naval history, and for him

Plymouth has added attractions. It didn't stop him making one comment when he was asked if he had expected wind and sea conditions like those of Monday night. He removed the cigar from his lips and drawled: 'Sure, you know it blows out there. If it hadn't been for a blow like that some years ago, you might all be speaking Spanish now.' Almost in the shadow of the statue of Drake on the Hoe this might have been too much to take from anyone of a lesser character than Turner.

By late afternoon it became obvious that there was no boat that could beat *Tenacious*. There was one awful moment for Ted when a retiring Class V boat was timed as a finisher and given a corrected time far better than that of *Tenacious*, but that was cleared up after a while. Turner and his crew could then celebrate the win they richly deserved, but even their celebrations were tinged with regret for those who had died. There was no denying Ted one thing: his name was on the Fastnet Cup.

Peter too was celebrating his own unique success. He was found with friends the next day having a 'quiet little drink' at the biennial gathering of ocean racing crews at the Greyhound close to the gates of Millbay Docks. At the subdued prizegiving at the Guildhall the following evening, Peter collected the Alf Loomis Trophy for the winning navigator but his moment really came six months later in Florida when Ted Turner and Chuck Kirsch presented him with the Golden Dividers Trophy to mark his triple crown.

CONDOR OF BERMUDA

Condor of Bermuda is a 78-foot sloop designed by John Sharp and built by Bowman Yachts at Emsworth. As *Heath's Condor* she was jointly skippered by Robin Knox-Johnston and Leslie Williams in the 1977/78 Whitbread Round-the-World Race. In that race she achieved some renown by being first home to Portsmouth but more by shedding her carbon-fibre mast off the west coast of Africa on the first leg. Since then she has been radically altered in the keel, stern sections and rig, to design modifications of David Pedrick.

For *Condor* and her crew the Fastnet Race was another opportunity for a head-to-head battle with her old and formidable rival *Kialoa*. Jim Kilroy's American 79-footer had been re-rigged as a sloop and had had stern modifications, also to designs by Pedrick. They had raced together in Antigua and in the Transatlantic Race and the honours were in

Kialoa's favour. Bob Bell, *Condor*'s owner, sought to redress the situation. There was also *Kialoa*'s course record of seventy-nine hours, eleven minutes and forty-eight seconds at stake and the maxi-raters always like to have a crack at records.

By the time they reached the Fastnet Rock, the schedule for the record was well behind. The passage out had been slow. The big boats don't like the light airs. *Kialoa* held the advantage; she went round the Rock at 1250 on Monday, forty-six hours and twenty minutes after leaving Cowes. At this time the Class V boats were just emerging from Mounts Bay to round Land's End. The maxis were nearly 200 miles ahead with 251 miles to go. To beat her own record *Kialoa* had to come home in under thirty-three hours, and this appeared out of the question with the light airs that they had at the time. The stronger winds hadn't even been forecast.

Condor was an hour and seven minutes behind the leader at the Rock. Peter Blake, her skipper, was not dispirited. He knew the American boat had the edge in light weather but he was certain the boot would be on the other foot if it blew hard. There were, he argued, low pressure areas coming across the Atlantic, and these would bring plenty of wind – if only it came in time.

There was a southerly wind blowing at about force 3 when *Condor* left the Rock. Blake believed that the wind, when it strengthened, would veer and so planned his strategy accordingly. Instead of sailing close-hauled he had the crew set the number one reacher with a genoa staysail and, with this double-head rig, close-reached to get maximum speed. Peter reckoned that the navigator was going to earn his keep on the leg back to the Bishop Rock. If his strategy was to work he needed to know exactly where he was at any time to plan his next move if and when the wind shifted.

Condor was therefore a long way back from the Rock when the wind began to blow hard. Peter called for gradual reduction in the sail plan as the wind increased. The staysail was the first to go and then came a reef in the mainsail followed by the number two genoa for the reacher. *Condor*'s twenty-four-man crew were working all the time. The sails were big and heavy and each one had to be flaked and bagged before it went down below.

Peter knew from the sky before dark that this was no ordinary blow coming on and made sure that all the storm gear was prepared. He checked out the spitfire staysail and the storm jib and all the emergency equipment.

Andrew Spedding, known to everyone as 'Spud', was *Condor*'s navigator. He is a very funny man but this was no time to test his humour. He was using the Consol beacon, Ploneis, near Quimper in Britanny, as a major part of his navigational plot together with the other direction-finder beacons to back his dead-reckoning. He had heard the weather forecasts and making his own prognoses realised that that night they would have more than enough wind.

The sails were progressively reduced until all that was set was the storm jib and a triple-reefed mainsail. *Condor* often had her lee rail under and was knocked flat on more than one occasion, but Peter says that there was nothing that gave him a great deal of anxiety. At times the sea conditions were worse than those of the Southern Oceans, but only because the waves were close together. Had she been cruising, Peter would have taken down the mainsail and replaced it with a trysail, but *Condor* was racing and there was a chance that she could take *Kialoa* and her record.

Racing these bigger boats is quite different from racing the Class V boats. The maxis are able to cope with more extreme conditions with greater ease and while it was tough going to race through the height of the Fastnet storm, it was more feasible for the big boats.

At the height of the storm, while *Condor* was on course for her rounding of the Bishop Rock, the pressures on navigator 'Spud' became heavier than usual. Not only was *Condor* travelling fast towards an unfriendly lee shore with low visibility but also, using her powerful radio transmitters, she was relaying distress calls from yachts to the rescue services.

It is ninety-nine miles from the Bishop Rock to the Fastnet Race finishing line off the breakwater at Plymouth. By the time she was on this leg it was obvious to all on board *Condor* that the race record was going to tumble. But her crew had no idea of where *Kialoa* was. All they could do was race as hard as possible. And that is what they did. Once inside the shelter of the Lizard, Peter piled on the pressure. *Condor* was on a very broad reach in a north-westerly wind. It was still blowing force 8 but the sea conditions were nowhere near as severe when Peter called for a spinnaker.

In her very adequate wardrobe *Condor* has a red, white and blue tri-radial spinnaker from the Butler Verner loft. Its nylon has very elastic properties and is therefore able to withstand strong gusts in a way that a newer, stretch-resistant nylon sail would not. Up it went and *Condor* took off, surfing down the waves at speeds well in excess of 20 knots.

It couldn't last, however, and it was certain that she would broach eventually. When she did she surprised everyone by the suddenness of the move and by the extent to which she went.

Peter Blake later described it as a 'three-point turn'. *Condor* turned round through 180° and the spinnaker was blown back on to the mast and spreaders. *Condor* started to make a sternboard and Peter reversed the wheel and steered *Condor* out of the situation backwards. The boat spun round, faced her proper course, the spinnaker filled and *Condor* was on her way again. Not a manoeuvre to be recommended.

The extra speed gained by hoisting the spinnaker was the telling factor in the *Condor* v. *Kialoa* duel. *Condor* pressed on through the driving rain and bad visibility and finally crossed the finishing line at 1355 on Tuesday, twenty-eight and a half minutes ahead of *Kialoa*. Her elapsed time of seventy-one hours, twenty-five minutes and twenty-three seconds was seven and threequarter hours better than *Kialoa*'s record. And to rub salt further into the wound, *Condor* also beat *Kialoa* on corrected time by six minutes, even with *Kialoa* claiming an age allowance in her handicap.

POLICE CAR

Police Car is one of the more extreme boats designed and built to the IOR. She is a two-tonner of light displacement, built in aluminium alloy with a threequarter rig. *Police Car* is owned and skippered by Peter Cantwell and was a member of the victorious Australian Admiral's Cup team. She was designed by Ed Dubois.

Peter had had a mixed season in Britain with *Police Car*, perhaps because she didn't appear to be as happy with light winds as she did with the fresher breezes, certainly her showing in the Two Ton Cup at Poole had not been what had been expected of her. But in the Admiral's Cup races prior to the Fastnet, she had found things very much to her liking. The fractional rig gave her more control downwind, whilst upwind her crew were able to adjust her large mainsail to suit the wind conditions far more quickly than those of her rivals. Before the Fastnet began Peter expressed the desire for a good blow to pull up the points that *Police Car* would need to beat *Eclipse* for the prize of best individual boat overall in the series.

Police Car cleared the Runnelstone off Land's End at 0110 on Monday and headed out on a rhumb-line course for the Fastnet Rock. She was two-sail reaching on port tack. The Seven Stones light was abeam at 0300 and there was little indication of what was in store. By 0715 the wind had freed sufficiently for the spinnaker to be hoisted but it moderated until it was 'quite soft'. Navigator Ron Packer recorded just over four nautical miles on the log and this speed continued until 1130. Then the wind began to strengthen to about as much as they could handle with full mainsail and spinnaker set on a close-reach, with the apparent wind at over 20 knots and 105° apparent angle to the bow.

Soon after Packer had listened to the 1355 shipping forecast the wind changed quite dramatically until *Police Car* was forced to take down her spinnaker and come hard on the wind on the opposite tack to steer 310°. Twenty minutes later she tacked on to starboard as the wind swung again and she held this tack until 1600 when she was able to tack back on to port and hold a course of 345°. By 1830 the wind and the boat speed were up. The wind had freed so that *Police Car* was now carrying a spinnaker and full mainsail and she was scudding along at 10 knots. This was what Peter and the crew had been waiting for. In these conditions *Police Car* was able to sail well above her handicap rating and, hopefully, gain on *Eclipse*.

In the hour to 2200 *Police Car* logged eleven and a half nautical miles and at times her speedometer was clocking 19 knots as she surfed on the faces of the waves. Packer recalls one prolonged surf of around twenty seconds at this speed as 'mind boggling'. At 2203 when he was preparing to report *Police Car*'s position on the radio, as requested for Admiral's Cup yachts, she dug her nose into a wave and green water came back across the deck; it was still about three feet deep when it passed the mast. *Police Car* almost stood on her bow. Kevin Williamson was on the spinnaker sheet and he let it fly to help the bow come out of the water. It did, but the snap shackle on the end of the spinnaker sheet had flogged itself undone and so the sail had to come down. This was no easy task on a pitching foredeck with the boat still hurtling along under full mainsail in more than 30 knots of wind. By using the lazy guy the crew were able to pull the sail down and stow it below.

There was considerable discussion as to what sail should be hoisted to replace the spinnaker; the wind had risen to the extent that there was no chance of putting the tri-radial blue and white spinnaker back up again. The first thought was to use the number two genoa, set as a spinnaker with the tack out at the pole end and the clew on the sheet. The bag came up through the hatch, but by then the wind was stronger and the decision changed to the number three set normally. While the sails were being exchanged through the hatch the decision was altered yet again and the call came for the number four genoa, the tiniest headsail apart from the storm jib. The final decision was that even this sail would be too much and it was about time the main was reefed. The extent of the increase in wind can be gauged by the action of *Police Car*'s crew at this time. They took in one reef and immediately took in another two as well. While they were lacing the unused part of the sail to the boom, somehow, in the darkness, the lower running backstay, which was slack, was laced in as well. No one noticed it at the time and *Police Car* thundered along on a close-reach at 9 knots.

By now the seas were building up to forty-foot waves. *Police Car* had very little sail up; the triple-reefed main was reduced to only thirty per cent of its original area. This was as much as she could carry and she might have been better off with a trysail only, but since the rules did not require one, she was not carrying this sail. The wind angle was 50-60° apparent and there were more than 50 knots across the deck by 2300. Ron had read the synoptic situation rather better than the forecasters and had warned the skipper and the two principal helmsmen, his brother Chris, and Chris Bouzaid, well in advance that they could expect at least force 9.

Navigation in these conditions was not easy and according to Ron, 'Finding the Rock in daylight in those seas would have been extremely difficult.' At night with its light the Rock was a little more obvious. Galley Head light was their first sighting and from its position a course to the Fastnet was laid. *Police Car* reached the Fastnet Rock at 0230. Waves were breaking all over the Rock and the lighthouse and the crew could see *Noryema* rounding at the same time.

As they tacked, the problem of the lower runner laced in with the mainsail became immediately apparent. A quick slash with a knife to the lacing freed it but it meant that the unused part of the mainsail had to be re-laced. With the apparent wind now further aft, the boat could carry more sail to advantage and the number four genoa was hoisted. Ron Packer said the boat was going fast without the genoa but 'simply flew' as soon as it was up and drawing. And she flew on for nearly three hours until Chris Packer, who was on the tiller at that time, decided that there was too much sail up and dropped the mainsail. The rest of the sail was lashed to the boom and the whole of it secured to the deck on the port side. Still *Police Car* romped along and then at

0550 the combination of a gust and a bad wave tipped the boat on its side. Ron recalls being thrown from his bunk across the short distance to the engine box; he then quickly made his way to the main hatch where Peter was trying to get out. *Police Car* righted herself very quickly, so fast in fact that Peter thought that the rig had broken. It hadn't and *Police Car* continued on her pell-mell way towards the Bishop Rock.

The mess below was fearful. A saucepan full of curry and rice, waiting for the crew to come off watch, had strewn its contents everywhere. The contents of the chart table drawer were spread around with food and gear. Miraculously only one jar (of pickles) had broken. Imagine the effect of a jar of instant coffee breaking; the thought did go through Ron's mind. He set-to to clear up the mess with Peter and John Blackman. On *Police Car* the off-watch crew's sleep is sacrosanct. The three men who had just come off-duty returned to their bunks to let Ron, Peter and John, who don't stand watches, get on with the job. John is the specialist foredeck crew and he, with Peter and Ron, answer the 'all hands' call of the on-watch crew. It is a system which works well. The watches rotate at three-hour intervals so that no one gets too tired.

Five out of the nine on board had been through weather similar to that which they were experiencing then. Chris Packer and John had been together in a yacht that had rolled over in the Indian Ocean while Chris Bouzaid is a veteran of the Southerly 'busters' of the Tasman Sea and the Bass Strait storms. He can also claim to have been picked up after going over the side at night in the One Ton Cup in Sardinia.

Half an hour after the first knockdown there was another and all the tidying up below had to be done again. *Police Car* righted herself quickly without damage but shortly did it all over again. A fourth knockdown came when Chris Bouzaid was steering and this time *Police Car* put her mast deep into the sea until she lay at $120°$ to her proper position. Once again she righted quickly and continued on track for the Bishop Rock.

By noon the wind began to moderate and the mainsail was hoisted, first with all the reefs in and they were later shaken out. Then it was discovered that there were hardly any winch handles left after the knockdown. They had all come out of the crew's pockets and fallen in the sea. There was one left on deck, which had been in a winch under the lashed down boom and mainsail, and another spare down below.

Police Car's crew rely on winches enormously; her mainsheet, for instance, is a two-part tackle with a winch on each end; without the handles they would have been embarrassed.

At 1530 they saw the French yacht *Jubilé* astern and this caused not a little consternation. *Jubilé* was a two-ton rival and in this race *Police Car* had to give her time. Up went the spinnaker to get more speed. *Police Car* was now running in big seas and a north-westerly wind. She had to gybe to get round the Bishop Rock and gybed back as she passed it at 2000 on Tuesday when the seas were 'quite dramatic'. Then the wind began to take off and the crew knew that the storm was over. They were on the last leg but the race was far from run.

With the big, left-over, sloppy sea and falling wind, downhill progress was not the easiest. *Police Car* was tacking downwind through 90° to keep up the best speed. She finished at lunchtime on Wednesday, fourth in the Admiral's Cup division, beaten by *Eclipse, Jubilé* and her team-mate *Impetuous*, giving her second best individual points score for the series.

Her crew did not see a flare throughout the storm. They were well to the west and to windward of the area where the most damage occurred, when it occurred. Ron says that the amount one sees in those conditions is minimal. Looking at the waves near the bow the spray stings the eyes, so the crew tend not to search the horizon all the time, only as a check in the immediate vicinity. Thus he felt there was little likelihood of their seeing flares from the distressed area. He had also had some difficulty in receiving radio transmissions and had had no communication with other yachts or the shore with either the VHF or the single-sideband transmitter that *Police Car* carried during the storm.

For navigation from the Fastnet to the Bishop Rock *Police Car* used the Consol beacon Ploneis at Quimper and had no difficulty in pinpointing the Bishop. On that leg she passed *Aries* and *Blizzard*, both much larger boats, because they had ended up very wide at the end of the leg and had to run in to the Bishop Rock from the west.

MORNING CLOUD

Morning Cloud is the best-known ocean racer in the world. Owned and skippered by former British Prime Minister, Edward Heath, the 44-foot *Morning Cloud* is scarcely ever out of the public gaze. In the Channel Race, which was held the weekend before the Fastnet Race, *Morning Cloud* made headlines by her enforced withdrawal when her carbon-fibre rudder broke. She had been the top points scorer in the British Admiral's Cup trials and Edward Heath was back again as captain of the team to defend the Cup.

Morning Cloud was designed by Ron Holland and built in 1977. That year she disappointed and did not make the Admiral's Cup team. In 1979 Owen Parker was back as sailing master and Edward Heath had invited a strongly talented crew to race with him.

At midnight on Monday *Morning Cloud* was broad-reaching for the Fastnet Rock, making her approach to the lighthouse from south of the rhumb line. The boat was surfing in the big seas under number four genoa and a triple-reefed mainsail. Peter Bateman was at the wheel. He had full control of the boat as the seas had yet to build up to the confused pattern that came with the veer in the wind, and for the next hour and three quarters it was relatively plain sailing as *Morning Cloud* closed with the Rock. There were five other boats in close proximity and these gave some trouble as they rounded the Fastnet just ahead of *Morning Cloud* forcing Peter to take avoiding action as the other boats came away from the Rock on starboard tack.

Starting the return passage *Morning Cloud* was close-hauled and racing hard; Peter continued to steer for another hour. The veer had begun and *Morning Cloud* was freed with it as the seas began to build into huge waves. Owen took over the steering from Peter who went below as Larry Marks came on deck. Larry and Peter were the two principal helmsmen in all the yacht's races for the season and it was not long after Larry came on deck that he took over the wheel from Owen. Owen's was an onerous job and he was beginning to tire.

Larry had been at the wheel for three quarters of an hour, with the seas continuing to build and becoming more confused as the secondary wave pattern became established, when one wave bigger than the others broke right alongside the yacht. It appeared as a vertical wall of water coming towards the boat and it broke over *Morning Cloud*. Larry saw water hit the top of the sails before it hit the deck and *Morning Cloud* was rolled over by it.

Chris Moody and Terry Leahy, who were on the weather side of the cockpit, were washed over the lee rails to the extent of their harness lines. Owen Parker went over the top of the wheel into the leeward rails and held on to them. Larry lost his grip on the wheel and was taken out over the stern pulpit which he bent. Luckily he just managed to grab the backstay as he was washed out astern. All were harnessed. *Morning Cloud* hung in the knocked down position for what seemed like eternity to those in the water but was probably no more than ten to fifteen seconds; then she flipped back quickly.

Terry and Chris crawled up the deck as they got back on board and Owen quickly grabbed the wheel. Larry felt himself being catapulted by the boat as it came upright and climbed back to the safety of the cockpit in double time. A quick head count revealed that no one was missing.

Down below the chaos was as bad, if not worse than it was on deck. Edward Heath, who had been working at the navigation table, was thrown across the boat and had gashed his leg. All the aluminium tubes that formed the bunk frames had come out of their cups and tipped out those sleeping. There was food everywhere. Cornflakes and eggs had redecorated the deckhead. Pat Lilley suffered the indignity of collecting four dozen eggs at once on his head. The contents of a pot of stew which had been on the stove were now splattered liberally around the cabin. The mess was appalling.

It was time for action. The spindle of the wheel had been bent due to a combination of Larry hanging on to it and Owen hitting it as the boat was knocked down, and while it was still possible to turn the wheel for the full traverse of the steering quadrant, it was not as easy as it should have been and there was doubt as to whether or not it would hold out. Confidence had been slightly shattered too.

Peter Bateman said of the incident, 'I don't know anyone on the boat who wasn't frightened and if you can show me one person who says that he wasn't frightened, from any of the boats out there that night, I will show you a liar.'

It was then around 0345 and the decision was made to take down the number four genoa and heave-to under the triple-reefed main until dawn. With the heavy overcast skies it didn't get light until around 0600 when the storm jib was set, the mainsail dropped and stowed and the trysail set. This took the best part of half an hour and *Morning Cloud* returned to course. While hove-to she had been making headway at 60° to her proper course, once the veer had been completed, but was making considerable leeway and the combination of these two factors kept her close to the rhumb line for the Bishop Rock.

Daylight brought some relief. Those on board were less fearful of the conditions although the storm was still raging. At least the helmsman could see the seas well in advance and could thus take avoiding action in good time. The boat was being cleaned up and thoughts were more generally in the direction of racing than purely of surviving.

Looking back on the hours of the storm Larry Marks says:
I was all right when I was committed in the action but no good
when I was down below thinking about it. I wouldn't, however,
have missed it for the world. I learned so much; I have so much
greater knowledge of how to deal with storms now that I feel
I can go to sea with greater confidence.

Chapter 5

THE STORM—
THE RESCUED SURVIVORS'
STORIES

'Nature cannot be ordered about, except by obeying her'

Francis Bacon
Novum Organon

FLASHLIGHT

Flashlight is an Ohlson 35 owned by the Royal Navy and in the charge of the Royal Naval Engineering College, Manadon. In the Fastnet she was skippered by Lt Commander Roger Gibbs with six crewmen. On Monday morning they were almost becalmed in Mounts Bay, drifting at first with a light genoa and full mainsail and then hoisting a floater spinnaker when an easterly breeze began. Around midday *Flashlight* and her crew rounded Land's End. Soon afterwards they peeled the ultra-light floater in favour of a tri-radial spinnaker as the wind began to increase. By 1430 they decided that, as there was a small hole or two in the tri-radial spinnaker, it would be best to peel that in favour of the star-cut and repair the holes. The wind was gradually freshening all the time. *Flashlight* was sailing a rhumb-line course for the Rock on port gybe. At 1900 the crew set the high clew reacher and doused the spinnaker. Progressively, as the wind increased, the crew reduced the amount of sail that the boat was carrying. First they put one reef in the main and changed the reacher for the number two genoa. Then they put a second reef in the main and while they were debating whether to change to the number three genoa, the wind rose more and a decision was made to put up the storm jib. By 2200 the only sail that *Flashlight* was carrying was a triple-reefed mainsail.

The seas were big, and down below Roger Gibbs found he had another problem with the yacht. The power from the batteries had fallen drastically. The engine was started but the batteries seemed unable to hold the charge — Gibbs believed that there was a massive leak to earth – and the yacht's electrics were all failing. The emergency navigation lights, which are powered by their own dry batteries, were rigged, and all power-draining instruments and lights switched off. Only the compass light was allowed to remain on and that, too, soon flickered and went out at 0200 on Monday. The loss of the log made navigation difficult. They were having to estimate position by guess-work and dead reckoning and they were beginning to suffer the worst of the storm. They pressed on towards the Rock all through the midnight to 0400 watch.

At the watch change Charlie Steavenson took over at the wheel and for an hour he had a tough job to stay there. Then the skipper made the decision to retire. The boat was not making much forward progress and weather conditions were appalling. He believed that in the shallower waters near the Rock itself, the seas would be too bad for *Flashlight* and that the most seamanlike thing to do would be to run off towards home. From their position fifteen miles south-east of the Fastnet Rock, it was a reaching course to Land's End. They reckoned they would have plenty of sea room for hours and planned to make a landfall in daylight.

Almost immediately a shackle in the mainsheet parted and the mainsail had to come down. The storm jib was hoisted and *Flashlight*, now with John Pennington at the wheel, reached on a south-easterly course for Land's End without incident.

At 0600 Pennington handed over the wheel to Steavenson and moved just in front of him on the starboard side to give the new helmsman some protection from the flying spray. He clipped his life-line on to the same D-ring as Steavenson's. As he looked over the starboard quarter he saw a massive rogue wave abeam (at the time the average wave height was thirty-five feet). There was no way to avoid it. Pennington shouted to Steavenson but almost instantly the boat began to pivot on the curling crest of the wave. *Flashlight* had no choice and two thirds of the way down the face of the wave, she was pooped. Pennington grabbed a winch with both hands and hung on, shouting 'Look out!' as the boat was pitchpoled.

He described the sensation as one of tumbling in the water and he had no idea of the position of the boat. Neither did any of the crew in the darkness below. He felt himself being dragged by his life-line and reached up to grab one of the pushpit rails as the boat came upright again.

At this time Roger Gibbs came up into the cockpit to help Pennington back on board. Pennington looked round for his two watchmates, helmsman Charlie Steavenson and Russell Brown. Both were in the water some way astern of the boat. It was quite light now and their brightly coloured oilskin jackets were easily visible. Steavenson's lifeline had parted one foot from where it was hooked on to the D-ring; Brown's was believed to have been clipped to a guard rail which had also parted.

The skipper called for all hands. Pennington, who was badly cut on the head, sat aft and kept his eyes firmly on the position of the two men overboard. Gibbs took the wheel and tried to bring the boat about, while Jim Mant and Derek Jones endeavoured to start the engine by hand. They tried unsuccessfully for a couple of minutes while Gibbs abandoned his attempts to tack *Flashlight* in favour of gybing round. John Wells went to give Jones a hand with the engine while Mant trimmed sheets. Two minutes later the diesel barked into life.

Flashlight was able to make headway back to the two men, but by now one of them had disappeared under the waves and was not seen again. The crew willed *Flashlight* back to the one survivor in the water. They were within five yards of him when a wave knocked the boat back and went over the top of the man in the water. As *Flashlight*'s crew watched, the man went under and did not re-appear. After a short search for the two missing men, Roger Gibbs had a hard decision to make: he had to abandon the search in order to preserve the lives of those still on board.

First, he had to patch up Pennington's cut on his head. By this time it was almost eight o'clock and Pennington was beginning to feel exposure symptoms. He was put below in a pilot berth on the port side after his cut had been attended to. Mant was trying to make some hot Oxo when the boat rolled 90° to leeward and then lurched back with a roll of 90° to windward. Pennington came right out of the pilot berth, fell across the cabin, and was pitched back into the bunk when the boat came upright. Mant's attempts at hot Oxo were somewhat strewn about.

This wild rolling put an S-bend in the mast which was only spotted when it was noticed that the port lower shroud had gone slack. At 0830 it was decided to lower the storm jib and lie-a-hull to prevent further rolling. The wheel was lashed amidships, and the five survivors went below and battened the hatches until 1600. The boat, meanwhile, was doing between 1 and 2 knots through the water and making 45° leeway.

Morale was at a low ebb. These men had seen two of their companions drown. They themselves had been badly shaken up physically. Fortunately the boat was not too badly damaged. When she had rolled right over, the storm boards had been in place and the companion hatch was shut so a minimum amount of water had gone below. They had been able to pump out this water without too much difficulty and it had never come above the level of the floorboards. But they were miserable about the two men who were lost and the fearful conditions on deck. Now, sitting down below, they had time to think about their lot.

At 1600 the wind had moderated sufficiently to get under way again. In fact it had done so earlier but they were too low to appreciate it. As they came up through the hatch they heard the sound of a helicopter and as soon as it came in sight, they fired off a red parachute flare to attract its attention and put out an orange smoke flare to pinpoint their position. The helicopter came overhead and the winchman, turning his thumbs upwards, asked if they wanted lifting off. Roger Gibbs agreed and Derek Jones was first to be lifted. He jumped into the water with a lifejacket on and as he was drifting away from the boat the winchman clipped him on and he was lifted into the helicopter. Because of fuel problems there was only time to take Jones and a second helicopter arrived half an hour later to take the other four to RNAS Culdrose.

Before they left *Flashlight*, her crew battened down the hatches and secured all her gear. She was later found by a Cornish fishing vessel and towed into Penzance before being returned to the Royal Navy and the Engineering College, Manadon.

CHARIOTEER

Charioteer was one of the eleven Doug Peterson designed OOD 34s built by Jeremy Rogers that took part in the Fastnet Race. She was owned and skippered by Dr John Coldrey and sailed with a seven man crew.

On Monday afternoon *Charioteer* was reaching towards the Fastnet Rock under a single-reefed mainsail and number two genoa in force 7 winds from the south-west. In the early evening the wind abated somewhat and the watch, consisting of Colin Rowley, Francis Williams and Keith Brimacombe, were able to shake out the reef and change up to the number one genoa. All of the crew were aware of the gale warning issued at 1755 and as Jeremy Heal, Aubrey Denton and Rod Newbolt-Young came on watch, the weather was such to make them wonder whether 'the Met. Office had pursued their summer practice of exaggerating wind strength for the sake of dithering yachtsmen', to use Jeremy's words. (This belief is shared by others. All too often the Meteorological Office shipping forecasts, broadcast on 1500 metres by the BBC, are seemingly an overstatement of wind strengths that do occur around the coast. Further out at sea they are more often than not correct and for this reason the shipping forecasts take the form they do; but it tends to make those who sail in coastal waters believe that the Meteorological Office does cry wolf.) At the time Jeremy believed that they had already experienced the weather which had been forecast but now admits 'We and the Met. Office were both wrong.'

Soon after the watch change it became apparent that there was too much sail up and the wind was increasing fast. One reef was put in the main and the number three genoa replaced the number one. *Charioteer* was screaming towards the Fastnet at 8 knots. As it grew dark, so the wind blew stronger and by 2330 Rod was pushing the skipper for a second reef in the main. John Coldrey hung on for a while; *Charioteer* was racing and he wanted to make the most of the favourable wind even if it meant pressing the boat for a while. Eventually, around midnight, the second reef had to go in and there were complications. The radar reflector had been hoisted up the backstay by the fixed-length topping lift and this topping lift was an essential part of the reefing procedure as the reefing pennants had been used for the flattening and first reefs. The topping lift was therefore needed when the crew were trying to get the reefing pennant into the second cringle on the leech.

Jeremy was steering while the skipper performed the difficult task of retrieving the topping lift and reeving the reef pennant. By the time he had got it all sorted out, the wind had increased further and so fast that there was no need for the mainsail at all. The watch changed, Keith, Francis and Colin coming on deck. After a while the wind strength had increased until the windspeed indicator was regularly showing 40 to 45 knots and *Charioteer* was once again carrying too much sail.

The storm jib replaced the number three and after a time that too came off as the skipper decided to lie a-hull. Immediately, the boat became more comfortable. The seas were enormous and broken but a fantastic sight. John and Jeremy both describe the phosphorescence in the spindrift and for John it was like 'so many green fireflies'. Down below the off-watch crew slept.

Then *Charioteer* suffered a series of knockdowns. In the first one Keith was washed out of the cockpit while not attached by his life-line and he saved himself by grabbing the main boom. Jeremy, aided he says by his young officer training in the Royal Marines, slept for most of his off-watch without being disturbed. When he woke, Rod and Aubrey were getting dressed when another wave hit the boat and produced a near knockdown which sent Aubrey, who was struggling with his sea-boots, across the cabin where he struck his head and back. John took one look at him and sent him back to his bunk as he appeared con-cussed. Rod and Jeremy went on deck to relieve Keith and Colin while Francis stayed at the tiller.

At this time the motor was running to charge the batteries and there was some discussion between the skipper and Aubrey (whose company makes the engines that go into the OOD 34s) as to the advisability of putting the engine in gear to hold a better heading and retiring from the race. The decision was taken to press on.

Jeremy was feeling decidedly queasy. During his last watch he had swallowed a considerable amount of sea water and its presence in his stomach was making itself felt. He asked for the seasick pills as he went on watch; they appeared from Colin's pocket. They were perhaps too late to be of real use; maybe a placebo would have been just as effective. The wind had now begun to scream in the rigging and it was pulling the skin on the faces of the crew as they looked into it.

During the remaining hours of darkness *Charioteer* was knocked down three more times. Those in the cockpit were washed or thrown to the leeward side of the boat. Jeremy was feeling badly sick by now; the battering in the cockpit was draining his reserves although not his morale. He says: 'I was sick once during this time and lifted to such a state of euphoria by the ecstatic relief of vomiting out the salt water that Rod and I were once caught respectively yelling and singing with exhilaration at the tops of our voices.'

Another yacht passed within fifty yards to windward. All that *Charioteer*'s crew saw of her was her navigation lights, her storm jib and her instrument lights as she swept past at great speed. Both Rod and Francis had been worried when they saw her navigation lights coming up from astern, believing her to be on a collision course with *Charioteer*; Francis went as far as to suggest putting the engine in gear to get out of her way.

The waves were by now at mast height — at least the biggest ones were — about forty feet. The wind was way off the scale of the wind-speed meter (it stops at 60 knots). Conditions were appalling but eventually dawn came bringing some comfort. *Charioteer* was sliding down the big waves like a Malibu surf board. At 0605 the yacht was fifty miles from the Fastnet, Jeremy was vomiting over the lee side (Rod had just checked his harness), Francis was on the tiller and Rod was on the weather side just forward of the helmsman.

It was then that *Charioteer* was overwhelmed. Rod describes it:
At this time I noticed a huge wave building to windward. It seemed to remain motionless just drawing water from in front of it and getting bigger . . . it seemed sheer with a white top and it seemed taller than the others, taller than the mast-head . . . I thought it would flatten but it just got bigger and steeper and then it came. I shouted a warning . . . it was a tremendous impact. We, in the cockpit were thrown headlong into the sea . . . everything went dark . . . I saw stars. I was being dragged underwater by my harness at a tremendous speed (I thought to the bottom) and then everything stopped and I was on the surface with the top of the mast in front of me. I thought at first that the boat had gone down and that I was the sole survivor but then I heard voices behind me and saw the boat upright, her mast snapped.
The skipper and the off-watch crew were down below. There was as much chaos there as on deck. John was hit on the back of the head and neck by the cooker which came adrift from its gimbals. He sustained a seven-inch gash to his head and was later found to have fractured a cervical vertebra.

The three crewmen in the bunks had been tipped out and thrown around badly. There were other hazards below. The batteries had torn themselves free of their containers and food and gear had come out of all the lockers. There was a lot of water in the cabin and one of the cabin windows had been knocked out complete with its mounting. All four made to get out of the hatch. For John, who was first on deck, it was frightening. At first he could not see his three crewmates in the water and thought they had all been washed away. He turned into the cabin from the companionway and said, 'Oh, my God! They've gone.' Francis shouted from the water and only then did the skipper realise that they were relatively all right.

'Relatively' is the correct word. *Charioteer* had performed a full 360° roll and with the mast broken in two places there was rigging around the boat. Rod was caught up in it and he had received a massive blow on the face which had split his lip and broken three of his teeth. Aubrey and John had been able to get Francis and Jeremy back on board while Rod shouted for help. He was trapped by his harness in the rigging of the broken mast and he feared that he would be crushed to death if the boat rolled again. Every movement applied an agonising pressure on his chest from the mast. Jeremy and John went to his aid and tried to undo the deck attachment of the harness but it was too tight. Eventually with some clearing of the rigging Rod was able to undo his harness and slip out of it to climb back on board.

Rod then remembered that he had seen the lights of a ship before the boat had rolled and called for a flare. Colin handed him one immediately – an emergency flare, one of the hand-held type. The container with the full quota of flares was then passed up from below and Jeremy began to fire parachute flares. Considering he had been trained in the use of flares by the Royal Marines, it was strange that he got the first one wrong. In his own words: 'Despite my following the instructions and my familiarity with that type of flare, the first I let off went straight into my foot, causing me my only injury, before doing several laps of honour around the cockpit.' The second one went skywards. Rod meantime was undoing the plastic wrappings of some hand flares with his broken teeth and after one false start when the striker went overboard, he had one of these alight. The nearby French trawler, *Massingy*, saw these and headed to give assistance.

On board *Charioteer* the crew prepared to be taken off. The life-raft was got ready as a possible means of transport to the trawler and the crew all donned lifejackets. Rod went below to get his wallet and was shocked by what he saw there.

It looked as if everything had come away from its fittings and just been dumped on the floor. The cooker had come away and was lying upside down on the floor and there was a hissing noise. The mast had come away from its stepping and was wagging around in the cabin, the heads bulkhead had come away and was just resting against something and the starboard forward cabin window was broken. However, the one thing that I will always remember was the ghastly stench below; it was a combination of whisky, gin, diesel, sulphuric acid, and blood; and that hissing noise.

Rod checked the gas safety tap and found it closed. He then went forward to retrieve his wallet from his jacket and found that all the clothing in the locker was bone dry. He couldn't resist trying on his jacket, but 'it wouldn't fit with lifejacket and all!' He went back on deck to find *Massingy* coming alongside.

All seven were successfully transferred to the trawler leaving *Charioteer* to the mercy of the waves. On the quarter deck of the trawler John looked at Jeremy and with a bloodied smile said something about £30,000 before they were whisked away down below to the crew's quarters.

Charioteer has not been found and is presumed to have sunk.

TROPHY

Trophy is an Oyster 37 designed by Holman & Pye, owned and skippered by Alan Bartlett. She is based at Burnham on Crouch and was sailed in the 1979 Fastnet with a crew of eight in Class III. *Trophy* was one of ten Oyster 37s that took part in the race.

Once they had cleared the calms off Land's End the crew were enjoying some good sailing with a perfect breeze and the spinnaker up. When they heard Monday's 1355 shipping forecast with its threat of force 7, they took note but felt that it was a little unreal in view of the conditions they were experiencing. They were even more amazed at the gale warning which they heard at 1505.

In the early evening a stronger breeze made its presence felt, and when the wind veered somewhat, it was decided to hand the spinnaker for the number one genoa and also to take one reef in the mainsail. At 2000, on the watch change, the wind increased and so quickly that the number one was exchanged for the number three and at the same time the mainsail was taken off, stowed on the boom and the boom lashed down to the deck on the starboard side. With just the number three genoa up, *Trophy* was making good progress towards the Fastnet Rock. Robin Bowyer, the navigator, John Puxley, Dick Mann and the skipper went below, off watch.

On deck were Simon Fleming, Derek Moreland, Russell Smith and Peter Everson. An hour after the watch change they saw a red parachute flare and shouted for all hands. Alan recalls that they didn't assume it was from a boat in distress, although the wind was now well over the 50 knots that their windspeed indicator registered, rather they felt that it was a case of someone overboard and immediately went to see if they could help.

It took them an hour to get to the area where the flare was fired; the big Perkins diesel engine was used to supplement the power of the number three genoa. When they reached the area they found it was *Allamanda* who had sent the flare. *Trophy* slowly manoeuvred in close enough to hail Michael Campbell and his crew and ascertained that there was no one missing.

Alan did not want to get too close as there was a danger of smashing the two boats together, but he held station off *Allamanda*. Shortly after he had hailed *Allamanda, Morningtown* arrived and both boats took up station so that they were well clear of each other.

The waves were getting very big; estimates of their height vary but conservatively they were more than thirty feet from trough to crest. *Trophy* went into one of them and was knocked backwards. The wheel went dead. Alan thought the steering wires had jumped the quadrant but an examination of these proved him wrong. Nevertheless, the emergency tiller was brought out and fitted. Only then was it realised that the rudder itself had sheared off.

With no steering, the only course of action open to Alan and his crew at the time, was to lie a-hull without the genoa set. This they did very successfully until midnight. On watch at that time were the skipper, Peter and Russell; the other five were sleeping down below. Despite the disablement of the yacht all on board were happy. Then one almighty wave hit *Trophy*.

Russell said afterwards that it broke above the masthead before it overwhelmed the boat, which means it must have been fifty foot high, at the very least. When it hit the yacht, it rolled her like a toy, turning her through 180°, and there she stayed for a few seconds. Just how long can only be judged by the fact that those below were able to stand and gain their balance on the deckhead before she righted herself.

Peter and Russell in the cockpit stayed where they were when the boat rolled and breathed the air trapped in the cockpit when the boat was upside down. Alan was clipped to the starboard toe-rail and was thrown clear of the boat as it rolled starboard over port. When the boat completed the roll, he was dragged under by his safety harness and surfaced close to the side of the boat. Simon and Derek, coming on deck, tried to help him on board through the life-lines. This was difficult because his safety line was over the top of the life-lines. Eventually they got him on board after unclipping his safety line.

Down below, the conditions were chaotic. There was about two feet of water in the cabin. Meanwhile the broken mast was banging against the side of the boat and in the big seas there seemed every chance that *Trophy* was going to roll again. Alan and members of the crew didn't think that she would survive another roll. They believed the yacht would sink, taking them with her to the bottom. The decision was then made to launch the life-raft.

When they went to board the raft they found that the entrance was on the far side, and boarding it through the observation hatch in full clothes with inflated lifejackets was far from easy. Alan had lost his lifejacket when he was pulled on board after the knockdown but all the others were wearing theirs. Dick Mann found three parachute flares before he boarded the raft and he stuck these in his foul weather jacket pocket. What they had lost, however, was all of *Trophy*'s torches, which had been in the cockpit when she had rolled.

They were now sitting in the life-raft, all clothed but unaware of where the gear was stowed in it. It was 0030 and almost immediately the raft came alongside *Morningtown*. *Trophy*'s crew were worried about getting out of the raft alongside the yacht as they feared that the raft would tip up. One of the crew of *Morningtown* tried without success to grab hold of the raft when it was alongside. Soon afterwards the crew of *Trophy* had their worst fears confirmed as the raft was capsized by a wave. They were quickly able to right it again but they had lost the water-activated light. Simon then deployed the drogue but it didn't last long; its line parted after only a few minutes. Almost immediately the raft turned over again and the top half separated from the bottom, the two parts held together only by a tiny lanyard. It was now after 0100.

All eight men climbed into the bottom half of the raft but this was far from a safe refuge. It had only half its former buoyancy and water was coming in so fast that it was constantly waterlogged. Crew members were often washed out and the raft frequently capsized. It tipped up once too often and John Puxley and Peter Everson were washed clear of the raft. Alan could see them twelve yards away and the crew made a concerted effort to get the raft to them but they were drifting away from the raft too fast and finally they were lost from view. The distance had been just too much for them to swim. Alan himself had been tossed three yards from the raft and had to make a superhuman effort to get back to it; twelve yards was too much for the weakened men.

An hour before dawn the raft tipped again and the two halves parted completely. Simon, who was clipped on to the lower part, drifted off on it while the other five clung to the top half from which the canopy was missing. It was a desperate situation. Shortly, their number was

73

reduced to four, as they watched Robin Bowyer die and drift away. Morale dropped to an all-time low but merely the sound of a Nimrod gave them fresh hope and with it new strength to hold on to what remained of the life-raft. They talked to each other, offering encouragement now that they were aware that help was at hand. However, they were getting very cold in the water.

Then they heard a helicopter and saw it go off to pick up someone else. It was Simon. The pilot had spotted his oilskin jacket out of the corner of his eye as he made his approach to the four clinging to the top half of the raft. Once Simon had been successfully winched to safety the helicopter came over to the four. It first lifted Alan, who was without a life jacket, but, as the *Overijssel* was close, left the other three to be rescued by her.

It was almost half an hour before Dick, Russell and Derek were pulled on board the Dutch warship with the aid of frogmen. All three have the highest regard for the handling of the *Overijssel* and the courage of the men who came into the water to rescue them.

Trophy stayed afloat and was finally towed into Falmouth by a Swedish yachtsman on his way to Spain.

GRIFFIN AND LORELEI

The stories of these two yachts merge as one; one which shows a combination of courage, seamanship and humanity. *Griffin* was an OOD 34 owned by the RORC and skippered by Neil Graham. *Lorelei* is a SHE 36, a production boat designed by Sparkman and Stephens and built by South Hants Marine. She is owned and skippered by Alain Catherineau out of La Rochelle in France.

Griffin was run in conjunction with the National Sailing Centre at Cowes. For the race Neil, an instructor at the centre, had with him two fellow instructors, Stuart Quarrie and Peter Conway, and four trainees with a reasonable amount of training and experience between them. In addition they had just completed a week's racing training at the National Sailing Centre. As might be expected of this yacht, which was the last of a line to bear the name *Griffin* as the RORC's own club yacht, all those on board were thoroughly familiar with the emergency equipment. All would have known, almost instinctively, where each individual item was stowed; something which every skipper should, but certainly did not, check on with his crew. It was to prove important to *Griffin*'s crew in the early hours of Tuesday, August 14th.

Griffin had been pressed hard from Land's End out towards the Fastnet Rock. Under Graham's leadership the crew were working well together. He had extra responsibilities to his crew but he had a wealth of experience of heavy weather sailing to draw on. As the going got tougher and the wind blew more strongly, *Griffin*'s sails were reduced in size until by midnight on Monday they were down to a storm jib and three reefs in the mainsail. Eventually, at 0130, even this was too much for *Griffin*. Neil decided that with such huge seas and winds of more than 60 knots, *Griffin* would be better off lying a-hull under bare poles and so all sail was taken down. The mainsail was firmly lashed to the boom and *Griffin* began to fore-reach, 60 to 70° off the wind.

The three instructors were in the cockpit at 0200, all clipped on with their safety harnesses. The four trainees were down below. *Griffin* was forty miles from the Fastnet Rock and a few miles to the west of the rhumb line. The wind was from the starboard side and Stuart noticed a huge wave building up to weather. There was no way to avoid it. Neil, using his Australian terminology, described it as 'a dumper'.

Griffin rolled. She went over through 180° and stayed there.

As she rolled, the three in the cockpit were thrown violently into the sea and dragged along by their harnesses. Stuart's harness clip opened and released him from the boat. He was twelve feet from the boat but could see the strobe light that is attached to the horseshoe life-buoy in the stern, flashing underwater. Now that it was in the upright position it had automatically switched on. The keel of *Griffin* was sticking up in the air.

Neil and Peter were still attached to the boat and were underneath it, breathing the air that was trapped in the cockpit. By taking deep breaths and diving deeply they were able to unclip their harnesses before the boat came upright. At the same time the four down below were standing on the coachroof. Water was pouring in through the companionway hatch. The washboards dropped out when the boat inverted and the sliding hatch was pulled back by the force of the water.

It took another big wave to knock the inverted *Griffin* from this stable condition and once the keel was no longer atop dead centre she began to right slowly, but the effect of the lead keel was not what might have been expected. As the boat came upright, Stuart, Neil and Peter clambered back on board. The boat had only just made it. There was no more than three inches of freeboard and she was not far off sinking.

Neil Graham examined the state of the boat quickly and decided for safety's sake that the right course of action would be to abandon ship. Stuart pulled the eight-man Avon life-raft from its stowage and began its inflation. The painter was tied to the backstay. One of the trainees went below to get the flare pack and to do this he had to swim through the cabin. Most of the crew were well clothed but one, who had been in his sleeping bag, had on only a tee shirt and oilskin trousers. There was no difficulty getting into the raft since *Griffin* had settled with very little freeboard and despite the rough seas the raft stayed firm by the boat.

All seven were soon in the raft and that was when they encountered their first problem. The painter on the Avon life-raft is not on the same side of the raft as the entrance hatch and to cut it free from *Griffin* it was necessary to lean over the top of the life-raft which, in those conditions, was extremely dangerous.

As soon as they were in the raft they fired one red parachute flare. They planned to fire flares at regular intervals as they had two sets available; one full container from the boat and another, emergency pack on the raft. After three quarters of an hour and with one of the crew being sick through the entrance hatch, the raft capsized. Two men were pitched into the water. Neil got the other four in the raft to move to one side so that the raft righted itself. At the same time, however, the canopy was ripped from the raft and the raft began to lose its circular shape; the seas were compressing it into a lozenge shape. The two men who had been pitched into the sea were recovered to the raft.

Bailing now became an essential and the best tool for the purpose was found to be the flare container. This meant that the flares, in their plastic wrappings, were now swilling about in the bottom of the raft. Once the raft was bailed they fired another red parachute flare and set about sorting the emergency gear in the raft. It was badly stowed in their opinion. The inessentials, like paddles and bailer, were on top and the really necessary items for immediate use, like the flares, were at the bottom.

Later they saw the lights of a boat and fired another parachute flare and some hand flares to attract attention. The man in the tee shirt was beginning to suffer from exposure and hypothermia was setting in; the rest were in relatively good shape. Then morale had a huge boost; they saw a yacht coming towards them. They realised that with this sea running it would be a huge task of seamanship for the yacht to come alongside the raft and pick them up, but they had hope.

The yacht was *Lorelei*. Alain Catherineau raced his yacht with his wife, Jacqueline, and four others, Gérard, Marc, Thierry and Philippe. At 0230 on Tuesday *Lorelei* had more than 50 knots on the windspeed indicator and the number four genoa was set with the mainsail with three reefs. She was close-reaching, the apparent wind was 70° off the bow and the boat was going well, nicely balanced. There was little effort needed on the tiller. Thierry was at the helm and for an hour *Lorelei* overtook several boats. The wind increased and a call went out to take down the jib. Alain and Marc went forward to do this and while they were there Thierry shouted that he had seen a red flare go up to windward. Alain and Marc struggled to remove the jib and finally stowed it in a cockpit locker.

Lorelei was heading north and Alain was intent on finding the source of the flare. He believed he was too far to the north and made an attempt to bring *Lorelei* about. It took four attempts before the boat swung to a southerly course. He saw a hand-held flare lighting up the sky from time to time when the wave patterns were right. Alain asked Thierry to go to the west of the lights, not knowing what sort of boat in distress they might find.

Under a deep-reefed mainsail, *Lorelei* was moving slowly to windward of the area where Alain thought the flares were coming from when he saw, some fifty yards to windward, two small lights which appeared to be water-activated distress lights. It was 0330 and dark. Under the two lights was a barely discernible black shape. Alain realised that it was a life-raft and to use his words, 'What a sighting'.

The boat's speed was around 4 knots and Alain took the yacht on another fifty yards before tacking. Then, after the tack, he headed for the life-raft and passed within four yards and attempted to get a line aboard. It failed and two of *Griffin*'s crew fell out of the raft as they tried to grab the rope.

Alain took over at the tiller; he believed he knew his own boat best. He kicked the motor into life and set it in forward gear. He had to make several attempts to come alongside the raft, during which *Lorelei* was once knocked down so that her mast head was in the water, but she came up again quickly.

Eventually Alain was able to manoeuvre the yacht into the same wave pattern as the life-raft. He could see it twenty-five yards away and came in close, putting the engine into reverse to stop the yacht. (*Lorelei* had a variable pitch propellor which went quickly into reverse to stop the yacht.) The raft was but a yard away and Alain was worried lest the crew should not be able to catch it. Ropes were thrown as the life-raft began to drift away from *Lorelei*. Two of the ropes did reach the crew members of *Griffin* and they began to haul the life-raft back towards the French yacht. *Lorelei* proved difficult to control with no way on in the seas and Alain struggled with the engine controls and the tiller. At last the raft came alongside the yacht, tucked in under the starboard quarter to leeward.

Four of the men in the life-raft scampered easily on board *Lorelei*; three remained in the raft clinging to the stern pulpit of *Lorelei*. The life-raft began to move away but one of its occupants grabbed a rope again and hauled it back to *Lorelei*. A few seconds later Alain saw the life-raft drifting off again, but this time it was empty. The last three were in the water at the stern of the *Lorelei*, clinging on for their lives.

The first four rescued by *Lorelei* were taken below by Jacqueline and found clothes and bedding. Two of the three men clinging to the stern were hauled aboard but the third had no strength left. Alain passed a rope around his harness, but the harness started to ride up. Philippe grabbed his tee shirt, now all that he had on, and, helped by four others, managed to get the weakened *Griffin* crewman on board.

Jacqueline, the ship's doctor, took him below, got him into a bunk and covered him up to warm him. She thought that he was going to die because his nails were showing symptoms of cyanosis and he was shaking with cold continuously.

Alain was exhausted. He had had very little sleep since the race had started but now he had difficult decisions to make. There were now thirteen people on his yacht. It was heavily overloaded and the storm was at its height. The wrong choice of sails or course could have been disastrous. One of the radio direction finder sets had gone out of action but the consol set was working and the Ploneis beacon was coming through clearly on it.

Lorelei heeled violently, almost a knockdown. With that Alain called for a course south, now with the wind and waves. It was 0630 and *Lorelei* appeared to be coming out of the worst weather. The motion was still not good but breakfast of marmalade sandwiches and tea brightened them all.

The storm jib went up to ease the motion and to help progress when the wind had moderated, and the rest of the day was spent resting and sailing for Land's End. The weather moderated and *Lorelei* sailed between the Scillies and Land's End with a number two genoa set and a reefed mainsail at 1100 on Wednesday morning. Alain decided that the time had come to clear up the inside of *Lorelei*, so all the clothes and bedding were brought out on deck to dry. It took them an hour to clean up the boat, after which Gérard and Marc prepared the sort of meal that only the French would do on board a yacht in a race. The rescued began to feel easier and to help.

Plymouth was reached at 2300 that night. The end of an ordeal for the seven from *Griffin* and of an adventure for the six Frenchmen. It was a sequence of events that none of the thirteen is ever likely to forget.

For rescuing the crew of *Griffin* and abandoning the race to do so, the RORC awarded *Lorelei* joint second place in her class.

For outstanding seamanship and courage, Alain Catherineau was awarded the British 'Yachtsman of the Year' trophy at the London International Boat Show at Earls Court in January 1980.

ARIADNE

Ariadne is a threequarter tonner, cold-moulded in wood to designs by Dick Carter. She was owned and skippered by Frank Ferris, an American resident in Britain, and sailed with a crew of six. The 35-footer was well prepared for ocean racing and considerable extra effort had been made to ensure that she was ready for the Fastnet.

Early on Monday morning *Ariadne* was becalmed near Land's End and it wasn't until 1030 that the wind picked up. With a spinnaker and full mainsail set *Ariadne* began a rhumb-line course from Land's End to the Fastnet Rock. In mid-afternoon the wind veered so that it was no longer possible to hold course and a spinnaker. The high clew reacher was hoisted and the spinnaker dropped. Under this rig *Ariadne* continued on port tack as the wind increased in the early evening. By 2200 *Ariadne* was on the limit of carrying this sail combination. The wind was stronger and the seas were bigger and both were building fast.

Just as the decision to change down was made, a wave lifted *Ariadne*'s stern and she spun round in a broach. It was an all-hands job to get the reacher down and replace it with the number three genoa and at the same time put a reef in the main. At this time the wind was increasing fast; progress became difficult so a second reef was taken in the mainsail. This was soon followed by a reef in the number three genoa.

At midnight the wind was up to 60 knots and *Ariadne* was becoming unmanageable. Down below, Frank Ferris and Bill Le Fevre listened to the 0015 shipping forecast and realised that this was going to be a bad storm and conditions were certainly not going to improve for twelve hours. The mainsail had ripped when the crew were trying to get the third reef in and the boat was now working to windward under a reefed number three genoa and the helmsman could not hold the course. The skipper decided that the best course of action would be to run off downwind into open water under bare poles.

The reefed number three headsail was taken down and *Ariadne* turned downwind to run before the storm in the darkness and driving spray. Matthew Hunt, a young medical student in the crew, remembers the stinging pain of the spray blown into the eyes. It hurt so much that it was impossible to take more than a quick glance into the wind.

There were a lot of other competing yachts about *Ariadne* as she began to run off. Navigation lights approached from the starboard side and stern lights disappeared to port. Many of these boats crossing were quite close, too close for comfort in the huge seas that had started to run. By now the waves were cresting forty to forty-five feet and had two boats hit they could have smashed each other to smithereens.

Ariadne had little control under bare poles, so the storm jib was hoisted in an effort to improve her stability and steerage. It went up all right but didn't last long. Before half an hour had passed, it had split away from the luff wire and the tack and blew out over the stern attached to the sheet and halyard. It was no easy job retrieving the flogging sail.

All the warps and spare sheets were streamed astern in an effort to make *Ariadne* more controllable as she was steered straight downwind. Matthew says that she became more comfortable, particularly when the helmsman had become accustomed to keeping the boat on track; not the simplest of tasks under the conditions. David Crisp on the tiller was hoping that dawn would soon break so that he could see the seas and be able to deal with them more effectively. He was on watch with Rob Gilder at 0430 when the first sign of dawn began to chase the sky. Frank, Bill, Matthew and Bob Robie were down below, getting what rest they could. Matthew was dozing in the quarter berth when he felt the boat roll more violently than it had before. Rob was standing in the cockpit lighting a cigarette when *Ariadne* was picked up by a bigger than usual wave which crested under her side and flipped the boat until she was totally inverted. She stayed there in a stable condition for a minute with water pouring in through the companion hatch.

Another wave helped *Ariadne* from the capsize position, completing her roll through 360°. In the process the mast broke and part of it lay alongside the hull dangerously butting its jagged end against the wood. As the boat righted both Rob and David found themselves in the cockpit. David said later that it was a combination of two waves that had caused *Ariadne* to capsize. The first had lifted her stern and made her broach and before she could recover from the broach the second wave had hit her broadside on when she was at her most vulnerable.

Down below, Matthew was lucky that he was wedged into the quarter berth. Bill was not so lucky; he was thrown across the cabin and struck his head, splitting his skull. He was only semi-conscious when the boat righted. There was loose gear all over the place and water was up to waist-level in the cabin.

The first consideration was to get the water out of the boat as it made her less stable and thus in far greater danger of being rolled again. Bill's condition gave cause for concern. He was losing blood rapidly from the gash in his head, but with the safety of all six at stake bailing the boat took pride of place. It was now 0445.

The cockpit drains were a problem. One person kept them free of debris and bailed the cockpit whilst another was on the bilge pump. The rest were busy with buckets and saucepans, clearing out the water in the cabin. After forty-five minutes of intensive effort the amount of water was dramatically reduced; it was now only up to mid-shin. The crew were in good spirits again. No one seemed too worried any more and the odd joke was being cracked. Then another wave rolled *Ariadne*.

This time the boat took only ten seconds to rotate through 360°. David was on the helm, Frank was clearing the cockpit while Bob attended to the bilge pump; all were clipped on by their harnesses. Matthew was in the companionway passing buckets while Rob and Bill were filling buckets down below. Matthew managed to hang on and was still in the companionway when the boat righted but all three who had been in the cockpit were in the water. Frank and David were still hanging on by their safety harnesses but Bob's webbing harness had broken and he had become detached from the boat. He tried to swim back but his efforts were in vain; the waves carried him away from *Ariadne* faster than he could swim.

Frank and David were pulled back on board and neither was in good shape. David had broken some ribs when the boat rolled and Frank was becoming exhausted. He was not a young man and he was tired, wet and cold. In addition they had seen one of their companions swept away to a certain death by drowning. Morale was low because more

81

water had gone into the cabin, water which they had all spent much time and energy in removing. Bill with his badly split skull had lost a considerable amount of blood and was exhausted. Only Matthew and Rob, the two youngest on board, were still fit and active.

The bailing began all over again, but the strength of those on board had been sapped. They had no flares, or thought they had none because the container had become wedged between the cabin roof and the mast when the boat was first knocked down. It was not until after the second knockdown that they were found, by which time it was impossible to get the container freed.

By 0630 the situation had not improved and Bill suggested that they would be better off in the life-raft. At least they would have shelter and flares in the raft's emergency pack. The thought was in the back of all their minds that *Ariadne* would sink and so the six-man Beaufort raft was quickly prepared and a small amount of gear loaded into it. All five were smartly into the raft as soon as it was inflated and the painter cut.

For two hours they drifted in the raft. All were complaining of the cold and they were bailing continuously. Rob peeled open the flap to bail more freely at 0830 and caught sight of a coaster nearby. Immediately he fired off a red flare which was seen aboard the German coaster *Nanna*. The 200-foot vessel turned to head for the raft but in the seas that were running, this cannot have been easy. Matthew described the skipper's handling of his coaster as 'an amazing piece of seamanship'.

Soon after sighting the coaster, *Ariadne*'s raft capsized. The five men were tipped into the water but rather than right the raft, they clipped on to the outside and climbed on to the bottom of it. *Nanna* had a pilot ladder down as she came alongside the raft. Rob jumped for the ladder and scrambled up. Frank jumped too and held on to the ladder but as the coaster and the raft parted, a wave swept him off the ladder into the sea. The skipper of the *Nanna* had to go around again to try to manoeuvre alongside the raft.

On the second pass the coaster was too far from the raft for anyone to attempt to make for the pilot ladder and *Nanna* went round again. This time the skipper was able to manoeuvre the coaster so that the raft came alongside the boat at the pilot ladder. Matthew shouted to the other two to make sure that they were unclipped. Both were in poor shape, Bill through loss of blood and David through the pain of his broken ribs. As the raft came alongside the coaster Matthew went first and was quickly up the ladder. Bill went next but was washed off by a wave and when David got on the ladder he found that he was still clipped to the life-raft. The next wave took him and the life-raft away from the side of the *Nanna*.

Bill went down the side of the coaster and it is believed that he was sucked into the propellor. David did not have the strength to get back on to the top of the raft himself and drowned, still attached to the life-raft. The *Nanna* made several passes to try to pick up David and the raft but finally lost sight of both and the skipper was loath to put his coaster at further risk.

Matthew and Rob were taken to the crew's quarters and given hot food and dry clothes. The coaster steamed towards Land's End and soon after midnight met the Lizard-Cadgwith lifeboat which landed the two survivors at 0155.

Ariadne weathered out the storm and was later towed in by a trawler. Frank Ferris, who had been swept away when attempting to board the coaster, was later spotted by a Sea King helicopter and winched aboard. Despite his ordeal he was still alive on recovery but he died before reaching hospital.

GRIMALKIN

Grimalkin is a Ron Holland designed half-tonner, a series production boat built by Camper & Nicholson. She is a sister-ship of *Silver Jubilee*, the highly successful yacht of 1977. *Grimalkin* was owned by David Sheahan and had the nucleus of a regular crew who knew the boat well. She was well found and fitted as Sheahan's own letter to his crew, a couple of weeks in advance of the race, will testify. Nothing in the preparation of *Grimalkin* for the Fastnet Race was left to chance.

Her crew were the right admixture for ocean racing; a combination of experience and youth. It was also the right combination for pleasure; David Sheahan's son Matthew was on the foredeck, and all were friends who knew each other's ways about the boat. Jobs had been allocated well in advance by the skipper and a rota of cooks nominated. Nick Ward had obviously shown a lack of talent in the galley for he got the first half-day there, when there is little harm that he can do to the food which has been pre-cooked ashore. But the leg pulling in Sheahan's pre-race instructions leave one in no doubt as to Nick Ward's ability to 'burn water' in the galley. (Not that Nick minds — he hates it down there and is far more valuable as a spinnaker trimmer.)

David Sheahan believed in good communications. Going off in a small yacht in a race of 600 miles would leave behind many apprehensive relatives and friends. Those with concern for the six aboard *Grimalkin* would nightly have their fears allayed for it was David's plan to use the VHF radio to telephone his wife Gaye each evening and she would then relay news to the nearest and dearest of the other crew members.

Grimalkin started the Fastnet well. She was first boat away in Class V, close to Brian and Pam Saffery-Cooper's *Green Dragon*, the outstanding British half-tonner of 1979. The early part of the race was slow and *Grimalkin* encountered a great deal of fog. David contacted Gaye through Start Point radio on the Sunday evening. *Grimalkin* cleared Land's End by 1000 on Monday and that afternoon Nick Ward was much in demand. His personal recollections of that part of the race record: 'Glorious spinnaker reach during the afternoon, doing 8-10 knots through the water.' He was in his element nursing the nylon sail to provide the greatest possible forward-making power.

The Wolf Rock was left five miles to port and, on a course of 330°, the Seven Sisters to starboard. *Grimalkin* was hustling along at the front of her class. When the wind began to increase the spinnaker had to be handed and there was some systematic changing down of headsails and reefing of the mainsail. Still *Grimalkin* pressed on into the night.

But then the weather deteriorated fast and so too did any vestige of comfort in this 30-footer. By midnight she was down to storm jib only and was making a close-hauled course at nearly 6 knots. Matthew and Nick lashed the main boom firmly to the deck. They checked that the mainsail was properly stowed and would not flap loose because, by now, *Grimalkin* was in full gale-force winds and the seas had built up to forty feet from trough to crest. Nick believes the worst ones were much bigger but from a small boat judging the height of waves is very difficult. The waves made living below extremely uncomfortable. David Sheahan was worried for his crew. They were getting a battering inside the cabin as *Grimalkin* was tossed about in the waves. Soon after midnight the cabin became untenable.

A decision was made to bring everyone up into the cockpit where, when they were clipped on, they would help to keep each other warm and would not suffer the physical damage they might have done down below. Gerry Winks, who was second in command to the skipper, was at the tiller as *Grimalkin* climbed the faces of these huge waves and, with almost a sigh of relief, surged down them. The wind was bitingly cold and the spray stung the exposed faces of the crew. Long periods of this could lead to the onset of hypothermia.

Indeed Gerry had the first symptoms when he was relieved from the helm at 0300 on Tuesday morning. He was tired, wet and cold and he went below to change into dry warm gear before joining the rest of the crew in the cockpit while Nick Ward steered. The wind continued to increase and by 0400 it was no longer possible to hold *Grimalkin* on course with the storm jib up; the anemometer was now showing more than 60 knots of wind.

David Sheahan felt sure that there was only one course of action open to them. The storm jib would have to come off and *Grimalkin* should run off under bare poles streaming warps. The seas were 'like blocks of flats' and he felt that *Grimalkin* would come to less harm running with these huge seas than trying to go to windward against them. Four to five hundred feet of warp was streamed from each quarter but *Grimalkin*'s progress was only partially checked. With the windage of the hull and spars, the 60-knot winds were able to propel her at nearly 8 knots with bursts of 10 knots as she slithered down the face of the waves. That was too fast and by 0500 *Grimalkin* had suffered four horizontal knockdowns.

Each time, the crew were thrown down to leeward, hurtling across the cockpit and into the guard rails on the leeward running backstay where they were totally immersed in the sea. Each time it was an energy- and morale-sapping experience. The boat behaved well after each knockdown, righting herself within seconds, but the cockpit was full of bitterly cold sea water which took at least five minutes to drain.

The fifth knockdown came at 0530 and was more violent than the rest — at least that is how it seemed to a much weakened crew. It sent Nick from the helmsman's position across the cockpit and over the wrong side of the stanchions. He had so far managed to avoid injury but now his shoulder had been twisted by his harness and his left leg was badly bruised. David and Matthew helped him back on board but he was unable to continue helming the boat. Dave Wheeler took over on the tiller; Mike Doyle and Nick were to leeward and Gerry was to windward eagerly searching the early morning sky for a Nimrod. Down below David and Matthew had raised *Morningtown* on the VHF radio and had organised a rendezvous with a Sea King helicopter. David believed then that the crew were not in good shape and while the boat just might survive, the crew could take very little more of the cold.

Grimalkin rolled yet again and in the cabin David struck his head, gashing his scalp badly. There was a comprehensive first-aid kit on board but all that the crew could do for the skipper was cover the gash with antiseptic lint and spray on plastic skin. It afforded him some protection with the addition of his balaclava and oilskin hood, but he was losing a considerable amount of blood.

The cabin was in a frightful state. The engine box was wrecked, the VHF radio smashed, the burden boards were everywhere. The chart table and the companion ladder were badly damaged but the hull was still sound.

The gash on David's head began to cause further concern; he kept losing consciousness and had to be supported. Gerry too had taken some heavy knocks around the head and with the probable onset of hypothermia had begun to show signs of distress. The opinion that the life-raft would provide a safer refuge was therefore appealing to many of them. Those that had been hurt in knockdowns were most receptive to the suggestion that the raft should be launched.

Everything was prepared. The raft was made ready to launch, the flares and other emergency gear collected. Then came the capsize. It happened fearfully quickly and with great violence. A sea came from abeam and inverted the boat. David and Mike were forced into the cabin, Dave and Matthew were thrown into the water to the extent of their harnesses while Nick and Gerry were trapped in the cockpit amid all the rigging which came into the cockpit when the mast parted. It took some time for *Grimalkin* to come upright.

When eventually she did right, David, whose life-line had been cut, was swept away by the seas. He could not get back to the boat and was drowned. Matthew had seen his father die. Gerry and Nick also appeared to have drowned when they were trapped underwater. They showed no signs of life, but perhaps the judgment of their crewmates may have been temporarily clouded by the preceding events.

Dave, Mike and Matthew decided to take to the life-raft without delay. They got into the raft convinced that *Grimalkin* would founder. They abandoned her with the two men they believed dead still on board. An hour later the occupants of the life-raft were lifted to safety by helicopter.

But neither Nick nor Gerry was yet dead; they were very deeply unconscious and badly hurt, but not dead. Some time later, and Nick has no idea how much later, the yacht rolled again and both men were tipped into the sea yet again. Nick then recovered consciousness. He came to in the water with the backstays and shrouds tangled around his arms and body. His thoughts were a complete blur; his head was beaten against the skeg and hull and he had to force his way to the surface — he could first feel the air with his arms. As soon as he surfaced he disentangled himself from the stays and crawled back on board. He thought then that he was the only survivor but quickly checking around he noticed Gerry over the side. Nick had no idea where the other four were or what had happened to them.

Using the genoa sheet winch to help him, he manhandled the unconscious Gerry back on board, a superhuman effort considering Nick's own physical state. He found that Gerry was still alive, but only just. He gave him artificial respiration, both by chest massage and mouth-to-mouth, and encouraged him to recover consciousness by these means. Gerry lived for another three quarters of an hour but the combination of his injuries, massive bruising and abrasions of the head, and hypothermia finally brought about his death. He was able to give Nick a message for his wife before he passed away.

The situation for Nick Ward was then very frightening. The life-raft had gone and so had the flares. He still didn't know whether these items had just drifted away when the boat capsized or not. He knew that the crew had been preparing to abandon ship because they believed that *Grimalkin* would founder and now she was his only chance of survival. He was tired, cold and wet; an ideal candidate for hypothermia. The boat was half full of water; the mast was over the side and there was a dead companion in the cockpit. The odds were firmly stacked against Nick Ward.

But Nick is an intelligent, ingenious and highly practical young man. He bailed, as best he could, with a small bucket and retrieved such food as he could. He found some milk and believes that kept him going. He formulated a watch system of an hour on and half an hour off, sleeping when he could in a water-logged quarter berth. He had little idea of time, he was intent on surviving. He listened for the sound of a Nimrod, or better still a helicopter. None came. When a Nimrod was sighted he had no way of attracting its attention.

On Tuesday afternoon the weather began to moderate and Nick's hopes were improving. He says that he prayed, not in the conventional manner he is quick to add but by raising his arms and eyes heavenwards and shouting to the Almighty, 'You don't want me yet, do you?' It was a question he really didn't want the answer to either.

He was down below, getting some rest on the quarter berth when he heard a spotter plane. By the time he got into the cockpit, the plane had gone. It was then 1730. He stayed in the cockpit, hoping for the plane to return. He was armed only with a foghorn and a whistle. Half an hour later the French threequarter-tonner, *Fragola*, came close by and Nick managed to attract its attention. *Fragola* had no VHF but, with flares, she attracted another yacht which summoned a helicopter from RNAS Culdrose. Transferring Nick from *Grimalkin* to either of these yachts was out of the question in the seas that were still running. By the time the radio call had gone off to RNAS Culdrose it was 2045 and it seemed likely that Nick would have to spend another night at sea.

That was one thing he didn't want to face. Luckily the clouds rolled away to give a clear sky and darkness held off. Nick admits weeping for joy when he heard the sound of the Sea King and knew that he was safe.

Gerry was lifted off first. Nick comments: 'A sad way to be taken by the sea. Not in vain, I hope.' Then it was his turn to be winched up. His own feelings at the time: '*Grimalkin* looked very small as I looked down on her, spinning on the retrieving line, safe at last. She had done her job, at least for me, providing a haven, and a safe one, for many hours.'

Grimalkin also survived. She was towed into the southern Ireland port of Waterford, damaged but repairable. It is planned that Matthew Sheahan will campaign her again as a racing boat; he feels that is what his father would have wanted.

GUNSLINGER

Gunslinger is a Hustler 32 owned by the National Westminster Bank Sailing Club and skippered in the Fastnet by Mike Flowers, whose experience in ocean racing goes back more than twenty years. The yacht had been campaigned throughout the season and was properly prepared. The rest of her crew had a mixture of experience and all were fit.

The 1355 shipping forecast on Monday gave this crew their first indication of what was to come. The forecast was for a depression of 992 mbs, a drop of 5 mbs indicating increasing wind. This increase began at around 2000 and, just before darkness fell, the crew changed headsails to the number two genoa. As the wind increased further, the sail was reduced so that by the time it was dark the storm jib was set, the mainsail taken down and the sail and boom securely lashed down.

Gunslinger was still romping along, making 6 or 7 knots on course for the Rock. This seemed perhaps imprudent and for a time Mike Flowers suggested that they try lying-a-hull but the motion was most uncomfortable and it was decided to sail on. At 2200 the crew on watch spotted a red flare off the port beam and Bob Lloyd received a Mayday radio call which he directed to *Morningtown*. It was a French yacht that had been dismasted and as soon as *Morningtown* had made contact, *Gunslinger* was released from the Mayday.

The 0015 shipping forecast issued warnings of force 10 and Mike Flowers held a short battle conference with Bob Lloyd and the decision was made to go for the maximum possible protection by gaining as much sea room as they could, without pushing the boat too hard. This meant a northerly course with as much westing in it as possible. The lee shore was the coast of Pembrokeshire, not one of the most friendly places in a storm.

Shortly before midnight there had been a watch change. Bob was on with Alex Antill and Eric Sharpen was steering. All were clipped on in the cockpit. Meanwhile Mike was offwatch with Paul Baldwin and Gordon Pickett. Around this time Bob had identified *Gunslinger* with *Morningtown* by flashing the mast-head lights on and off while in VHF radio communication.

The wind blew very hard now and in the cockpit they were discussing lying a-hull once again. Then the rudder fractured. Naturally enough Eric was the first to notice something amiss. Bob, at the forward end of the cockpit on the starboard side, let go the jib halyard, opening the main hatch at the same time to call for help. It was at this moment that the rudderless boat broached and laid over at 90°. As she went over to the horizontal position Bob was thrown over the guard rails and into the water. He could see the hatch was open but the boat was floating with the hatchway well clear of the water.

A second wave, estimated by Bob to have been all of forty feet high, hit the hull as the boat tried to right herself and pitched it over to 180°, full inversion. Bob could see the keel in the air and that the rudder was completely missing. *Gunslinger* began slowly to right herself. Bob saw the cockpit grating and the life-raft floating nearby. The life-raft was still in its container and attached to the yacht. Then the righting became faster and Bob was dragged into the boat and deposited across the starboard life-line as it came upright. Alex and Eric, who had been attached to the port toe-rail were pulled straight into the cockpit by their harnesses when the boat righted. They then helped Bob into the relative safety of the cockpit.

Down below, as *Gunslinger* rolled over, Mike was thrown across the boat and landed on his neck, badly injuring his shoulder. With the boat in full inversion, water poured in through the open hatch until she righted. Bob had thought that *Gunslinger* was going to settle in the inverted position and sink. He could see things quite clearly; the cabin lights were still on and there were strobe lights from the lifebuoys that were activated.

The mess down below was almost indescribable. Loose gear was floating about in water that was up to the level of the settee berths and it appeared to be getting deeper. The lights were still on, the batteries (remarkably) still supporting them. Paul started to bail the water out from the cabin but it appeared to be gaining on him. Later the crew believed that much of this additional water was trapped higher up in the boat and was not coming in from outside or through the rudder shaft, which they most feared. It did appear, however, that the boat would founder and the skipper ordered the life-raft to be launched. It had only recently been recovered from the sea in its container.

Bob Lloyd asked for a sail to be passed up from down below to stream it from the bows on a warp to hold the bows head to wind while the life-raft and spare gear were prepared. Mike, Eric and Alex recovered the raft and prepared it for launching while Bob, Paul and Gordon collected the safety equipment and continued to bail *Gunslinger*. Torches, flares and emergency dry packs were collected and at the same time Bob used the Callbuoy emergency radio to send out a Mayday. Unfortunately, a wave hit the boat, knocking Bob sideways and fracturing the base of the brittle aerial of the Callbuoy. The Callbuoy was out of action.

With everything set against the survival of *Gunslinger*, a decision was made to abandon the yacht in favour of the life-raft. There seemed to be only a few minutes before the yacht would sink. Alex triggered off the life-raft and launched it over the starboard side. There were two other yachts in the vicinity and it was felt that the best way to get to them was to drift downwind in the life-raft as it would have been impossible for them to come alongside in the heavy seas. Paul got into the life-raft and began loading the emergency stores.

With Paul inside it the life-raft was capsized by a breaking wave. It was pulled out of the hands of those who were holding it alongside and out to the extent of its painter. Paul switched on a waterproof light and this could be seen clearly by those in the cockpit of *Gunslinger*. Alex tried to haul in the painter but the strength of the seas and the drag of the upturned raft were too much for him and his hands were badly burned by the rope.

Paul came out from under the life-raft with his lifejacket inflated and a McMurdo strobe light in his hand. Just at that moment another wave came, separating Paul from the raft and causing the painter holding the raft to the yacht to snap. Paul could still be seen and a heaving line was thrown to him, but he couldn't quite reach it. Paul's only hope was to reach the life-raft again, and that he didn't manage.

The morale on *Gunslinger* can never have been lower than it was then. One of the crew had gone and all on board realised that he hadn't the slightest chance of survival; for that matter their future didn't look bright either. They were in a rudderless yacht with little in the way of emergency gear, and they believed the yacht was leaking so fast that it could not stay afloat much longer. On top of that the skipper, Mike, had a badly injured shoulder and Alex's hands were painfully rope-burned. In addition, Eric had a dislocated thumb.

Bob and Eric began to bail with the bucket. It wasn't easy. They had to sort out the floating debris down below — some of it might be useful — and they had to open the hatch each time a bucket was passed up to keep more water from going down below. Bob thinks he bailed for two hours — time seemed quite immaterial. Eventually he could feel that the water, at first up to his waist, was beginning to recede. He began to believe that they had a fighting chance for survival. The boat was stable and there was little coming down the hatch. Alex tried to take over the bailing. He and Gordon had been in the cockpit clearing the drains and bailing with the aid of a sail. Alex's hands were in a bad state and he could not lift the bucket out through the hatch so he returned to the cockpit job while Gordon and Bob continued with the bailing.

Slowly, oh so slowly, the level inside the boat went down. Mike was put on a bunk and swaddled in a wet sleeping bag in an attempt to protect him from exposure. His back and shoulder were giving him great pain. The water inside was now down to ankle level and from somewhere Gordon found some dry matches and lit the stove to make some hot drinks. The crew were exhausted. After a hot drink they rested until daylight.

Once it was light they began to assess the situation more clearly. The boat now seemed buoyant enough. It was dried out as far as was possible and tidied so that an inventory could be taken. The bottom of the starboard quarter berth was turned into an SOS signal. Food was basic; hot tea and biscuits seemed favourite, palatable and easy to produce.

Just before noon on Tuesday the Class II yacht *Nick Nack* was seen on the port quarter. It was pointless for her to attempt to come alongside *Gunslinger* but she came close enough for Bob to hail her and ask her to relay a Mayday for him.

Gunslinger was streaming a long grass warp and all the synthetic warps that the crew could find. These they buoyed with lifejackets to slow their downwind progress under bare poles. The yacht lay almost beam-on to the sea and as the waves hit they swung her stern with a relatively easy motion. It appeared that if conditions remained the same, the yacht had sea room for at least another thirty hours' safety. The crew began to assemble the emergency rudder but the sea conditions were still too severe for it to be shipped.

The radar reflector was hoisted together with the code flag hoist NC. In addition, a blue and red sleeping bag was hoisted up the mast to aid recognition. At around 1400 a Nimrod was in the vicinity and *Gunslinger* put her blooper into the sea with a fender at the tack and clew, and the head lashed to the boat. The brightly coloured blooper gave the Nimrod crew a better chance to spot the stricken yacht. Two hours later a Sea King helicopter arrived and arrangements were made to take off Mike Flowers to get him to hospital for treatment for his injured back and shoulder.

Bob Lloyd took over the skipper's responsibility. Radio reports told him that the general situation had now reached disaster proportions. With *Gunslinger* in no immediate danger of sinking, he asked the rest of the crew if they would stay on board provided the helicopter crew did not consider it dangerous for them to do so. The crew unanimously opted to stay, so the helicopter could be released for more rescue work. Mike was floated off wearing a lifejacket and eased away with a line attached to a horseshoe life-ring. He was soon hoisted into the Sea King.

Morale lowered a little as the helicopter disappeared over the horizon, but the wind was easing, sea conditions were quietening and visibility was good. There was plenty to be done on board as well. It was obvious that rescue would not take place until morning but there might be boats to warn off and there were no flares on *Gunslinger*. Down below, the crew made flares by soaking rolls of kitchen paper in diesel fuel. In addition they rigged an emergency light for the cabin using a six-volt dry battery and the chart table light. The ship's batteries were now dead.

Much more had now dried out below. Watches in the cockpit were shared among the four in half-hour segments and every effort was made to defeat exposure and hypothermia. The crew kept themselves wrapped in sleeping bags on watch, while the stove was kept alight down below to provide a little warmth.

During the night several vessels were seen and the paper and diesel flares lit on the end of a bunk pole. The flares burned brightly but no vessel came near enough to attract attention. At first light a Nimrod flew over and dropped a smoke flare. Two hours later the Dutch trawler *Alida* came within hail. Bob decided that the wisest course of action would be to transfer the crew to the trawler and take *Gunslinger* in tow. The effects of shock and exposure were beginning to be seen.

The transfer of all four began as soon as the yacht was taken in tow in accordance with the Lloyds' open salvage agreement. *Gunslinger* suffered very little damage in her tow to Cork Harbour, although when she was transferred to a harbour launch there was a little more sustained to her guard rails. She had survived when all on board thought she was going to sink and one of the crew was lost when preparing the life-raft.

Chapter 6

THE RESCUE SERVICES

'You don't want me yet, do you?'

Nick Ward, Survivor, *Grimalkin*

There has never been a search and rescue operation of the proportions of that caused by the storm which hit the 1979 Fastnet Race fleet. Some idea of the vastness of the operation can be gauged by the fact that over 10,000 messages were passed between HM Coastguard and yachts, ships and other authorities in the period 2000 August 13th to 0800 August 16th.

The search and rescue operation was co-ordinated by the Marine Rescue Co-ordination Centre (MRCC) at Shannon in southern Ireland and HM Coastguard Marine Rescue Sub Centre (MRSC) Land's End. It involved the Royal Navy, the Royal Netherlands Navy, the Royal Air Force, the Royal National Lifeboat Institution, HM Coastguard, the Royal Ocean Racing Club and several merchant and fishing vessels.

The RNLI is responsible for the lifeboats of Britain and Eire and thirteen of them were involved in the operation. The record boards in their lifeboat houses testify that, between them, they rescued sixty lives and towed or escorted twenty yachts to safety. For their crews there was an intensive thirty-six hours of activity during which they displayed great endurance and endeavour.

The first of the lifeboats to be launched was *The Robert* from Baltimore. She was called into action by the lighthouse keeper on the Fastnet Rock. He telephoned the secretary of the Baltimore lifeboat at 2205 on Monday to report a yacht in trouble near the Rock. It was the Irish Admiral's Cupper *Regardless*, which had lost her carbon-fibre rudder. Going in to the Fastnet, *Regardless* had been top points scorer in the Admiral's Cup. She is a 40-footer designed by Ron Holland and built by Kiwi Yachts in Florida.

The Robert was launched at 2215 when the southerly wind was reaching force 7. The seas were very rough and soon after the Baltimore lifeboat had put to sea the wind veered to the south-west and increased to force 9. *The Robert* searched the area around the Fastnet Rock for some time but drew a blank. She was returning home when she received a message from MRCC Shannon giving her *Regardless*'s position. She found *Regardless* to the south-east of the Rock and managed to get a tow rope on to her after a great deal of difficulty in the very big seas that were running. She began a slow and painful tow with the yacht yawing about astern, to Baltimore where she tied up at 0815 after ten hours at sea. All nine members of *Regardless*'s crew were safe.

The day's work was far from over for *The Robert*'s crew. Her coxswain, John Collins, put his men on standby following a request from MRCC Shannon and the lifeboat was only in harbour for fifty minutes before she put to sea again to assist another yacht in trouble. This time it was another Ron Holland design with a carbon-fibre rudder failure – the 46-foot *Marionette*, reserve boat for the British Admiral's Cup team. She gave her position as south-east of the Stags.

It took *The Robert* five and threequarter hours to locate *Marionette*, by which time she had drifted to a position twenty-five miles south of Galley Head. Once again, getting a tow line on board was difficult but after a while *Marionette* was secured and towed back to Baltimore in six hours. *The Robert* had been at sea for another twelve hours but twelve more lives had been saved.

At Courtmacsherry there was a relief lifeboat on temporary duty, the *Sir Samuel Kelly*. She was first launched at 0240 on Tuesday to go to the aid of *Wild Goose*, a member of the Singapore Admiral's Cup team which was twenty-seven miles south of Old Head of Kinsale. Forty minutes after she had left her station the *Sir Samuel Kelly* was diverted to go to the assistance of *Pepsi*, thirty miles south of Galley Head. It was hard going for the lifeboat. The winds were up to force 10 from the west and the *Sir Samuel Kelly* was taking the huge seas right on the nose. With full power the 47-foot lifeboat was only able to make 6½ knots against the elements. She reached *Pepsi*'s reported position at 0840 but there was no sign of the yacht.

A square search was instituted and air support sought because of extremely poor visibility due to the height of the seas. Coxswain Stephen Mearns continued to search for an hour and a half until the *Sir Samuel Kelly* was again diverted, this time to assist *Casse Tete V*, another casualty with a broken carbon-fibre rudder. *Casse Tete V* was lying twenty-six miles south of Galley Head and Mearns considered that it would take the best part of an hour and a half before he would reach her. The two boats maintained VHF radio contact.

Two other yachts in the race were sighted by the Courtmacsherry lifeboat but both were found to be under full control and still racing. When the *Sir Samuel Kelly* reached the area where *Casse Tete V* had been, there was no sign of her. Mearns called *Casse Tete V*'s skipper, Dave Johnson, on the VHF radio and the lifeboat fired a parachute flare for identification. Johnson took a bearing on the flare which he reported to Coxswain Mearns. The lifeboat then steamed down on a reciprocal bearing to find the yacht.

The lifeboat approached *Casse Tete V* to windward abeam and the tow line was passed by heaving line. It was quickly secured and the tow back to Courtmacsherry began at 1145. The rudderless *Casse Tete V* made a difficult tow. She yawed and surfed in the huge seas and progress was extremely slow; just over two knots was the best speed the *Sir Samuel Kelly* could make and it took more than twelve hours for the lifeboat to return to her home port. Coxswain Mearns and his men had been at sea for twenty-two hours to rescue the yacht's crew of ten.

Another relief lifeboat, the *Joseph Hiram Chadwick*, was on temporary duty at Ballycotton. She first put to sea to escort into Cork Harbour the French two-tonner *Accanito*. *Accanito* was another rudder casualty but she was steering with a blade of wood added to her spinnaker booms over the stern.

As soon as *Accanito* was deemed safe in Cork, the Ballycotton lifeboat returned to sea to search for *Wild Goose*. During the search, the lifeboat sighted the French half-tonner *Ossian* which was dismasted. The lifeboat succeeded in getting a tow line on board and she towed the yacht and her six-man crew to Ballycotton. It was another long haul, taking seven hours.

At 0300 on Monday the St Mary's lifeboat, the *Guy and Clare Hunter*, left her base in the Scilly Isles to go to the aid of *Magic*, which was in trouble forty miles west of Round Island lighthouse. Five hours later when the lifeboat was eight miles from this position, she received information from a helicopter that there was a dismasted yacht about seven miles downwind. The *Guy and Clare Hunter* altered course to see if this was *Magic*, but before she arrived she was informed that it was not *Magic* but a different yacht, whose crew had all been taken off. Coxswain Matthew Lethbridge continued to search for *Magic* and at 1045 encountered the yacht *Victride*, a French Class III boat which was

The Fastnet Rock and its lighthouse off the southern coast of Ireland, the outward turning mark that gives the 605-mile race its name. (*Photo:* Ambrose Greenway, Popperfoto)

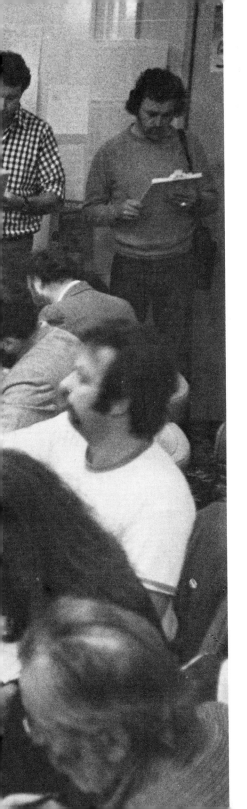

The press centre in the Duke of Cornwall Hotel, Plymouth. Roger Ware (in sleeveless check shirt) holds one of his hourly briefings on the state of the rescue operations. (*Photo:* Jonathan Eastland, Ajax News Photos)

Jolie Brise, a converted Le Havre pilot cutter, winner of the first Fastnet Race in 1925. (*Photo:* Beken of Cowes)

Tenacious, winner of the 1979 Fastnet, a 61-foot Sparkman & Stephens designed sloop, owned and skippered by Ted Turner. (*Photo:* Beken of Cowes)

HNLMS *Overijssel*, the Dutch frigate which acted as guard ship to the Fastnet fleet and which picked up fifteen survivors at the height of the storm. (*Photo:* Jonathan Eastland, Ajax News Photos)

Camargue, designed by the Bridgewater Navigation and Steamship Company, a 34-footer whose steering pedestal broke causing her crew to abandon ship. The last member is in the companionway awaiting rescue by helicopter. (*Photo*: Steven Pratt, RNAS Culdrose)

Above: The 47-foot Watson lifeboat *Guy and Clare Hunter* from St Mary's in the Scilly Isles, heading out in search of *Magic,* early on Tuesday morning, 14th August. (*Photo:* Steven Pratt, RNAS Culdrose)

Above right: Crew members of the 44-foot *Casse Tete V* making fast the tow line from the Courtmacsherry lifeboat, *Sir Samuel Kelly,* a 47-foot Watson on temporary duty at that station. *Casse Tete V* had fractured her carbon-fibre rudder. (*Photo:* Ambrose Greenway, Popperfoto)

A Wessex Mark V helicopter of 771 Squadron, her winch-man in the water, prepares to lift one of the survivors from *Camargue*. In order to be rescued, survivors had to jump into the water, as it was not possible for the helicopters to lift them directly from the yachts. (*Photo:* Steven Pratt, RNAS Culdrose)

Opposite page: Help at last for Nick Ward on board *Grimalkin*, as Midshipman Harrison, the winch-man of a Sea King helicopter of 819 Squadron, prepares to lift him from the stricken yacht. With *Grimalkin's* mast gone, a direct lift from the yacht was possible. (*Photo:* Steven Pratt, RNAS Culdrose)

Above: Petty Officer Roy Henshaw passes a lifting strop around the chest of Frank Ferris, owner-skipper of *Ariadne*. Frank Ferris died of a combination of hypothermia and drowning on his way to hospital. (*Photo:* Steven Pratt, RNAS Culdrose)

The abandoned hull of the
Dick Carter designed threequarter-tonner *Ariadne*. Her
mast broken and hatches still
open, the hull survived the
storm but four of her crew
did not. (*Photo:* Steven Pratt,
RNAS Culdrose)

A Sea King helicopter hovers
over the top half of the life-
raft of the yacht *Trophy*
prior to lifting skipper Alan
Bartlett to safety. Bartlett
had survived for five hours
without a lifejacket. (*Photo:*
Peter Webster)

The top half of *Trophy's* life-raft with Dick Mann, Russell Smith and Derek Moreland, coming alongside the *Overijssel*. To rescue the survivors frogmen had to go into the water to assist them to board the frigate. (*Photo:* Peter Webster)

Moonstone, one of the OOD 34s, limps home after retiring from the race with clothing and bedding drying out. (*Photo:* Colin Davey, London Express Pictures)

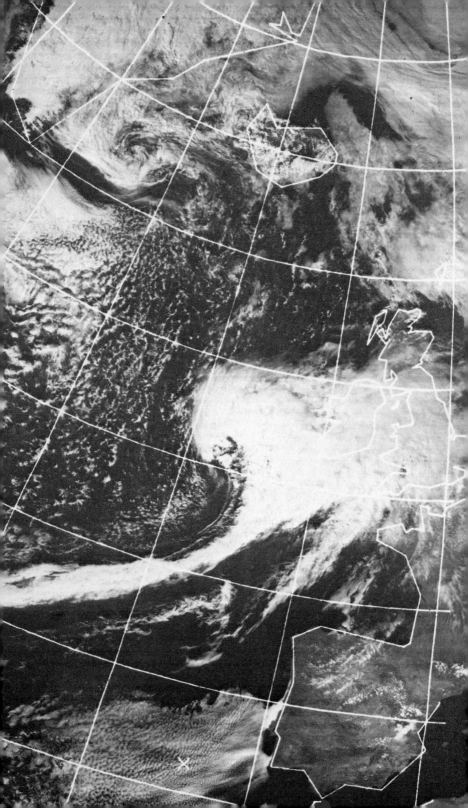

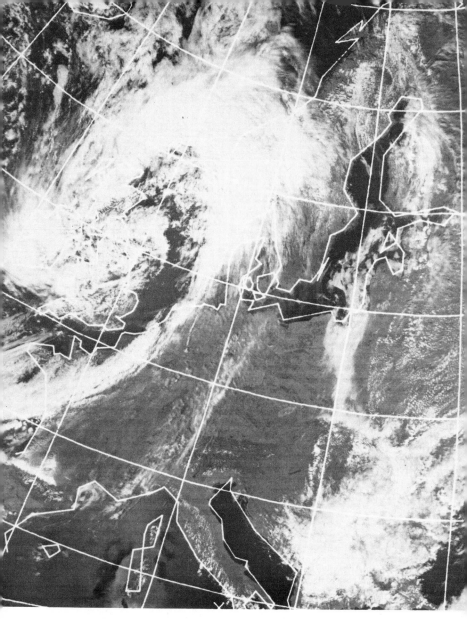

Opposite page: The Tiros N satellite picture at 1537 GMT on Monday 13th August, showing the storm centre 400 miles from the south-west tip of Ireland. (*Photo:* Dundee University)

Above: The Tiros N satellite picture at 1345 GMT on Tuesday 14th August, the storm having past over the race area and into the North Sea between Scotland and Norway. (*Photo:* Dundee University)

About a quarter of the personnel at RNAS Culdrose who were involved in the Fastnet search and rescue operation. (*Photo:* RNAS Culdrose)

taking part in the race. Although she was making heavy weather, all appeared well on board and the St Mary's lifeboat continued on her way. Twenty-five minutes later, however, *Victride* requested help. Her main hatch had split and she was taking in a great deal of water. The lifeboat stood by and began to escort her to St Mary's.

When the tow began, *Victride* and the lifeboat were forty-seven miles north-north-west of Round Island and the storm was at its height. The wind was full force 11 and the seas extremely rough. As soon as the St Mary's lifeboat had begun to escort *Victride*, she received a call for help from the Contention 33 class yacht *Pegasus*. She too required escorting and as she did not appear to be in any immediate danger, Coxswain Lethbridge gave her a course which would enable her to converge with the lifeboat and *Victride*.

The seas were particularly vicious as the St Mary's lifeboat and *Victride* headed for port. Twice *Victride* broached and was laid flat, but twice she staggered up. The lifeboat was continuously shipping heavy seas and, on one occasion, a sea ran straight through the wheel-house, carrying three crew members clean off their feet to the extent of their harness lines. The two boats met with *Pegasus* at 1800 and two hours later they were all alongside at St Mary's. The lifeboat had been out for seventeen hours and there were two boats with grateful crews.

But there was no respite for the crew of the lifeboat. They were able to change into dry clothes while other helpers refuelled the lifeboat. *Festina Tertia*, a Contessa 35, had been reported by the coastguard as being in difficulties twelve miles west of Round Island. By 2100 the yacht was three miles west of New Grimsby entrance and twenty-five minutes later she was sighted by the lifeboat and taken in tow. Two hours later she too was alongside in the little Scillies port. Now there were six more crew men who had reason to be grateful to the men of the RNLI.

Sennen Cove's lifeboat, the *Diana White*, had nearly twelve hours at sea. She was launched at 0700 on Tuesday into the teeth of the storm to search for two yachts sixty miles from her station. Her mission became unnecessary after four hours when helicopters reported that they had dealt with these two boats. The *Diana White* then diverted to search for *Azenora II*, a French yacht that was taking part in the *L'Aurore* Singlehanded race. She sighted nothing and was recalled for refuelling at 1300, arriving home at 1630.

Azenora II was found by the St Ives' lifeboat, drifting with a broken mast. She was taken in tow and arrived at St Ives at much the same time that the *Diana White* arrived back at Sennen Cove.

The search was still on for *Wild Goose* to which both the Ballycotton and Courtmacsherry lifeboats had been called. At 0900 on Tuesday, the Dunmore East lifeboat went out to join the search when *Wild Goose*'s position was reported as being fifty miles south of the tiny walled harbour where the *St Patrick* was berthed. Three hours after she had been launched her crew heard that the oil-rig service vessel, *Gulf Link 18* was in the area where *Wild Goose* had recently been reported, forty-five miles south of Minehead. The *Gulf Link 18* had picked up seven survivors from another yacht and was continuing the search for *Wild Goose*. At 1425 *Gulf Link 18* reported that she had taken *Wild Goose* in tow and was making for Cork Harbour.

The *St Patrick*'s crew continued to comb the area and sighted the S & S 34 *Korsar*, which appeared to be in no trouble. Then they spoke with the skipper of *Autonomy*, Edward Bourne, whose 36-foot Holman & Pye design had broken her steering, and with Andy Cassell, skipper of the J 30 *Juggernaut*, which had no power or lights and a broken boom. *St Patrick* then took *Autonomy* in tow and escorted *Juggernaut* to Dunmore East harbour shortly after midnight after fifteen hours at sea.

The Padstow lifeboat, *James and Catherine Macfarlane*, was launched at 1900 on Tuesday to take the station's medical adviser to an injured man aboard *Tamasin II*, a Nicholson 30.

An hour later the lifeboat met the yacht but even though the wind had moderated to force 8, the seas were still huge and prevented the doctor from getting on board the yacht until they were in the lee of Stepper Point. Once the yacht was safe in Padstow harbour, the lifeboat returned to sea to take over the tow of the Contention 30 *Tarantula*, from the French trawler *Petit Poisson*. That accomplished, she returned to help the Shamrock half-tonner *Mosika Alma* and finally berthed after eighteen hours at sea.

Lifeboats from outside the area were drafted in to help. The Clovelly lifeboat assisted in searches and the Falmouth lifeboat, a fast 52-foot Arun-class boat, left her berth at 2200 on Tuesday to search west of the Scillies. She didn't arrive in the search area for eight hours but immediately began to work with HMS *Broadsword*. She was asked to patrol from forty-two miles north-west of the Scillies back towards the Scillies and Land's End. At 0725 she was asked by *Broadsword* to investigate a yacht reported by a helicopter to be twelve miles to the west of the Bishop Rock. It was the Swedish Admiral's Cupper *Big*

Shadow, another which had suffered the loss of her rudder. The Falmouth lifeboat took *Big Shadow* in tow to St Mary's at 1100 and an hour later, after refuelling, the Falmouth lifeboat, *Elizabeth Ann*, was at sea again.

Elizabeth Ann met again with *Broadsword* at 1525 and took over the tow of the 45-foot Irish Admiral's Cup yacht, *Golden Apple of the Sun*, which had been abandoned by her crew when they had been offered the safety of a helicopter instead of the doubtful pleasure of another night in a rudderless yacht. *Golden Apple*'s tow line parted twice on the way to Newlyn and was re-secured by members of the lifeboat's crew who boarded the yacht. *Elizabeth Ann* arrived at Newlyn with her tow at 0115 on Thursday.

Angle lifeboat escorted two boats, *Caval* and *Animal*, into Milford Haven in the early hours of Wednesday morning. At the same time the relief lifeboat at Lizard-Cadgwith, *Euphrosyne Kendal*, rendezvoused with the coaster *Nanna* to take off the two survivors from *Ariadne*, Matthew Hunt and Rob Gilder. The final lifeboat launching associated with the Fastnet Race was that of the Penlee boat at 0415 on Thursday. This boat went to take over the tow of the dismasted Class V yacht *Gan*, all of whose crew had been taken by helicopter to RNAS Culdrose and believed that the boat had sunk. The Penlee lifeboat took over the tow from the coaster *Marianna V* and arrived at Newlyn at 0645.

The lifeboats formed one part of the sea-borne rescue effort; another part was played by the Royal Netherlands Navy ship, *Overijssel*, the official guard ship for the race. Her Commanding Officer, Kapitein-luitenant Smit, and crew rescued six survivors from *Polar Bear* and six from *Callirhoe*. In addition, they rescued three men from *Trophy*'s life-raft and brought back the bodies of two others who perished from that yacht.

Overijssel was working in conjunction with the 39-foot yacht *Morningtown*, a motor-sailor owned and skippered by Rodney Hill. *Morningtown* was the junior radio-relay escort vessel whose skipper was well versed in the sport of ocean racing. *Morningtown* left Cowes on the Friday before the race began in company with *Overijssel* and headed for Lyme Bay.

Morningtown and *Overijssel* were to take the twice-daily radio reports from the Admiral's Cup yachts and four other yachts which had volunteered to give their positions. The reporting was to be on VHF channels M or 72 and the reason for having the two boats was that when the fleet became spread out it was necessary to have *Overijssel* and *Morningtown* widely spaced to cover the relatively short range of the sets on the reporting yachts. The two radio-relay vessels also had MF radios for communicating with each other and for transmitting the yachts' reported positions to the shore.

On Monday evening *Morningtown* was hove-to in position 50°42N, 8°12W. At 2100 she received a message from *Accanito* that the yacht had lost her rudder and was proposing to steer to Kinsale using her spinnaker booms as a rudder. Rodney Hill on *Morningtown* advised the French yacht against this as she would be running into a rocky entrance on a lee shore. He suggested instead that she run off for a position ten miles off Cork Harbour where she could rendezvous with a lifeboat from Ireland. *Accanito* agreed and *Morningtown* relayed the situation to Land's End Coastguard (MRSC) and the rescue services were alerted.

It was a long procedure, and immediately after dealing with *Accanito* the same sort of messages had to be relayed concerning *Scaldis*, a 56-foot Class II yacht from Holland which was making for Cork with a broken rudder. The effect of working the radio desk with a lot of head movements and concentration made Rodney violently seasick. Nigel Wood therefore took over as radio operator for the 2200 position reports from the yachts.

At 0100 on Tuesday there was an 'all hands' call. Red and white parachute flares had been seen to westward of *Morningtown*'s position. They were answered by the radio-relay boat with a white Very light. All sails were taken in and *Morningtown* motored in towards the position of the casualty. Nigel spoke on VHF to other yachts who had run towards the stricken yacht but had been unable to hold position. It took *Morningtown* an hour to get near and identify the yacht as *Allamanda*, an OOD 34. Her mast was broken and *Morningtown* stood by at half a mile to rig a search-light. After twenty minutes *Allamanda* fired more flares and *Morningtown* returned to her.

Crew members of the OOD 34 shouted that their yacht was out of control and their life-raft had overturned alongside but a crewman on the foredeck was trying to right it. On *Morningtown* the tow line was prepared but attempts to take *Allamanda* in tow had to be abandoned because of the heavy seas. Her crew were observed huddled in the cockpit. The lights were on and the life-raft was now righted and riding in the lee of the yacht.

100

At 0302 another red parachute flare was seen a mile away to the east, so *Morningtown* left *Allamanda*, to investigate. Steering and control of the 39-foot boat were extremely difficult because of the high and confused seas that were running. After fifteen minutes a red flare was observed close by to the west. *Morningtown* turned to head in that direction.

She found *Allamanda* with her lights extinguished and the raft gone. She assumed (incorrectly as it happened) that her crew had abandoned her for the life-raft. She then sighted a raft, again believing it to be from *Allamanda*, and saw several men in it giving a thumbs-up sign. It later transpired that this was *Trophy*'s raft. After some manoeuvring, *Morningtown* re-established contact with this raft and endeavoured to bring it alongside. Due to the lack of hand holds, her crew found it impossible to get the raft alongside with the canopy flap on the correct aspect, and the *Trophy* crew were naturally unwilling to come out of the raft without the hatch in the right place. The raft drifted away.

At this time the steering wires jumped off the quadrant on *Morningtown* and Rodney and Nigel had to repair the steering. Their first repair was ineffective, so Nigel, together with Grant Walker, repaired it again.

Meanwhile, the radio traffic was heavy. Rodney first took a Mayday on Channel 16 from *Grimalkin*. David Sheahan was working the radio and doing it in copybook style despite the obvious state of distress. He managed to establish the yacht's position with *Morningtown* after the latter had passed the Mayday on to Land's End Coastguard. Sheahan gave his 1730 position and details of his log from then, in order that the rescue services would know best where to look for *Grimalkin* as he was unsure as to his exact position.

Innovation was the next yacht to radio in, requesting that she be recorded as retired and heading for home. In view of the amount of calls that followed immediately, it is not surprising that this one was overlooked. First *Dasher*, a Services Nicholson 55, came on to relay a Mayday from *Malligawa III*, a French half-tonner. Then *Morningtown* called her own report requesting aircraft assistance at first light; this was passed by the operator on the Gas Platform A in the Kinsale Field as the MF/HF antenna on *Morningtown* had been broken and was in the process of being repaired. *Overijssel* came into a three-way link with the Gas Platform to confirm that there were more than one or two life-rafts in the area and also that she had passed information concerning *Wild Goose*.

Rodney Hill was now unsure of his position. All the manoeuvring he had done during the night had made dead-reckoning plotting almost impossible, so he asked for some navigational assistance from *Overijssel* and received a bearing from the Dutch warship on her MF transmissions. With dawn came the first contact with the Nimrod aircraft and for the next hour the radio desk of *Morningtown* was busy with radio traffic with the aircraft and *Overijssel*. It was now rescue routine radio traffic and a busy day for all the radio operators.

The next scheduled report from the Admiral's Cup yachts was at 1500 that afternoon and fifteen of them answered. To a request for all Fastnet yachts to report their positions, another six replied. Ten minutes later the Executive Officer of the *Overijssel* asked *Morningtown* if the RORC had cancelled the race and commented that he thought they should have. Rodney Hill replied that the decision was not his to make but he would contact the race office. This took time and the obvious answer was slow in coming. The RORC is unswerving in its justifiable attitude that the responsibility of continuing in the race is entirely that of the skippers and crews and that also to cancel a race once it has been started would be impracticable.

Early in the evening came news from HMS *Broadsword* that a helicopter had lifted the entire crew of Michael Campbell's *Allamanda*, and that *Big Shadow* was calling for assistance from a position forty miles north-west of the Bishop Rock. She too had steering problems and required a tow.

The radio traffic on board *Morningtown* had been continuous and it was not until the early hours of Wednesday morning that Rodney had the chance to put in a link call through Land's End Radio, to his home, to inform the relatives of those on board *Morningtown* that they were safe and well. His own heat-of-the-moment comments, made on the Thursday, include one very pertinent statement:

> The hithero excellent safety record of the RORC is now shown to have contained a modicum of luck. My impression was that the conditions were no worse than the 1961 Fastnet or the 1972 Bermuda Races [both of which he took part in]. Storms of this nature will occur again. In this case the fleet was in deep water — but quickly accessible to most competent and practiced air/sea rescue services.

He felt that his own contribution in the rescue service was confined only to radio reporting procedures and that the attempts his boat made to render physical assistance were worthless. He does point out that had they had a scrambling net aboard, some lives would have been saved from *Trophy*'s life-raft; but there are few who would have foreseen the need for that equipment.

The Royal Navy are naturally reticent about the enormous part its men and ships played in the rescues. *Anglesey, Broadsword* and *Scylla* were joined by the *Dierdre* from the Irish Navy. *Anglesey* left Plymouth on Monday morning to act as a Fisheries Protection Vessel and headed initially for Jones Bank (49°50N, 8°00W). She first became involved with the rescue when she was relayed a Mayday from *Magic* through MRSC at 0300 on Tuesday and headed for the yacht, fifty miles to the north. On the way she was joined by the St Mary's lifeboat. The force of the storm can be judged by the fact that the *Anglesey* was several times knocked over to 50°.

At 0825, at a position 50°32N, 6°37W, *Anglesey* manoeuvred close to the Ohlson 35 *Bonaventure II*, a Royal Naval yacht in the race. As she was stranded, her crew were told to abandon and take to the life-raft. *Anglesey* manoeuvred upwind to blow down on the raft. One of the seven survivors had a broken arm and had to be lifted aboard in a sling, but all were saved. For the rest of the day *Anglesey* passed calls for help and kept a weather eye for the racing fleet.

Anglesey spent Wednesday checking the abandoned yachts in an area forty-five miles by thirty miles. Her crewmen boarded six yachts — *Grimalkin, Callirhoe III, Allamanda, Gan, Tiderace IV* and *Kestrel II* — battened them down and removed personal possessions which were later handed to the RORC for onward transit to their owners. The following day she patrolled a designated area looking for stragglers and after the search had been called off at 1435, she took the abandoned *Trophy* in tow. The tow parted the next day at 0515 in a force 9 gale.

HMS *Broadsword*'s role was one of rescue co-ordination. She was placed in charge of the search of the area and was thus responsible for the control of all rescue assets: fixed-wing aircraft, helicopters and surface ships. To do this she stationed herself in the middle of the area and directed the aircraft to search for and pick up survivors based on information that she received from a number of sources.

HSM *Scylla* was carrying out anti-submarine exercises south of Portland when she was called into the rescue operation on the Wednesday. She was joined in a 'sweeping' operation by *Olna, Robust* and *Rollicker* and, together with *Broadsword, Anglesey* and *Overijssel*, they effectively combed the main rescue area. The final stages of the operation were routine and provided excellent training. Scylla used her own Wasp helicopter in the search and logged sightings of ten yachts in her small area to the south and west of the Scillies. It was this mopping-up operation which took much of the £350,000 which the Exchequer provided.

August is a holiday month, and thus many of the helicopter pilots and crews at the Royal Naval Air Station at Culdrose were on leave on Tuesday 14th August 1979. Only a skeleton aircrew were on duty at Culdrose when the call came to search and rescue. With it came a call to those on leave to return to help in what was certainly the most hectic three days that the station has ever known. During that time the six Sea Kings, five Wessex and two Lynx helicopters flew 62 sorties, totalling 194 hours airborne, to rescue 75 competitors in the Fastnet Race.

The first information to Culdrose came from SRCC Plymouth and in hindsight it seems like just the tip of an iceberg. The Air Officer of the day at RNAS Culdrose realised that to be the case at the time and took action accordingly. The three separate incidents to which the SRCC message referred were a Mayday from the yacht *Magic*; a report from MRCC Land's End of yachts aground on the Scillies, and of four people on a raft at 50.40°N, 8.10°W. SRCC requested helicopter assistance. The message was timed at 0405Z, or 0505 BST.

Thirty minutes later the first Wessex was airborne and heading for the Scillies. Ten minutes after that the first Sea King took off to aid the crew of *Magic* and a second Sea King was brought up to immediate readiness.

Then the pressure began to build. The up-date from MRCC Land's End at 0500Z added *Grimalkin* capsized thirty miles north-west of Land's End and a Mayday from *Mulligatawny* at 50.50°N, 07.30°W. The Wessex was detailed to look for survivors from *Grimalkin* after her search of the Scillies and the second Sea King went to investigate *Mulligatawny*. Still more distress calls were reported from MRCC. The Nimrod reports of men in a life-raft and of red flares at 51.00°N, 07.10°W were noted and added to the rapidly growing list of casualties.

A second Wessex was airborne as soon as the first one landed; it headed off to search for the survivors of *Grimalkin*. The first lift was at 0746Z when an injured man was taken off *Tarantula*. Less than two hours later a Wessex and a Sea King were on their way back to base with survivors. The Wessex had all five members of *Magic*'s crew on board while the Sea King had three from *Grimalkin*'s life-raft and two from the split life-raft of *Trophy*. The Sea King also reported that there were a further three survivors being picked up by the *Overijssel*. All ten of these survivors were handed over to the sick bay on arrival at Culdrose at 0948Z.

Half an hour later a Wessex radioed that she was returning with all eight members of *Carmargue*'s crew and a Sea King that she had one crewman from *Ariadne* who was in a bad way. The Sea King was diverted directly to Treliske Hospital, Truro. She had hardly got there when a Wessex arrived with the five survivors from the abandoned Belgian yacht *Skidbladner*. All five of the crew had taken to the life-raft when they believed the yacht would sink.

Another Sea King was fully laden on its return soon after midday. On board were the complete six-man crews from each of *Hestrul II* and *Gan*. Another Sea King was lifting all seven of the crew of the sinking *Gringo* at 50.56°N, 07.30°W. As these two helicopters landed a request was made for two Lynx helicopters from Yeovilton to assist in the operation. As soon as the helicopters were refuelled they were airborne again as more distress requests were passed on to Culdrose from MRCC Land's End and SRCC Plymouth.

A Wessex answered the call for help from *Festina Tertia*, one of whose crew was suffering from the effects of the cold. One man had been lost overboard and her skipper, Neil Mooney, felt it was best to get the sick man ashore as quickly as possible.

By mid-afternoon there were four Sea Kings, two Wessex and two Lynx helicopters in the air. One of the Sea Kings lifted from *Gunslinger* Mike Flowers who had injured his shoulder. Soon after it picked up Derek Jones from *Flashlight* but could not lift the rest of the crew because it was running out of fuel. An hour later a Wessex lifted the other four off *Flashlight*. Elsewhere another Wessex took all ten off *Golden Apple of the Sun*, which was drifting rudderless. The sick bay at Culdrose was becoming crowded.

Throughout this time the weather had been bad although the visibility had cleared during the day. The force 10 storm had moderated to severe gale force 9 and the sea state officially 8. RAF crews reported wave heights of fifty to sixty feet and the helicopters were often in the troughs between two crests of these huge waves. Skilful handling of the aircraft was essential not only to rescue the survivors from the yachts and life-rafts but also for the safety of the helicopters and their crews.

At 1755Z a Sea King picked up Michael Campbell and the crew of *Allamanda II*. The yacht was dismasted and damaged and its life-raft

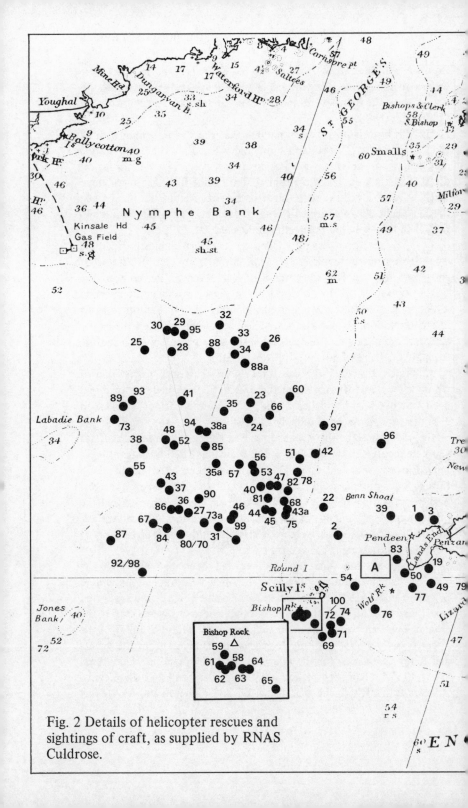

Fig. 2 Details of helicopter rescues and sightings of craft, as supplied by RNAS Culdrose.

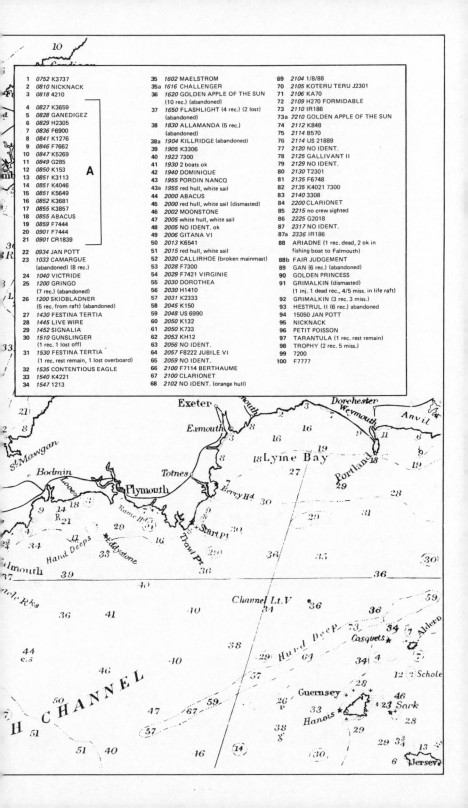

1	0752 K3737	
2	0810 NICKNACK	
3	0818 4210	
4	0827 K3659	
5	0828 GANEDIGEZ	
6	0829 H2305	
7	0836 F6900	
8	0841 K1276	
9	0846 F7662	
10	0847 K5269	
11	0849 G285	
12	0850 K153	**A**
13	0851 K3113	
14	0851 K4046	
15	0851 K5649	
16	0852 K3681	
17	0855 K3857	
18	0855 ABACUS	
19	0859 F7444	
20	0901 F7444	
21	0901 CR1839	
22	0934 JAN POTT	
23	1033 CAMARGUE (abandoned) (8 rec.)	
24	1040 VICTRIDE	
25	1200 GRINGO (7 rec.) (abandoned)	
26	1200 SKIDBLADNER (5 rec. from raft) (abandoned)	
27	1430 FESTINA TERTIA	
28	1445 LIVE WIRE	
29	1452 SIGNALIA	
30	1510 GUNSLINGER (1 rec. 1 lost off)	
31	1530 FESTINA TERTIA (1 rec. rest remain, 1 lost overboard)	
32	1535 CONTENTIOUS EAGLE	
33	1540 K4221	
34	1547 1213	

35	1602 MAELSTROM	
35a	1616 CHALLENGER	
36	1620 GOLDEN APPLE OF THE SUN (10 rec.) (abandoned)	
37	1650 FLASHLIGHT (4 rec.) (2 lost) (abandoned)	
38	1830 ALLAMANDA (5 rec.) (abandoned)	
38a	1904 KILLRIDGE (abandoned)	
39	1905 K3306	
40	1923 7300	
41	1930 2 boats ok	
42	1940 DOMINIQUE	
43	1955 PORDIN NANCQ	
43a	1955 red hull, white sail	
44	2000 ABACUS	
45	2000 red hull, white sail (dismasted)	
46	2002 MOONSTONE	
47	2005 white hull, white sail	
48	2005 NO IDENT. ok	
49	2006 GITANA VI	
50	2013 K6541	
51	2015 red hull, white sail	
52	2020 CALLIRHOE (broken mainmast)	
53	2028 F7300	
54	2029 F7421 VIRGINIE	
55	2030 DOROTHEA	
56	2030 H1410	
57	2031 K2333	
58	2045 K150	
59	2048 US 6990	
60	2050 K132	
61	2050 K733	
62	2053 KH12	
63	2056 NO IDENT.	
64	2057 F8222 JUBILE VI	
65	2059 NO IDENT.	
66	2100 F7114 BERTHAUME	
67	2100 CLARIONET	
68	2102 NO IDENT. (orange hull)	

69	2104 1/8/88	
70	2105 KOTERU TERU J2301	
71	2106 KA70	
72	2109 H270 FORMIDABLE	
73	2110 IR186	
73a	2210 GOLDEN APPLE OF THE SUN	
74	2112 K848	
75	2114 B570	
76	2114 US 21889	
77	2120 NO IDENT.	
78	2125 GALLIVANT II	
79	2129 NO IDENT.	
80	2130 T2301	
81	2135 F6748	
82	2135 K4021 7300	
83	2140 3308	
84	2200 CLARIONET	
85	2215 no crew sighted	
86	2225 G2018	
87	2317 NO IDENT.	
87a	2336 IR186	
88	ARIADNE (1 rec. dead, 2 ok in fishing boat to Falmouth)	
88b	FAIR JUDGEMENT	
89	GAN (6 rec.) (abandoned)	
90	GOLDEN PRINCESS	
91	GRIMALKIN (dismasted) (1 inj. 1 dead rec., 4/5 miss. in life raft)	
92	GRIMALKIN (3 rec. 3 miss.)	
93	HESTRUL II (6 rec.) abandoned	
94	15050 JAN POTT	
95	NICKNACK	
96	PETIT POISSON	
97	TARANTULA (1 rec. rest remain)	
98	TROPHY (2 rec. 5 miss.)	
99	7200	
100	F7777	

had been blown away. Ten miles to the north, at 50.40°N, 07.30°W, this same Sea King winched to safety the six members of the French yacht *Billy Bones* and then headed for home.

The final lift of the day was that of Nick Ward and the body of Gerry Winks from *Grimalkin*. Nick Ward sums up the relief of all of those who were rescued when he described how he 'cried for joy' when he heard the helicopter coming to him.

But the day was far from over for the pilots and crews of the helicopters. They were still airborne, searching the area and checking reports of life-rafts, yachts and lifejackets until after dark. The final landing was that of a Sea King at 0030Z the next morning; but at 0504Z the helicopters were in the air again, continuing the search. Now it was a clearing-up operation and on Wednesday only one pick-up was made, that of a body in the sea, but a similar number of hours were flown that day.

By Thursday the heat was off. Nevertheless the helicopters flew many hours checking the area. They also brought ashore a *Bonaventure* crewman who had broken his arm. Abandoned yachts were checked and where possible battened down after personal possessions had been removed for return to their owners through the RORC. The search and rescue operation was finally called off for all the helicopters at 2000Z.

Throughout this vast search and rescue operation the helicopters were aided by the search ability of RAF Nimrods from Kinloss and St Mawgan. Nimrods perform long-range search and rescue tasks around the shores of the United Kingdom and their job is first to locate boats or people in distress by means of radar, radio or visual look-out and then to relay positional information to rescue co-ordination centres and to ships and helicopters that may be assisting in the rescue. Also, Nimrods carry in their bomb-bays, multi-seat dinghies and survival equipment that can be dropped to survivors. In addition to the Nimrods which flew a total of 110 hours in the three days, there was one sortie by a French Atlantique aircraft which is equipped for a similar rôle, and six sorties by Irish Beech King fixed-wing aircraft.

Chapter 7

THE RORC'S ROLE IN THE DISASTER

'For should professional traveller come,
Asked at the fireside he is dumb,
Declining with a secret smile,
And all the while
Conjectures on our maps grow stranger
And threaten danger.'

W.H. Auden
No Change of Place

The overall responsibility of the yachts and the sailors who compete in the Fastnet Race is morally, if not legally, that of the RORC, the organisers. The responsibility for the safety of the yachts and their crews is very definitely that of the skippers. Each skipper chooses his own crew and decides whether a yacht is seaworthy enough to tackle the race in question. The owner must in no way shirk his responsibility or seek redress from the Club in the event of a mishap. Those who race must be made aware of these responsibilities and of the sort of conditions they might encounter.

To this end, on the 26th July 1979, David Sheahan, skipper of the ill-fated *Grimalkin*, sent each member of the crew detailed information of his rôle in the race. Sheahan informed them as to the make-up of the crew together with the special watch system and their specialist duties on board. He listed the extra insurance cover, details of the check on the safety gear that was to be carried out by Camper & Nicholson, of the extra watertanks that would be fitted and of the amount of fuel to be carried. Clothing, medical matters, food and provisions were all itemised and there was even provision for contact with the shore. He concluded: 'We have maintained a high standard of personal safety on

109

board, let's retain it for this event.' David Sheahan took *Grimalkin* to the Fastnet as well prepared as he knew how.

The RORC for their part provide a stringent set of safety regulations and comprehensive sailing instructions. It has always been a qualification requirement that a full crew list with addresses and contact telephone numbers is submitted by the skipper of each competing yacht. Indeed the sailing instructions are not issued until this has been done. In this way the RORC knows exactly who is involved in the race and on which boat, in case of an emergency.

The owner's responsibility is clearly stated in the RORC Special Regulations. Item 2.1 states:

> The safety of a yacht and her crew is the sole and inescapable responsibility of the owner, who must do his best to ensure that the yacht is fully found, thoroughly seaworthy and manned by an experienced crew who are physically fit to face bad weather[1]. He must be satisfied as to the soundness of hull, spars, rigging, sails and all gear[2]. He must ensure that all safety equipment is properly maintained[3] and stowed[4] and that the crew know where it is kept and how it is to be used[5]. (The numbered check points are intended as an aid.)

In making this statement the RORC in no way frees itself of its responsibility. Without a regulation of this kind there could be lesser vigilance on the part of some owners. Most of those who race offshore, even for the first time, are aware that this can be a dangerous sport. In fact it is all the more challenging because of the potential dangers, but these can be minimised by the deliberate action of the individuals who take part.

The plans for the 1979 Fastnet Race for the organisation of the communications and for the results were co-ordinated by the RORC firstly from their headquarters in London and then in temporary offices established in Groves & Gutteridge Marina at Cowes and in Jewson's Building, Millbay Dock, Plymouth. Crew lists were collected and sailing instructions issued at Cowes and as soon as the fleet had started from the Royal Yacht Squadron line, the secretariat moved to Plymouth.

Unlike the Sydney-Hobart Race where there is a mandatory, thrice-daily radio schedule for every yacht to maintain, the Fastnet Race radio reporting requirements applied only to the fifty-seven Admiral's Cup yachts. These entailed twice-daily calls, at 1500 and 2200 hours, with back-up schedules an hour later if necessary. In addition, four other yachts had agreed to make radio reports. The yachts concerned were required to have a VHF transceiver working on channels 37 and 72 with a minimum transmitting power of 25 watts. The Royal Netherlands Navy Ship *Overijssel* and the yacht *Morningtown* would act as radio-relay vessels.

Prior to the storm the rôle of the RORC was simply routine. The Club was working with volunteers from the Royal Western Yacht Club, logging all sightings from coastguard stations as the fleet headed westwards past Land's End. It was ready to receive the radio reports from the Admiral's Cup yachts and *Siska, Mistress Quickly, Tula* and *Xaviera.* For the rest of the fleet there would be sightings from commercial shipping, aircraft sightings from the eager press and more importantly reports from the lighthouse keepers on the roundings of the Fastnet Rock and the Bishop Rock.

Monitoring the race was a daunting task, but the RORC had the basic tools to deal with the problem. It was at the centre of a fine communications network and worked in co-operation with rescue services. In addition it had the services of a computer which had been programmed to formulate the race results.

The early radio schedules were excellent and the path of the Admiral's Cup fleet was plotted together with all the other boats that had been spotted from coastguard stations. Only when the storm broke did the regular radio reporting cease; with so many vessels in distress the rescue services had greater need of the VHF frequencies.

Early in the morning of Tuesday, 14th August the rôle of the RORC changed. The computer was reprogrammed to keep a tally on all the yachts and the Datawest Computer Services team worked round the clock keeping the information up to date. All the yachts that had entered the Fastnet Race were listed alphabetically. Their sail numbers, class, whether an Admiral's Cup team, preceded their status in the race. This might have been in the form of the last sighting, giving the source; the number of people rescued; the casualties; gear failure; or the finishing time together with the elapsed and corrected times. As each new piece of information came into the Race Control Centre, it was fed into the computer.

Regular print-outs from the computer were supplied to those who had the unenviable job of answering the incessant telephone inquiries.

Alan Green was in charge of the RORC operation in Plymouth. The size of the available offices and the restricted number of telephone lines was limiting but, with assistance, Green was able to maintain a reliable, up-to-date information service for the press and for those seeking news of relatives and friends afloat.

Much of Green's liaison with the outside was through Roger Ware. It was through Ware that the press conferences were arranged. Mostly these were difficult occasions as Green was under pressure to defend the action of the RORC in continuing the race after the storm had struck. Green had a difficult task endeavouring to explain to a partly hostile audience why it would have been impossible to cancel the race, pointing to the relevant clauses in the Club's Special Regulations which stressed owners' responsibility. He handled each question with the same careful consideration. He was aware that if he got one phrase out of line, there would be further undue, and probably unjust, criticism of the sport of ocean racing.

Initially he was on his own. The RORC is a club whose Flag Officers and Committee are actively engaged in the sport. Only John Clothier, one of the Rear Commodores, who had been prevented from going on the race by business pressures and whose yacht was believed for a long time to be sunk, was available to help Green in this crucial rôle. Even so the bulk of the responsibility fell on Green's shoulders.

Questions were being asked in the House of Commons and some journalists sought out Green's comments for the Club on these. They varied from the advisability of ocean racing unrestricted by law to the cost of the rescue services. Members of Parliament in the Department of Trade appeared somewhat perplexed at the questions they received at the time, particularly with a most notable sailing Member taking part in the race. The answers given in the House in no way satisfied the journalists or their editors and for some there were really no answers from Green that would have satisfied them either. Other, more militant inquirers were equally dissatisfied that the Secretary of the RORC should take the predictable line that he did. Green was their whipping boy and no one was more aware of it than he was.

It is interesting to note that one of the questions that Green was asked concerned the cost, or at least the estimated additional costs to the Exchequer, of the rescue services. The same question was asked of the Secretary of State for Trade but the answer was not forthcoming until a written reply from Mr Norman Tebbit, MP appeared in *Hansard* on 22nd October, over two months after the question had been posed. It stated that the estimated additional cost to the Exchequer was in the region of £350,000 of which the bulk, £310,000, was for helicopters and fixed-wing aircraft and the rest for Her Majesty's ships.

The very next question in *Hansard* that day concerned the manning of the coastguard station at Rame Head, the last headland on the Fastnet course before the finish.

Green was always reluctant to sit on information but nothing was issued until he was satisfied that it had been checked. He was the voice of the RORC and his attention to detail and devotion to duty made him a respected figure. He drew on all the help possible to elaborate on the conditions that were experienced in the race, taking with him to the press conferences all the latest arrivals, be they finishers, off retired boats or, on occasion, survivors. No one was left in any doubt that the RORC was trying to help everyone concerned with the race.

Following the race, it was the RORC as organisers who were, together with the RYA as the national authority, given the task of preparing an inquiry document into the disaster. The Inquiry team was headed by Sir Hugh Forbes, Sir Maurice Laing and Lt Col James Myatt, and the findings of the Inquiry form the basis of the rest of this book. It is a comprehensive document but it is criticised for avoiding certain issues, notably that of the design of boats and the trends towards lighter displacement boats. There are those who see these developments as being entirely responsible for the loss of lives in the Fastnet Race. These factions are, in the main, regarded with scepticism by the more authoritative members of ocean racing circles. There are counter factions that will go further the other way and suggest that had a storm of these proportions hit a fleet of this size composed of the boats that were raced twenty years previously, the toll would have been far higher. The RORC/RYA Report seeks to avoid this type of controversy.

Chapter 8

THE METEOROLOGICAL STORY

'The glass is falling hour by hour, the glass will fall for ever,
But if you break the bloody glass you won't hold up the weather'

Louis Macneice
Bagpipe Music

Peter Bowker was walking down York Street at Cowes early on the Saturday morning before the race. He crossed into the High Street by the Duke of York, memories of a few pints causing a smile to add a few lines around his eyes. His mind was on one thing — how to win the Fastnet Race, the win that had so far eluded him.

Bowker's eyes chanced on a weather forecast stuck up in the showroom window of Offshore Instruments. It was a long (Bowker suggests medium) range forecast for the Celtic Sea. Reading it revealed that there was a prediction for a north-westerly force 8 gale to pass through the Fastnet area at midnight on Monday. The forecast had originated from the Southampton Weather Centre and Bowker, a thorough navigator, made a note of it.

After the race Bowker said he was surprised that there was not greater distribution of this forecast. He saw no further amendment to it and was thus none too astonished when the gale appeared right on schedule. Indeed he was 'impressed by the prescience of the forecaster, despite the fact that it came from the south-west'. Yet more amazing, to his way of thinking, is that this forecast is not considered in the inquiry report. The relevant paragraph of the report (2.22) states that the forecast was issued on the morning of 12th August, the Sunday, when Bowker was at sea. In the previous paragraph of the report mention is made of the last medium-range forecast covering the period to 2359 on 13th August making no reference to gales and storms. The forecast that Bowker saw in the window of Offshore Instruments was dated 1700 Friday, August 10th.

114

In forecasting the winds for an ocean race a navigator has but few facilities at his disposal. To win a race the knowledge of what the wind is going to do is just as important as being able to sail the boat well. The navigational equipment must include (by Special Regulations) a radio receiver capable of obtaining weather forecasts. The average ocean racer will consider the BBC's shipping forecasts enough but the real competitor knows of the forecasts available from the Direction de la Météorologie, Ministère des Transports in Paris and which are broadcast on France Inter and Brest le Conquet. In addition there should be an accurate barometer. The check of forecast pressure against actual pressure and the note of rate of change are vitally important to a navigator's own forecasting. Wind direction, too, and its changes in strength are necessities for accurate prediction.

Whatever method of forecasting was being used by the Fastnet's yachtsmen in 1979, the storm caught almost all of them in some way unprepared. It surprised many of the professional forecasters and the reasons are that the rate of change of the windspeed was rather unexpected and the veer, in the area where many of the boats were, was fast. The building southerly winds which, during the second half of August 13th, went from force 4 to force 8 plus, created one wave pattern. The new north-westerly gale-force winds which came after the veer had time to build up another wave pattern on their way to the area. It was the combination of these waves — seas of similar wavelengths — that built up the fearful cross-seas that were the wreakers of damage in this race.

For many years yachtsmen have considered that the effect of the shallowing over the Labadie Bank would cause greater confusion of the seas. According to oceanographic experts this is not so. The Labadie Bank, which is on average 45 fathoms deep, with a shallowest point of 34 fathoms, would not have a significant effect on the wavelength of the seas in these wind conditions. Lawrence Draper of the Institute of Oceanographic Sciences has calculated that the effect of the Labadie Bank would be to reduce the wavelength by no more than 4 per cent with an appropriate increase in the wave height; not a significant amount. The waves, therefore, were wind generated.

Prior to the start of the race there had been much talk in the bars of the pubs and clubs of Cowes about the possibility of strong winds for the Fastnet Race. The discussions had begun along the lines of the probability because there had been no strong winds for several years — 1971 was the last time that there had been what many of them referred to as a 'real blow'. Then came the strong winds of Cowes Week and the Admiral's Cup and the bar talk became stronger. Meanwhile Peter Bowker and the like were consulting the Atlantic charts and noticing that there was a row of three lows out there waiting to come across. Certainly there was wind to come, but much depended on how deep those depressions got and exactly what path they took.

The cause of the storm was a depression identified as Low Y. At 0100 on Sunday 12th August, Y was a small secondary depression with central pressure 1006 mbs situated close to the south of Newfoundland. In the next twenty-four hours it moved rapidly north-eastwards across the Atlantic but remained at the same pressure. In the next eighteen hours, Y moved towards the south-west tip of Ireland and deepened. By 1900 on Monday 13th its centre was 200 miles south-west of Valentia with a central pressure of 984 mbs and by 0100 the next day it had deepened further to 978 mbs and moved immediately to the west of Valentia. It continued north-east over Ireland crossing the east coast near Dublin about 0830 moving on to a more northerly path, filling slightly until by 0100 on 15th August it was 986 mbs 100 miles north of the Shetlands.

It was not a storm without precedent. Nine years before, on 15/16th August 1970 (a non Fastnet year), a very similar depression had moved in the same path. There have been deeper depressions over Britain at this time of the year and gusts have been recorded inland reaching 69 knots (force 12), but these have been exceptional as the storm associated with Low Y can also be described.

Strangely, a very high proportion (34 per cent) of the competitors claimed that they had experienced weather conditions as bad as these before. In sheer wind strength alone it is doubtful whether as high a percentage had been afloat in comparable conditions. Certainly few of them can have experienced seas such as they encountered in the early hours of Tuesday 14th August resulting from the rapid veer which combined with darkness and lack of conformity of the wind and seas. Most of those who had raced in the Southern Oceans on fully crewed boats in Round-the-World Races said that they had never encountered seas like those off the Fastnet that night. David Birchenough, who had rounded the Horn aboard *King's Legend* and did both the Southern Ocean legs of the 1977/8 Whitbread Race and was on the Bermuda Race in 1972 when a hurricane crossed the path of the fleet, said that conditions were the worst he had ever experienced. He was racing on the 79-foot *Kialoa* which was second into Millbay Dock and added

116

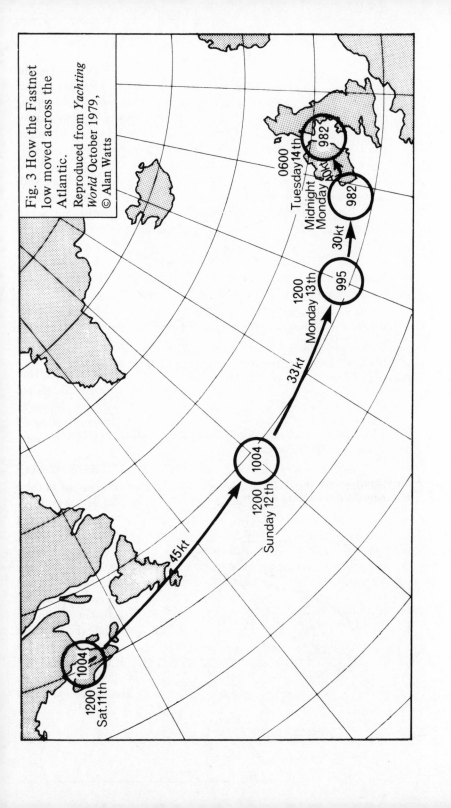

Fig. 3 How the Fastnet low moved across the Atlantic. Reproduced from *Yachting World* October 1979, © Alan Watts

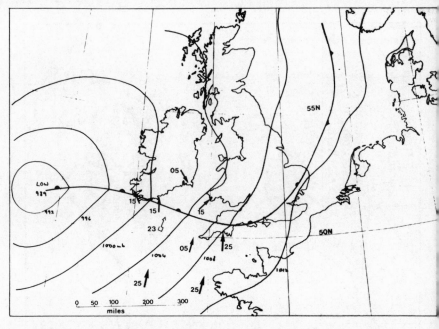

Fig. 4 The weather map for 1900 Monday. The calm before the storm
– Scilly had 5 knots and strangely in Wexford the light wind was
blowing contrary to the trend in the isobars.

Fig. 5 The storm corridor develops with surface winds above 60 knots
off the Fastnet (0100 Tuesday).

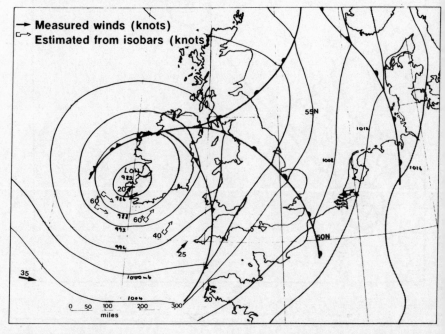

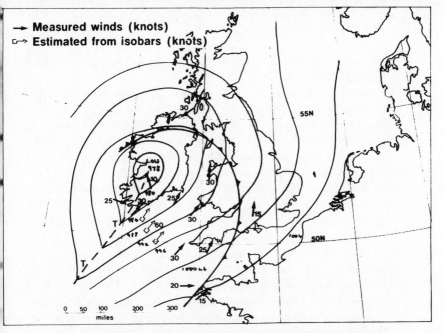

Fig. 6 The height of the storm (0400) when the violent storm-force winds (force 11) had spread across much of the fleet. All land stations fail to record anything above 30 knots mean speed. A trough-line (T) with a 90° shift on it begins to move across the area.

Fig. 7 Off the Rock the wind shifts and relents, but it still blows storm to violent storm force over the rescue operation. The wind drops to force 10 behind the trough.

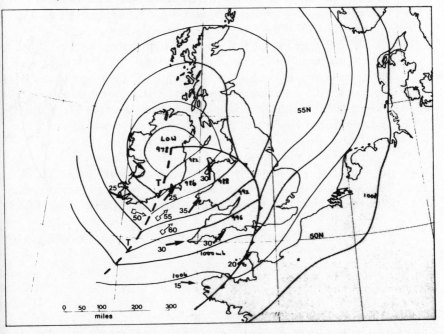

that the conditions on the Fastnet were far worse than those of the Bermuda hurricane.

The most important aspect was how the competitors reacted to the forecasts that they did receive. The first gale forecast for the area was issued by the Meteorological Office at 1355 13th August at the same time that the shipping forecast was being broadcast on Radio 4 on 1500 metres, and which did not get broadcast until 1505. The forecast which was issued an hour earlier contained:

'The general synopsis at 0700. Complex low, 300 miles south-west of Iceland, 986 mbs, moving slowly south-east. Cold front with shallow waves, Viking, Lundy, north Finisterre expected Fisher, Dover tomorrow. Low 300 miles west of Sole, 1002, expected Scotland 994 by the same time, with associated cold front through northern England to central Finisterre. The area forecasts for the next twenty-four hours:

Sole, Lundy, Fastnet: South-westerly 4 or 5, increasing 6 or 7 for a time, veering westerly later. Occasional rain or showers.

Coastal station reports:

Scilly: south by west 5, . . . 1013 falling.

Valentia: south 4, . . . 1009 falling slowly.

Ronaldsway: south-west by south 4, . . . 1011 falling slowly.

Malin Head: west by south 3, . . . 1008 falling slowly.'

There was nothing untoward about that forecast. The promise of force 6 or 7 for a time should not make any ocean racing sailor apprehensive, just aware of what he might have to do to use the winds to the best possible advantage. The veer would have indicated a need to stay to the south of the rhumb line course to the Fastnet.

The gale warning was first broadcast just over an hour later, when few would have been listening to the radio and thus its value was lost to the majority. It was for Sole, Fastnet and Shannon and warned of south-westerly gales, force 8, imminent. At the coastal stations there was little barometric evidence of this impending storm. The pressure was not falling rapidly enough to induce a state of concern and there were some anomalies about this throughout the storm.

It needs a barometric drop of 10 mbs/hr to indicate a force 8 with any certainty, but only once, at Valentia, between 0100 and 0200, did the barometer show a fall like this and then only briefly. In general the fall was no more than 6 mbs/hr at Valentia, about the right rate of fall for force 6.

The next BBC shipping forecast was at 1750, a bulletin which had been issued at 1705. It gave warnings of gales in Plymouth, Finisterre, Sole, Lundy, Fastnet, Irish Sea, Shannon. The general synopsis at 1300 was of a low north Cromarty, 1005, moving steadily north, deepening slowly. Low Y 250 miles west of Fastnet sea area, 998, expected Carlisle area, 993 by 1300 Tuesday. The relative area forecasts for the next twenty-four hours were:

Lundy, Fastnet, Irish sea:

Mainly southerly 4 locally 6, increasing 6 locally gale 8, becoming mainly northwesterly later . . .

The coastal station reports at 1600 were:

Scilly: south-west 4 . . . 1010 falling more slowly.

Valentia: south by West 3 . . . 1005, falling.

Ronaldsway: south 3 . . . 1009 falling.

Malin Head: east by north 3 . . . 1006 falling.

There was enough in this forecast for some concern but there was a feeling among many of those who were sailing that they had had more bad forecasting than bad forecasts come true. The wind force at the coastal stations tended to contradict the forecast and although the wind had begun to rise it was doubtful that at this time there were more than a very few who were worried. At the Meteorological Office however, there was greater concern. The availability of the 'Tiros N' satellite pictures of the gathering storm brought a further gale warning, issued just ten minutes after the shipping forecast had been broadcast. It was for sea area Finisterre, Sole and Fastnet: 'South-westerly gales force 8, increasing severe gale force 9, imminent.'

Once again most of the fleet would have missed this when it was broadcast at 1830 and again at 1905. After all, one of the reasons for sailing is to get away from the interferences of life, like radio, and the majority tune in to 1500 metres just for the shipping forecast and turn the radio off immediately afterwards.

The seriousness of the warning can be gauged by the decision to broadcast the gale warning twice within thirty-five minutes and this leads to possible consideration of more 'scheduled' gale warnings when they are necessary. The BBC might, in future, be prepared to have 'hot spots' where gale warnings would be re-broadcast if any were in operation.

The next move from the forecasters came while they were preparing the chart at 2200. The isobars were tightening fast and it became inevitable that there would be force 10 in the Fastnet area. This necessitated a further warning to be broadcast and one was issued at

2245 which the BBC transmitted at 2300. The BBC was, by now, well alert to the gravity of the situation in pure weather terms although it is doubtful if anyone concerned with weather broadcasts was aware that 303 yachts were racing in the areas that were affected by these gales. But at 2300 when the following bulletin was issued — Fastnet: south-westerly severe gales force 9, increasing storm force 10, imminent — the winds were already blowing that strongly. Richard Matthews, skipper of *Oystercatcher 79*, a 40-foot one tonner, reported that at 2300 he was 50 miles south of the Fastnet Rock and the winds were between 45 and 50 knots (force 9—10).

The strong winds associated with Low Y, hit the fleet faster than the Meteorological Office could forecast them. Indeed there was never a forecast of force 11 although it can be argued that there is little difference in tackling this extra strength of wind in yachts the size of those that were racing. The first opportunity of receiving a forecast of force 9 for the Fastnet area was at 1830, yet there are many reports that by 2000 boats were in winds that had begun to top 40 knots. Not only that, the direction of the force 10 winds was inaccurately forecast and it was this that caused the waves to build up enormously.

The earliest forecast of gales that was broadcast came in the France Inter forecast at 0740 on Monday 13th August. This predicted gales in the Fastnet area for the night of 13/14th and on the day of the 14th August. The 1733 forecast from Brest on the 13th, forecast winds of force 8 with strong gusts (by implication, force 9—10).

While earlier forecasting would not have lessened the effect of the storm for those racing, it would have given greater opportunity to prepare for it. On board many of the yachts there would have been more attention to the details of stowing gear above and, particularly, below decks. Crews could have made sure that storm sails were available and that other very necessary items of gear, like bolt croppers, were to hand. It was already obvious that there would be strong winds during the hours of darkness but the forecasts hung back too long for the crews to make the fullest use of the daylight hours for their preparation. Had some of the skippers been aware of the probability of force 10, let alone force 11, they would have run for shelter. If they had done so as a result of the late forecasts, it would have caused them to hazard their yachts for they would have arrived close to the coast when the storm was rising to its full height.

It must be admitted that the forecasters were hampered in their duty by the lack of numbers of ships in the eastern Atlantic and in the south-western approaches when Low Y was heading for the Fastnet area, so that the Central Forecast Office was unaware of the fact that Low Y was deepening on Sunday 12th August. Had this fact been available to them, the forecasters would have had gale warnings out considerably earlier. In addition to this, two ship reports that were received were inaccurate; the pressures that they sent were wrong. And it does seem unfortunate that those ships which do send reports in through Portishead, appear to give up when they reach the coastal areas (in their case some fifty miles from the land).

Chapter 9

SURVIVAL

'Dear God, be good to me. The sea is so wide and my boat is so small'

Old Breton Fisherman's Prayer

Survival, like any other technique, must be learned. Many of those who were forced to survive in the Fastnet Race had no idea of the principles of survival and survived through luck rather than considered judgment. That some survived at all is nothing short of miraculous because they were hideously ill-prepared for the rigours of survival at sea.

'You are not a survivor until you have been rescued.' This is the maxim by which Joe Cross, Principal Instructor at the Offshore Survival Centre in Aberdeen, runs his courses. For him 'rescued' means safe refuge aboard another vessel, recovery to a non-hostile environment. Most of those who attend courses at the Centre are from the oil industry or are fishermen — both high on the list of potential survivors. Whatever their occupation, they face the same hazards as yachtsmen once the decision has been made to abandon their rig or vessel; they must use everything at their disposal to promote their chances of being rescued. Knowing the right way to tackle the problems lessens the dangers, and subsequent events have proved that those who have taken a course at the Offshore Survival Centre have survived in critical situations where those who have not taken the course have perished.

Thus it was that fifteen people died in the 1979 Fastnet Race: they had not been properly prepared to survive. Had they been aware of the principles of survival, there would have been very few casualties in the race. Unfortunately yachtsmen tend to take a blinkered attitude towards the possibilities of having to survive if their yacht sinks. Far too many placed implicit faith in the ability of the life-raft to protect them without knowing how to protect the life-raft or even how to use it properly.

Cold is a killer. Man is a tropical animal and cannot survive in a temperate climate without clothes. Heat loss by conduction is twenty-six times greater in water than it is in air. In water of 6°C a man dressed in conventional clothes has a survival time of only two hours. He must therefore make deliberate efforts to improve his chances. Wind will accelerate heat loss; a gentle breeze of 10 knots makes the effect of a 12°C air temperature one of 10°C in still air. The force 11 storm winds of the Fastnet Race would have effectively dropped the air temperature by around 10°C.

It therefore becomes rapidly apparent that to survive man must endeavour to keep himself warm and dry and must select the best haven to do so. Which refuge he chooses must be that which offers him the best protection against the elements; it may not be the most comfortable. The decision to take to the life-raft rather than stay with the boat was made on more than one occasion in the Fastnet Race, on the basis that it would be more comfortable in the raft than in a boat which rolled and made life below unbearable. The crew of *Grimalkin* had taken a mid-line course by staying huddled together in the cockpit rather than remaining below where injuries seemed likely.

In retrospect there are competitors who say they should have made greater efforts to make it possible to stay below, by ditching or securing any loose gear that was likely to cause injuries, and by securing themselves firmly to bunks so that they would be capable of surviving a B2 knockdown. In retrospect they agree that this sort of decision is easier to make in the light of experience but at the time they were motivated by fear.

It is the opinion of survival experts that no one should have left their yacht until it was sinking under them. It is also their opinion that there were very few who understood the order of importance of the essentials for survival when abandoning the yacht became necessary. The education of yachtsmen in the use of safety equipment is poor. Almost every one of them would have to read the instructions on the pack at the time that they need to use it, losing valuable seconds doing so. Their knowledge of the use of pyrotechnics is lamentable, restricted probably to the ignition of out-of-date flares on Guy Fawkes' night. Even a former Royal Marine officer, well versed in the use of this type of pyrotechnics, managed, at the height of the Fastnet storm, to fire a parachute flare at his feet rather than into the sky, injuring himself and, just as important, wasting a flare.

Above all it is the yachtsman's distressing ignorance concerning hypothermia which causes the greatest anguish among the survival experts.

The normal human core temperature is 36.9°C. Hypothermia begins at 35°C and death is inevitable if the body reaches 24°C. At the lower limit severe hypothermia is often indistinguishable from death and it must be everyone's duty to endeavour to resuscitate what appears to be a corpse apparently dead from hypothermia.

To avoid heat loss it is imperative to slow down one's actions particularly when in water. If taking to the life-raft it is better to enter it dry but this is often not possible and certainly was not for many of those who took to rafts in the Fastnet. Those who had to swim to a raft were at an immediate disadvantage, both from being wet and from having to speed up their movements in the water. The *Griffin* crewman who had only oilskin trousers and a tee shirt to wear was at an even greater disadvantage than any of the others who survived in a life-raft.

In the extreme case of abandoning ship, the first priority should be to put on plenty of warm clothes, with as many wind-proof layers as possible, topping it all with water-proof clothing and essentially a life-jacket. The importance of the lifejacket must never be underestimated; to start with it enables the wearer to remain still in the water and thus conserve body heat.

Hypothermia is insidious; it creeps up unawares. The first symptoms are those of vasoconstriction; the blood vessels of the skin close up and the skin takes a pallor. There is some mental disturbance and the will to survive begins to recede; the casualty becomes introverted. Then shivering begins. This is the body's reflex action when the core temperature is down to around 35°C. Shivering continues for a drop of another two degrees, after which the victim becomes semi-conscious. Shivering produces heat for the body, the sort of heat equivalent to running at 8-9 miles an hour; and burns up the same amount of energy. At rest the human body produces 0.1kW of heat and at its maximum in strenuous exercise it can produce 1.5kW. The action of shivering produces 0.7kW.

When a state of semi-consciousness is reached, deterioration becomes more rapid. Someone who has begun to shiver needs the help of others. The length of time that the sufferer can go on shivering and raising his core temperature in this way is limited — limited to the amount of time that he could continue to run at 8-9 miles per hour. The time from semi-consciousness to death in hypothermia is very short; the heart rate drops dramatically and the breathing rate follows it.

126

Hypothermia killed some of those who died on the Fastnet and some of those deaths could have been avoided.

If taking to the life-raft is inevitable and all on board the yacht are aware of the necessary action, there are some vital steps that must be taken. At best the crew will have boarded the life-raft properly clothed and dry. At worst, they are wet and have only a few clothes. Whatever the situation, they must preserve body heat, huddling together if necessary.

The first deliberate action must be to cut the painter which secures the life-raft to the yacht. Each raft is equipped with a knife, stowed near to the point of attachment of the painter, specifically for this purpose. Then the sea anchor or drogue must be streamed. Unless the drogue is deployed the life-raft can drift at an amazing rate, more than 6 knots in extreme conditions. Obviously this provides the search and rescue operation with a larger area to search. In the 1979 Fastnet there were reports of drogues becoming detached from rafts and this also contributed to their instability.

The drogue also keeps the life-raft at the right aspect to the elements. The entrance, which is the most vulnerable part of the canopy, is kept downwind and away from the waves. The canopy should be kept closed at all times to preserve all possible heat and the floor should be inflated with each of the chambers maintained at the correct pressure. Without the floor inflated there is no good insulation against the coldness of the sea water.

The secondary actions of good life-raft usage must also be implemented immediately. Leadership is important; without it the morale will lessen quickly and the psychological aspects of survival are as important as the physical ones. The will to survive must be there. The injured, if there are any, must be treated. The responsibility towards them is high. Loss of blood can contribute towards early suffering from hypothermia. Any water inside the raft must be bailed out and someone should be kept permanently at that task. Water must be sponged out in an effort to keep the life-raft dry.

Routine tasks should be split up into short watches. A look-out should be posted but he should not stand watch for more than a quarter of an hour at any time because he will get cold. Someone must look at the food and water stores available and decide how these should be rationed. Another person must be in charge of repairs to the raft and these must be made at the first sign of damage. The fabric from which the raft is made has been known to fail: *Trophy*'s raft parted between the upper and lower chambers and finally the two halves became separated. The pyrotechnics must be used sparingly and only when there is a reasonable chance of them being seen.

As soon as possible after entering the raft, everyone should take seasick pills. Even the hardiest of stomachs are likely to react badly to the motion of a life-raft. The loss of food by vomiting means a loss of body fuel to combat hypothermia; it also causes an immediate drop in the body temperature.

Location of a drifting life-raft can be aided. In addition to the sparing use of pyrotechnics the crew should have endeavoured to take an emergency radio transmitter with them. These should be used with some care to preserve the batteries. The operator should be aware of the fixed listening times for the frequency of his transmitter. When trying to attract attention the life-raft crew should use everything at their disposal; whistles and waved bright clothing all help to attract possible rescue craft.

When rationing food and water it is worth remembering that the human body can go without water for ten days and without food for fifty. Such food as is eaten should be examined to see if it needs a lot of water to assist digestion. For this reason one should avoid protein which needs an equal amount of water for digestion and if this is not available as drinking water, then it will be lost from the body itself resulting in dehydration. Fats and carbohydrates need very little water for digestion and thus are excellent foods to be consumed in a raft.

Rescue is another difficult phase and lives were lost in the Fastnet Race just when it seemed that all was well. Only two of the five people in *Ariadne*'s life-raft made it to the deck of *Nanna*. They were weakened by the cold and by injuries when they tried to get up a ladder on the side of the boat. A rope thrown to them, which they might have made fast to themselves, would have saved all three of these men.

Perhaps the most dangerous time to be rescued is in the hours of darkness. Certainly one should never beach a life-raft on a strange shore in the dark; there are too many recorded incidents of people being pounded to death on rocks when life-rafts have been brought into the shore at night.

When trying to survive, the crew has to work together better than at any other time. The will to survive must be there and he who has it strongest must spread the gospel and keep the crew in a state of hope.

The good skipper will give his crew a better chance of survival in the case of the yacht sinking if he maintains his safety gear in tip-top condition and instructs all his crew in the proper use of it. Even then he may find the fates turned against him. The four-year-old eight-man life-raft of the yacht *Trophy* had been serviced specially for the Fastnet Race and that came apart around the middle. The four men who clung to the top half of that life-raft were perhaps the luckiest survivors of the 1979 Fastnet Race.

Chapter 10

AFTERMATH

'And all that noise, as of a rushing crowd,
With groans, and tremulous shudderings – all is over –
It tells another tale, with sounds less deep and loud!'

Samuel Taylor Coleridge
Dejection

A race which claims the lives of fifteen competitors is certain to attract sufficient adverse criticism to necessitate a major inquiry. The RORC together with the RYA was determined that this inquiry should be as thorough as possible and began its investigations before all the boats had retired or returned to Plymouth. Those who finished were debriefed by members of the Club's Committee and from these early investigations it was possible to draw up a questionnaire to issue to all the yachtsmen who took part in the race.

In addition, the inquiry sought information from coastguards; the RNLI; the Royal Navy and RAF crews of the helicopters and fixed-wing aircraft; the staff of the Southern Rescue Co-ordination Centre; the Meteorological Office and its French equivalent; Southampton University's Wolfson Unit for Marine Technology; the Commanding Officers of HNLMS *Overijssel* and the other Royal Navy vessels; the Institute of Oceanographic Sciences; as well as numerous yacht designers and individuals concerned with the sport. The inquiry explored every avenue.

Replies to the questionnaire were received from 235 yachts. These replies were computer analysed. In addition replies were received from thirty other yachts, twenty-one of which were not at sea during the storm. Replies from a further nine yachts were received too late for inclusion in the computer analysis.

Of the 909 questionnaires despatched to competitors, 669 were returned. The working party dealing with the inquiry considered this to be a very high degree of response. From the 85 yachts which finished the race, replies from 64 were included for analysis; 148 of the 194 who retired, and all but one of the 24 which were abandoned, also provided information for the computer analysis.

Table 1. Race statistics for 1979 Fastnet

Class	Rating Limits	Started	Finished	Retired
0	42.1-70	14	13	1
I	33-42	56	36	19
II	29-32.9	53	23	30
III	25.5-28.9	64	6	52
IV	23-25.4	58	6	44
V	21-22.9	58	1	48
TOTAL		303	85	194

Class	No. of Crew Lost	Yachts Abandoned	
		Since Recovered	Lost Believed Sunk
0	—	—	—
I	—	1	—
II	—	—	—
III	6	4	2
IV	6	7	1
V	3	7	2
TOTAL	15	19	5

The inquiry at first dealt with the background to the Fastnet Race and the policy adopted by the organisers. The race is handicapped under the measurement system of the International Offshore Rule, whose custodian is the Offshore Racing Council (ORC). The Council consists of members nominated by national authorities for ocean racing together with two members nominated by the International Yacht Racing Union. Thus its constitution ensures broad representation with a reputation for impartiality with the power to authoritatively amend the Rule whenever it considers it necessary.

The design of offshore racers has always been influenced by whatever handicap measurement rule is in force. The ORC acknowledges this in the introduction to the Rule:

131

RULE MANAGEMENT POLICY

IOR exists to provide ratings for a diverse group of yachts. The Council will manage the Rule, changing it as necessary to permit the development of seaworthy offshore racing yachts.

In changing the Rule, the Council will endeavour to protect the value of the majority of the existing IOR fleet from rapid obsolescence caused by design trends, loopholes in the Rule, and other developments which produce increased performance without corresponding increases in ratings. The Council will act to discourage developments which lead to excessive costs, or reduce safety or the suitability of yachts for cruising. It will attempt to manage Rule changes to minimise disruption to the existing fleet.

The Council will act promptly to close loopholes as they are discovered. It will control and moderate design trends by penalising design features which depart significantly from fleet norms while affecting as little as possible boats near the norms.

The Council will provide retrospective rating credits to extend the competitive life of older boats and reduce the impact on the fleet of gradual improvements in design.

The Council recognises that there will be conflict among these objectives and will do its best to achieve a balance that will ensure the long-term vitality of IOR.

In 1978 the ORC decided that the trends of light displacement, broad beam, shallow-hull form and large sail area were becoming undesirable. Designers were going too far in these directions to produce fast boats; far beyond the proportions which the ORC felt was in keeping with the spirit and intent of the Rule and thus made to legislate against the trends. The Rule was amended to penalise boats of very light displacement and those which were potentially unstable were excluded from racing. Large sail areas, too, were penalised at this time.

The Inquiry Report analyses the ability of the yachts to withstand the storm with particular reference to the design parameters imposed by the IOR. The figures of boats involved in knockdowns were high: 48 per cent of the fleet (112 boats) were knocked down to the horizontal (B1 knockdown) on one or more occasions and, of those, 77 boats (33 per cent) were knocked down to well beyond the horizontal including total inversion (B2 knockdown). B1 knockdowns have always been accepted as a fact of life for cruising and racing yachts, a potential danger that can occur in strong winds and heavy seas. The B2 knockdown, however, is a rare and more serious occurrence and all the available information of the boats involved was carefully calibrated.

It showed that the smaller classes were more susceptible but then this is an obviously accepted fact. Smaller, and therefore lighter, boats are much more at the mercy of the waves than larger, heavier ones. What might not have been such a readily acceptable fact was the lack of relationship between ballast ratio or indeed length/displacement ratio, to vulnerability to knockdowns. What did tend to increase the vulnerability to B2 knockdowns were lack of initial stability, indicated by a high tenderness ratio, and a low negative screening value. The tenderness ratio is derived from a measurement of the inclining moment required to heel the yacht through one degree. The lower the value the more stable the yacht. The screening value is calculated from the tenderness ratio and other hull measurements to ensure that the yacht is self-righting at 90° of heel. A negative value indicates that the yacht has positive self-righting tendencies at 90° of heel and those boats with a positive figure must undergo a test to show that they are self-righting with weights attached to the mast.

Where concern for the stability of the modern ocean racing yacht has been expressed is in the configuration of the underwater profile and in the apparent lack of directional stability and the tendency to broach. There are factions which endeavour to relate these. The IOR does not, however, measure or control the underwater profile and the moves have been to develop yachts with short fin keels because designers believe this to produce the fastest yachts. Modern keel shapes are highly efficient in their lift/drag ratios but they do not add to the directional stability of a yacht in the way that a longer keel does by increasing the radius of a yacht's turning circle. Neither does the fin keel act to damp the rolling motion in the same way that the long keel profile is generally believed to do.

Somewhat regrettably there were too few long-keel boats racing in the 1979 Fastnet for adequate comparisons to be made. The data that has been made available about the modern yachts does not indicate that there is any need for a special study in connection with yachts' ability to survive storm conditions in the open sea, at least in the eyes of the Committee responsible for the Inquiry Report. In the eyes of many yachtsmen, however, this is perhaps one of the more important studies that are required. The dangers of wildly broaching boats cannot be overstated: one death in the SORC of 1979 and one serious and one other injury in one of the inshore races of the Admiral's Cup of the same year would endorse this gravity. In view of the way which the Report has dismissed it, the only course open to those yachtsmen concerned about this increasingly dangerous characteristic of modern ocean racing yachts is to bombard their national authorities with requests for action. Until they do, it is possible for the ORC to dismiss the problem as well.

What the Report does show about B2 knockdowns is that the characteristics of a yacht which would appear to increase its tendency to go past 90° to the horizontal are a lack of initial stability indicated by a high tenderness ratio and a low negative screening value; and a wide, shallow-hull form indicated by a high-rated beam/centre mid-depth immersed ratio. In addition there would appear to be a slight indication that wide beam, as shown by a low rated length/rated beam ratio, is a contributory cause. As a rider to these indications, the Report states: 'It must be stressed that while these tabulations appear to indicate trends towards, for instance, wide boats being prone to knock-downs past 90°, they do not constitute proof that all wide boats will inevitably suffer knockdowns.'

Statistics alone are bound to produce bad results. One must appreciate that the beam/immersed depth and length/beam ratios of smaller boats are respectively in the higher and lower areas which have proved more vulnerable and that it is perhaps the boat-size to wave-size ratio that is the most important factor which controls the ultimate vulnerability of yachts to a B2 knockdown. Almost half of the boats in Classes III to V suffered at least one B2 knockdown, whereas the percentage in the three bigger boat classes (0 to II) was only eleven.

One class of yacht did show particular susceptibility to B2 knock-downs. Of the eleven OOD 34s that were racing, nine suffered at least one B2. The Report grants that from the material available the OOD 34 does appear to have been particularly vulnerable but goes on to state that it is impossible to say whether this is due to the design or the fact that boats of this size and speed encountered 'particularly severe sea conditions'. It is now generally agreed that all the yachts in the Fastnet Race encountered much the same severe sea conditions, so perhaps the OOD 34s should not be excused on this count. The Report further attempts to excuse the OOD 34 by saying that eleven boats is not a sufficiently large sample to be 'statistically reliable'. Yet it must be noted that of those eleven boats, two, *Charioteer* and *Griffin*, were among the five that were sunk (and one of the other three went down under tow) and another abandoned (out of a total of nineteen). Those figures would point to some design or constructional deficiency and although it is not necessarily the duty of the Committee responsible for the Inquiry Report to single out the OOD 34 for further investigation, it must be the responsibility of the designer, builder and indeed the owners to examine how the OOD 34 can be improved to prevent a recurrence of this high proportion of failure.

Jeremy Rogers, the builders of the OOD 34, were determined to correct any faults that might have been their responsibility. After considerable research they determined that there were five places in which the OOD 34 could be improved and these improvements were immediately incorporated in the boats that were being built in their Lymington yard and in all future OOD 34s. All the owners of OOD 34s were informed by Jeremy Rogers of the alterations which the builders intended to make and were offered the facility of having them made to their boats for a small fixed charge (one which was well below cost).

Only one of these improvements was specifically needed for the OOD 34, the rest apply to many of the cruiser/racers that are manufactured all over the world. The particular modification was to the lid of the cockpit locker which has been re-designed to make it totally waterproof. The washboards of the main companionway, which fell out when the yachts were totally inverted, thus allowing huge quantities of water to go down below, have been re-designed to incorporate a locking device which is operable from either the cockpit side or from down below. There is no key; the device is permanently in place. Only human error, in not closing the lock, will result in the washboards falling out.

One dangerous aspect down below resulted from the cooker being able to leave the gimbals. Decklights were broken when the cooker came adrift in B2 situations allowing more water to flood in down below. The gimbal rod of the cooker is now pinned so that the cooker can rotate through 360 degrees. The batteries, too, presented problems when the yacht was inverted as they were able to come free from their box. A modification has now been made to have a locking bar across the top of them which, though it does present a minor difficulty when the time comes to remove the batteries altogether, does keep them in place even if the yacht is upside down.

Loose gear is a frightful hazard; it was this that forced the crew of *Grimalkin* to the decision that they were safer harnessed in to the cockpit than they were down below. Much loose gear can come from the lockers under the bunks. Jeremy Rogers have made the modifica-

135

tion to all the OOD 34s of having small turnbuckles on the plywood access hatches to the under-bunk lockers so that they can be locked in place, thus preventing all the gear that is stowed in these lockers from hurtling around the cabin. Tins of food can cause considerable damage to a boat and its crew members, if the tins are flying around under storm conditions.

It is, of course, not only the designers and builders of the OOD 34 who have learned from the horrors of the Fastnet disaster. Many other designers and builders must have been made aware of the shortcomings that were becoming standard in modern offshore boats. It is the owners of all cruiser/racers that should benefit from the lessons learned.

Knockdowns were significant in producing damage to the boats. Of the 77 boats which were knocked below the horizontal only 20 had no serious damage as a result. Easily the most singularly significant figure was that of the yachts dismasted by B2 knockdowns. Twelve yachts were dismasted after B2 knockdowns and a total of 29 of the 77 had significant damage to the rig. Only 12 of the 136 who were not victims of a B2 had any significant damage to the rig. The greatest percentage of damage was in the three smaller classes. Almost 80 per cent of the skippers whose yachts suffered bad rig damage believed that no matter how many extra pre-race checks, this damage would not have been avoided.

On the whole the damage to rigs was caused largely by the weight of water rather than the pressure of the wind. Many skippers did report that they had had difficulty in cutting through the rigging after the yacht had been dismasted in order to prevent the mast from puncturing the hull of the yacht. One crew deliberately left the rig alongside the boat and said that it acted well as a sea anchor.

Bolt-croppers, which are usually carried aboard yachts for the purpose of severing rigging in an emergency, found little favour among those that had to use them in this race. It was found that bolt-croppers had very little effect in cutting through stainless-steel rod rigging and, in any case, needed two-handed operation which was considered by many to be unsafe in the bad sea conditions. The arguments about bolt-croppers will doubtless continue and one must point to their original purpose which is the severance of various thicknesses of bar stock of many materials. They should be capable of cutting through rod rigging and yachtsmen may find that the way that they are adapted commercially to deal with heavy bar stock by extending the length of the handles with pipe, may be beneficial to them. These extensions, however, should have some simple form of locking to the bolt-croppers or there is a danger of the tool being lost overboard.

RORC Special Regulation 10.4 demands 'adequate means to disconnect or sever the standing rigging from the hull in emergency'. Bolt-croppers or hacksaws have been the usual answer to this requirement and at least one crew did use hacksaws for this purpose. The members of that crew felt that since four people could work simultaneously, four hacksaw frames should be carried. In addition, they recommended that at least six spare blades should be carried for each frame as the breakage rate was high, and even if the blades didn't break, they blunted very quickly when cutting through stainless-steel rod rigging. A more popular proposal was that one frame and at least a dozen blades should be carried.

Another crew took a more positive approach to the situation and disconnected the rigging by removing the clevis pins from the bottle screws at the chain plates. This is possibly one of the fastest ways of getting rid of the mast and rigging. The comment of this crew was that the whole operation would have been easier if the split pins had simply been splayed rather than bent back through 180 degrees.

But the severance of the standing rigging does not necessarily free the mast from a yacht. Some found they had further difficulties clearing the halyards and pole lifts, and the electrical wiring that went up inside the mast; and for this there was no real substitute for small bolt-croppers. Hacksaws are not particularly efficient for cutting through flexible wire rope.

It was felt that as most of the spar failures were due to knockdowns there would be little point in introducing legislation requiring the construction of rigs which could withstand the very large forces involved. These would only lead to more strongly constructed, and therefore heavier, hulls to support them and in turn this would lead to an escalation of rig size to drive them. In general the damage to the rigs was 'much as would be expected in yachts subjected to violent accelerations and enormous forces involved in a bad knockdown, total inversion or 360-degree roll.'

In the race, knockdowns were responsible for the loss of six lives and twenty-six injuries of which twelve were serious. Five lives were lost when crew members were washed overboard in a knockdown, including one when a man's harness was released to enable him to gain the surface from an upturned yacht. The sixth fatality occurred after a crewman had been trapped in the cockpit of an upturned boat. Although revived by artificial respiration, he died about three-quarters of an hour later from a combination of injuries and hypothermia.

Among the crews there was mixed reaction to the use of lifejackets and buoyancy aids. Several crews were adamant that under no circumstances would they use either, finding them restrictive to movement. Some experienced sailors with many miles of ocean racing behind them in deep waters far from land, were also totally against lifejackets. They felt that if their safety harnesses failed and they went over the side in adverse conditions, there was absolutely no hope of being picked up again. Given the choice they would prefer a quick death by drowning rather than a lingering one through hypothermia. It is a view which has been expressed by ocean racers at other times.

Keith Lorence, who was on board *Sayula II* when she had a B2 knockdown in the middle of the Southern Ocean during the second leg of the first Whitbread Round-the-World Race, was clear on this matter on his arrival in Sydney. He was certain that if any of the crew had gone over the side and been parted from the boat in those seas there would have been no chance of recovering him. The loss of three lives, in exactly those circumstances in that race, tends to bear out his theories. So too do subsequent losses from other yachts; but one must point to the recovery of one man by *Heath's Condor* in the second Whitbread Race but that was in only moderate seas; conditions not dissimilar to those when Tom Curnow was lost overboard from *Pirana* in the Ocean Triangle Race of the 1979 SORC. There is very little time available to a crew to recover a man overboard and as often as not the crew puts the boat and themselves at risk to do so. Those who do not advocate the wearing of lifejackets in storms may well be considered foolish, but often they are among the most experienced. At the back of their thoughts is the fact that if the boat has to be turned round in an attempt to rescue someone, there is a potential danger of the boat and its entire crew being lost. It is a hard decision to make as to whether or not one wears a lifejacket in force 10 and more and one which has to be left to personal preference.

There were crews who found secondary benefits to wearing buoyancy aids. They found that they gave them useful protection from injuries that they might otherwise have sustained by being thrown about the boat while down below in the cabin. Some crews rigged safety lines down below to prevent injuries of this nature. Forty-five per cent of those injured felt that their injuries were inevitable but the feeling was widespread that there were insufficient hand holds and 'crash bars' down below. Certainly the lack of severe weather in races for the past few years has made designers and builders somewhat dilatory in their duty to provide the necessary facilities down below to enable crew members to move around and to stay in one place. The possible exception is in the type of bunks which have achieved popularity recently which are raised and lowered on the inboard side by blocks and tackles. These will keep their occupants in situ to very large angles of heel, certainly to a 90 degree knockdown, but even they will not protect the crewman in the case of a total inversion.

Five of the boats which suffered B2 knockdowns reported that they had spent periods of inversion of between thirty seconds and five minutes. At this time the average frequency of the waves was thirteen seconds and the inference is that these five yachts achieved positive inverted stability for more than three waves; possibly the most serious situation which occurred during this Fastnet Race. All five yachts did eventually right themselves and all were subsequently abandoned although only one of the five later sank.

The seriousness of the concern for boats which could remain for long periods in positive inverted stability provoked the Committee of Inquiry to commission a report from the Wolfson Unit for Marine Technology and Industrial Aerodynamics at Southampton University on the stability conditions of two yachts; one which had shown very rapid self-righting and one of a type which had reportedly remained inverted for more than five minutes. The results of this analysis are in Appendix 2.

The Report admits, somewhat reluctantly, that the incidence of bad knockdowns was unacceptably high, yet in hindsight only one skipper who was knocked down thought that it was due to a basic defect in the design of his yacht. On the other hand 87 per cent thought that any boat of a similar size would have suffered a knockdown in the same circumstances, and only one of those who had been through a B2 had doubts about the self-righting ability of his yacht because of the length of recovery time. Most of the sailors, therefore, thought that under the circumstances, with force-10-plus winds and huge confused seas, capsizes were inevitable, even for fixed-keel cruiser racers — a far cry from the competitors in the Fastnet Races of the 1920s.

Insecurity of gear, particularly heavy items, is one area in which the competitors appear to have failed to observe the RORC Special Regulations, or basic seamanship, and possibly where the RORC Special Regulations might be extended in future. Special Regulation 7.31

specifically states that the cooking stove shall be securely installed – it makes sense since a loose one could sever gas pipes and fill the bilges with dangerous gas in addition to being a hazard to crew members or the boat itself by flying around in the confined space of the cabin.

Batteries, too, are lethal items if they come adrift, and many did. Like cookers, the stowage of batteries appears to have required gravity acting downwards from the deck towards the keel to keep them in place. Fully sealed batteries are now available, which does remove the potential hazard of acid spillage but further thought is necessary to ensure that batteries are 'properly secured in the boat'.

Special Regulation 10.3 was probably one of the least well observed of all. It simply states that the yacht shall have emergency steering equipment. In the case of boats steered by a wheel system, there are owners who feel that this regulation simply means that they shall have an emergency tiller which can be fitted to the rudder stock should the wheel system break down. From 1st January 1980 the rule was extended and notice of its extending clause was given in the 1979 regulations. It requires that owners have emergency steering in the event of a *full* breakdown of the normal steering system. It also states that inspectors may require that the emergency method of steering be demonstrated.

Eleven per cent of the yachts suffered significant damage to the steering gear and fourteen of them lost steering due to the failure of a carbon-fibre rudder or the weakness of another type which broke. It was among these that the emergency systems were found wanting too. The abandonment of the Class I yacht *Golden Apple of the Sun* would not have been necessary had an adequate emergency steering system been available but she, like a quarter of the boats whose main steering had failed, was unable to rig a satisfactory emergency system. Few owners seem to have realised that when the emergency system is required, the conditions will be such that it will have to be stronger than the normal one or a lower degree of directional control will have to be accepted. The problem is greater for the bigger boats proportionally; Class V yachts can make do quite adequately with a steering oar rigged over the stern. Larger boats often rig jury steering using the spinnaker boom or booms with or without a floorboard lashed to them. This proved to be only just workable for Edward Heath and his crew on *Morning Cloud* when her carbon-fibre rudder sheared off during the Channel Race in relatively moderate conditions – a pointer that was ignored by all those who went on the Fastnet Race a week later. It is certainly time that the ORC made more specific regulations for emergency steering of all yachts; with all yachts so required there would be no disadvantage due to weight particularly if the requirement was for the emergency steering gear to be on board when the in-water measurements are taken.

Designers' views of rudder construction may well have been altered by the events in the Fastnet. Certainly the attitude of the company that made many of the carbon-fibre rudders which failed has changed. Gary Carlin and David Kilponen, of Kiwi Boats Inc., Florida, issued a press release in Cowes shortly after the Channel Race. In it they gave the probable reasons for the failure of *Morning Cloud*'s rudder and revealed their philosophy concerning these new 'state of the art' rudders for racing yachts.

They explained that the rudder stock, which was an aluminium tube encased in wrapped carbon fibre, had been machined to enable the old steering quadrant to fit and this had substantially reduced the torsional strength of the carbon fibre causing progressive fibre breakage which had eventually ended in fracture. Moodys of Bursledon, the yard which had fitted the new carbon-fibre rudder to *Morning Cloud*, denied the allegations that the rudder stock had been machined to fit the old quadrant.

The pair from Kiwi Boats went on to say that, in their view, the extreme lightness of carbon-fibre rudders reduced the pitching moment of a yacht and allowed a rating advantage as well as saving some 100 lbs in the very stern of the yacht. The press release continued:

As all failures have been examined carefully and no inherent weakness has been found, the manufacturers stress that the development of this equipment will continue. Kiwi Boats has produced over fifty of these rudders with only three unrelated failures and believe that the current concern in the ocean racing fraternity is unwarranted in an era when all new yachts are commissioned seeking an 'edge'.

That statement was made before the Fastnet Race and subsequent to it appears trite. Kiwi Boats, on the other hand, have altered their attitude and though they are continuing their research into the use of carbon fibre in rudders, their scantlings are somewhat greater than they were in the pre-Fastnet Race era.

In 1956 following a storm in the Channel Race the RORC issued a questionnaire to all competitors and this revealed that the majority had had serious problems with water getting into the boat through openings not normally under water, including cockpit lockers, ventilators and hatches. After the Fastnet, 33 per cent of the boats reported that they had had problems of this nature and 11 per cent admitted that the amount of water in the boat affected the decisions that were made. What is perhaps important is that the length/displacement ratio appears to have nothing to do with the lack of watertight integrity, the fault stretching equally across the board.

Companionways were the worst offenders with ninety-eight boats reporting them as significant water-entry points. This was far more than any other recorded fault and the moves of Jeremy Rogers and other builders may do much to rectify this. Cockpit lockers were next most numerous offenders with mast coats and hatches taking third place equally, leaving only ventilators as a major worry.

Crews themselves admit some of the responsibility for the failure of the watertightness of companionways. They felt that communication between those below and those in the cockpit was essential and because of this the top washboard, at least, had been left out. If the boat was inverted the washboards would probably have fallen out and been swept away. On other boats it was discovered that the only effective way to secure the washboards in place was to lock the hatch over them. However, crews were reluctant to do this as it effectively trapped those down below in the cabin.

Many felt that companionways with heavily angled sides were a bad design. It meant that the washboards had only to lift a small amount before they fell out completely. Universally, crews believed that washboards and hatches must be capable of being secured from both inside and out. Those who lost washboards were, in many cases, able to close the aperture with a bagged sail.

While crews had strong views about hatches and washboards, stressing that these were of major importance, several boats that were abandoned with the washboards out and the main hatch open were later found floating and were subsequently recovered. The worst of the storm may have passed and the abandoned yachts may not have been rolled to a B2 knockdown again, which is when the watertight integrity of the companionway is of the greatest importance. It does, however, point to the truth in the statement made by one member of the RORC earlier in the year, when he suggested that the best life-raft was the yacht itself and that maybe the most efficient means of preserving life would be in having large emergency flotation bags in the hull of a stricken yacht rather than committing the crew to the hazards of a life-raft. This would have undoubtedly reduced the number of fatalities in the 1979 Fastnet Race.

'There is no more effective method of bailing a boat than a bucket in the hands of a frightened man' — an oft-quoted maxim but one which was in the back of people's minds when they prepared their boats for the Fastnet Race. At present there is no Special Regulation which requires yachts to carry buckets with strong lanyards, yet there are many yachtsmen who think there should be. Twenty per cent of the fleet found that bailing through the bilge pumps was unsatisfactory and, in hindsight, 45 per cent would make alterations to their pumping arrangements.

Regulations are desirable to encourage owners in the proper use of their basic equipment. Some had chosen to nominate the lavatory pump as the second bilge pump and in practice found this far from satisfactory. Special Regulation 8.21 requires: 'Bilge pumps, at least two, manually operated, one of which must be operable with all cockpit seats and all hatches and companionways closed. At least one of the bilge pumps shall be securely fixed to the yacht's structure.' The requirement that a bilge pump shall be operable with all hatches etc. closed means that it shall be operable from the cockpit and not from down below, yet it would be no bad thing if the Regulation insisted that one should be operable from there as well. There were times during the Fastnet storm when most of the crews should have been, and in many cases were, down below with only a minimum number on watch in the cockpit. Those ostensibly on watch down below could then have pumped the bilges. Those who attempted to use the lavatory pump felt that it was in the wrong part of the hull, too far forward with insufficient space to work. In addition, the complicated nature of the plumbing, a necessary part of the equipment for its primary purpose, made it inefficient for pumping the bilges.

Pumps which discharged into the cockpit were found on occasion to be inefficient. With a large amount of water in the hull, the cockpit drains were ineffective and the cockpit had to be bailed to cope with the flow of water from the pumps.

Modern yacht design has eliminated the sump from the bilges of many boats and this lack caused much annoyance. Without a sump one needs very little water down below before the boat is capable of giving a good impression of a washing machine. What water there is down below is thrown around liberally, wetting bedding and clothing. This is bound to lower morale and increase the risk of hypothermia. And this is a persistent fault as without a sump it is impossible to remove the last few gallons when pumping the bilge. A hand pump with a length of hose is the best tool for clearing the water from a boat with shallow bilges and for draining any water which becomes trapped and will not run down into the main bilge.

Twenty-nine per cent of the fleet used buckets to bail and all found them effective. A further 12 per cent agreed afterwards that they would carry buckets in future. The value of bailing buckets cannot be overstressed. It was reported by Butch Dalrymple-Smith after *Sayula II* suffered a B2 knockdown in the Southern Oceans during the first Whitbread Round-the-World Race, that the bilge pumps very quickly became clogged with food that had spilled into the bilges and that they had used buckets to get the water out of their Swan 65 which they believed initially to be holed. Small-boat sailors are generally much more aware of the efficacy of buckets and any who progress to ocean racing are usually among those with adequate bailing buckets on board.

There were a few failings in the deck arrangements of the yachts. Thirty-eight boats reported that there were insufficient hand-holds and safety harness attachment points and 28 per cent of the fleet reported that with hindsight they would make changes in the points used for harness attachment. This is a significant figure and points to the need for greater education in the use of safety harnesses and in the installation of their attachment points, possibly for designers and builders as well as for those who go to sea.

Harness failure or that of the attachment points accounted for six deaths. Twenty-six boats reported instances of harness failure. Of these, ten were in the failure of the harness itself, five of hook failure and two of the line; six more were due to the failure of the attachment point. There can be very little excuse for any failure in this department. It is the last-ditch line of defence and as such should be 100 per cent effective. Very few manufacturers offer harnesses which conform to the standards required by the British Standards Institute to meet BS 4224 and carry the BS kitemark. Full compliance to BS 4224 adds considerably to the cost of a harness and many of the yachting public, before the Fastnet disaster, did not consider the additional cost to be worth the guarantee of reliability which a BS requirement should confer on a harness. Many may have subsequently changed their minds and there is definite effort on the part of those manufacturers whose products do not conform to BS 4224 to alter their equipment. Not that all of them will bring their harnesses up to BS 4224 but an improvement in the design of hooks could save many lives.

One criticism of the standard harnesses which are made of webbing is that without a crotch strap they are useless to a man who has gone overboard. The natural reaction is to grasp the safety line in this situation and in doing so both arms are raised above the head. This simple movement is sufficient to allow the webbing harness to come off over the head and render it totally ineffective. Self-preservation leads to self-destruction.

Another harness of this type suffers buckle slip if the harness is put on inside out. This is all too easy to do, particularly at night. The manufacturers of this particular harness (So'wester) have asked owners to return them in order that they can be supplied with a newer model fitted with a buckle which the manufacturers claim to be more secure.

The RORC Special Regulations, while requiring a safety harness to be carried on board for each member of the crew, do not require that the harnesses shall be to BS 4224. It does, however, recommend owners to consult that Standard.

Some competitors reported that the harnesses which they carried were to their own design or modifications of standard models. Many had made what they considered to be a major modification in having two safety lines each with an independent hook. This enables the wearer to clip on to a new base before unclipping his old line when working his way up the deck, thereby giving himself complete safety.

One criticism of harnesses still exists: that they are difficult to put on in many cases. When a harness is needed it is often required at a moment's notice and the webbing ones, taken from a cave locker down below, generally need to be untangled before they are put on. The jacket type does not suffer from this problem. The incompatibility of a harness with a lifejacket has also received unfavourable comment. If a harness is put on over a lifejacket, then the latter is rendered inefficient as it is impossible to inflate it properly. If a harness is put on before the lifejacket, its use is impeded by the lifejacket over it. Those who used a combined lifejacket/harness commented favourably about them.

A very wide range of harnesses are available on the market and there was no general trend towards any particular manufacturer's product in the Fastnet fleet. One man has particular gratitude for a Kim safety harness (they were the most popular, with thirty-six boats using them) which he tested for the makers under the most severe conditions. Maurice Ridley is 6 ft 5 ins tall and weighs 18½ stone. He is a fit rugby player from Gosport and was crewing on the Swan 57, *Whirlwind*. On the way back from the Rock, the yacht broached and Ridley was thrown from the weather rail, across the cockpit, over the life-lines and into the sea. He broke his elbow in the fall but was brought up by his safety line. With his one good arm he heaved himself back on board when the boat heeled towards him. When it was heeled to windward Ridley was suspended over the top life-line by his harness line. After the race Ridley asked his skipper, Noel Lister, if he might keep that particular harness as it was thoroughly tested by him, had definitely saved his life and he was confident that it wouldn't let him down. The request was, of course, granted.

Three men went overboard wearing jacket-type harnesses; two were lost. One was lost as the result of the line between the harness and the clip breaking — a failure which has occurred before. The other was lost because he had clipped his safety line to a guard rail and that had failed.

The belt of another jacket/harness pulled out. The webbing belt and the line remained attached to the yacht but the crewman was lost. In the same knockdown at which this life was lost another crewman wearing an identical jacket/harness was washed overboard but remained attached. In another incident two crewmen were washed over the side wearing harnesses: one remained attached, the other failed. In a further knockdown the stainless-steel hook of one harness line straightened by ¼ inch and released itself. The yacht was inverted long enough for the crewman to swim back to the boat and secure a hand hold. In another case a safety line broke where there was a knot in it.

The ring of one safety harness failed and luckily the man was saved. The ring failure was brought to light by the boat's owner who is a physicist. He claims that the ring was made of poor quality bronze and was chrome-plated to cover its lack of quality.

It would appear that there is tremendous unconformity with safety harnesses; unconformity that is leading to danger. With more than twenty manufacturers offering their products in Britain alone there is an inconsistency in quality which could lead to a bad decision being made at the time of purchase. If a consumer survey was made of safety harnesses, it would help to weed out the unsafe ones and possibly promote the idea that those manufactured to BS 4224 are better than those which do not conform to this Standard.

Consideration might be given to the re-naming of life-rafts. They are the very last resort and as such would perhaps be better named emergency rafts. In practice in this race the life-rafts did save lives but lives were also lost due to their failure and in some cases due to the implicit belief that they were the safest place to be; a proven fallacy in at least three cases where fatalities occurred.

RORC Special Regulation 11.41 which covers the requirements for life-rafts states:

Life-rafts capable of carrying the entire crew and meeting the following requirements:

1. Must be carried on deck (not under a dinghy) or in a special stowage opening immediately to the deck, containing life-rafts only. Each life-raft shall be stowed so that one person can get it to the life lines in 10 seconds.

2. Must be designed and used solely for saving life at sea.

3. Must have at least two separate buoyancy compartments, each of which must be automatically inflatable; each life-raft must be capable of carrying its rated capacity with one compartment deflated.

4. Must have a self-erecting canopy to cover the occupants.

5. Must have been inspected, tested and approved within one year by the manufacturer or other competent authority and each life-raft shall have a valid annual certificate; this or a copy must be kept on board the yacht.

6. Must have the following equipment appropriately secured to each raft:

   1 Sea anchor or drogue
   1 Bellows, pump or other means for maintaining the inflation
      of air chambers
   1 Signalling light
   3 Hand flares
   1 Bailer
   1 Repair kit
   2 Paddles
   1 Knife

7. The number of crew shall not exceed the official capacity of the life-raft(s) as specified by the manufacturer.

While it is generally believed that all the owners considered that they complied to Special Regulation 11.41 in regard to the stowage of their life-rafts, at least in the spirit of the Regulation, it became clear that in storm conditions many did not. Of the fifteen that were used, four took more than two minutes to launch and five took between sixteen seconds and under a minute. In addition, twelve life-rafts were washed overboard, eight from the cockpit and four which were stowed on deck. In the cases of those lost from the cockpit, the common failing appears to have been the fact that they were stowed in a locker which opened when the yachts were rolled over and the life-raft fell out of its stowage, or was washed out. One of those lost from the deck was washed away with its chocks still attached. On one boat a crewman complained of not being able to use either of the life-rafts; one which was stowed on deck was washed away and the other which was stowed under the cabin sole could not be extracted because the floorboards had jammed.

Some of these criticisms add fuel to the argument that the best place to stow the life-raft is down below in the cabin. There is certainly less chance of it being lost inadvertently. In addition it is in greater evidence for the crew and can be better cared for. It has been the case in the past that life-rafts which are stowed in specially constructed lockers in the cockpit have suffered severe abrasion during the season which has gone unnoticed and that this abrasion has been sufficiently severe to impair the working of the life-raft. Stowage in the cabin would eliminate this and it was proved during the race that a life-raft that was taken into the cabin as a precautionary measure could be launched and inflated in just over two minutes.

There was only one crew which believed that the life-raft was stowed too securely. Yet that raft was used and it was estimated that from the time the decision was made to launch it until all the crew were safely on board the raft, was only five minutes. It is reckoned that even the smallest yacht in the race would have taken longer than that to sink with a foot-square hole in the side.

Some rafts inflated upside down and had to be righted before the crew could board them. At least three gave this problem. Otherwise those that were inflated gave little difficulty and allowed the crews to board them without first going into the sea. There was one tragic exception to this. Paul Baldwin was the only man on board the life-raft of *Gunslinger*, loading emergency stores, when it capsized whilst still attached to the yacht. He swam out from under the life-raft and was preparing to get back into it when the painter snapped as it was jerked by a wave. Baldwin was thrown a heaving line, which was carried out of his grasp by the wind. He failed to reach the life-raft as it drifted away and was drowned.

One of the major complaints about the life-rafts that were used was that the painter was on the opposite side to the access hatch making boarding the raft unnecessarily difficult as well as cutting the painter free when all the crew had boarded it. One crew boarded the raft through the observation hatch – a difficult feat in lifejackets – because of this anomaly.

The use of drogues appeared to cause some problems. In one raft where a sea anchor was not used, a capsize occurred when the raft had been in use for only fifteen minutes. All the crew were attached to the life-raft by harnesses and they were able to right the raft fairly easily and climb back in. They had, however, lost all the survival gear from the raft. Two hours later the raft capsized again and this time it was much more difficult to right as the crew were cold and tired. By this time, too, the canopy had begun to tear and it was four hours more before they were rescued.

One six-man raft was in use for eight hours, the longest time any raft was used. It did not capsize and the crew that used it made these comments about the use of their drogue:

The drogue was deployed when the raft was cut adrift from the yacht. It lasted between half and one hour and then carried away apparently at two points – one at the drogue and the other at one of the yoke lines to the raft. A second drogue was made from materials on board but this too failed after some hours.

The drogue performs three functions:

1. To reduce the rate of drift.
2. To stabilise the raft's attitude to the wind.
3. To stabilise the attitude of the bottom pockets of the raft to the sea.

The skipper continued about the attitude of the raft and the desirability of deploying a drogue:

I do not know what, if any, stability pockets were fitted to the bottom of the raft. In any event, it did not capsize although it was 'banana'd' on several occasions and half filled with water by the breaking waves. On each occasion the hoops over-pressurised and vented off and consequently needed pumping up by hand. The attitude of the raft to the sea therefore seems to be un-important.

It is desirable that the fixed side of the raft cover be held to the wind not only to keep the wind out but breaking seas also. This relieves the strain on the fastenings. However, if these are secure, this aspect too becomes of less importance. Finally, one is left with the desirability or otherwise of reducing the rate of drift, and I am led to the conclusion that in storm conditions, if there is sufficient sea room, life is more comfortable and the raft less at risk if it is allowed to drift at the same rate as the waves.

Certainly this crew had good experience and this was borne out by the crew of another yacht in a six-man life-raft. They, at first, streamed their drogue without problem but with it in use the raft appeared to be sluggish and waves were breaking over it. The skipper feared that the raft might capsize and decided to haul in the drogue and allow the raft to go with the waves rather than struggle against them. Immediately the raft became more lively and buoyant and it felt safer to those in it. It continued to ride out the storm for an hour, without capsizing, before the crew were rescued. In consultation with the manufacturers of the raft at a later date, the skipper was told that in the prevailing conditions the life-raft would have ridden better without a drogue.

There were life-raft failures. One six-man raft capsized when a crewman was lighting a flare in the doorway. An eight-man raft capsized as soon as the crew were inside it. They righted it and it capsized again. At this time the bottom ring and the floor broke away from the top ring and the canopy and they were held together only by a thin ring and a lanyard. It was when the top ring overturned that two of the crew were swept clear and drowned. The remaining six members of the crew were left hanging on to the two sections of the life-raft with life harness lines wrapped around the top ring, which was the only one with handgrips. One member was in the bottom section which broke clear, while five clung to the top ring; one of these could hold on no longer and was swept away and drowned. These four were sighted at first light by helicopter and the other man in the bottom section was found by the same helicopter shortly afterwards.

Another eight-man life-raft inflated upside down, was righted and capsized again after three quarters of an hour's use. At this time the canopy broke away.

Cold and exposure were the major problems of those who were in life-rafts that held together. Crews maintained that there was a lack of protection from the sea and from the cold and that this was a fault which should be corrected. Hypothermia was a big worry and the construction of the rafts did little to alleviate the problem. The securing arrangements for the canopy accesses were considered by most to be thoroughly inadequate and it was considered that this was far more important than keeping the access to leeward by means of a drogue.

The cold was the greatest hazard. Many of the crews who had been in the rafts suggested that foil 'space blankets' might have been used to advantage but when these were tested some years previously it was found that they were of little use in a life-raft. Their insulation to heat loss by radiation was good but the heat loss suffered by survivors in a life-raft is by conduction through the bottom of the raft and against this the foil blanket would provide little protection.

The cold in these circumstances is aggravated by the cooling effect of the 50-knot-plus winds and the stinging spray that this whips up. One suggestion that came from many of the crews was that heat loss through the floor of the raft could be minimised if the floor were inflatable. This unfortunately would reduce the initial stability of the raft but might be a feasible feature if the floor were pumped up separately after the crew had boarded the life-raft.

The lack of security of the survival equipment in the rafts and the order in which it was stowed came under fire as well. There were instances of the survival equipment being lost when rafts capsized. Flares were at the bottom of the pack rather than at the top where they should be, as they are the first things that are needed when a life-raft is launched. One other deficiency that crews commented about was the relative lack of hand holds on the rafts. For the crew of *Trophy* there were none on the bottom ring of their raft when it split from the top ring. For the crew of *Morningtown*, used as a support craft to the race, there were no hand holds on the outside of *Trophy*'s raft when it was alongside them earlier. Had they been able to hold it then, three lives would have been saved.

The Inquiry Report's section on life-rafts concludes:

Life-rafts clearly failed to provide the safe refuge which many crews expected. Seven lives were lost in incidents associated with rafts of which three were directly attributable to the failure of the raft, and the yachts which these seven people abandoned were subsequently found afloat and towed into harbour. However, fourteen lives were saved in incidents in which survivors took to rafts from yachts which have not been recovered. Many crews used rafts successfully to transfer from yachts to helicopters or other vessels. It is asking a great deal of any small craft to expect it to provide safe refuge in conditions which overwhelm a large yacht but this is what life-rafts are expected to do.

It is those seven lives that were lost which have caused the greatest concern because they were lost unnecessarily. One of the overriding fundamentals of seamanship was disregarded in not staying with the ship. The proof is now greater that it is best to stay with a yacht rather than take to a life-raft. Highly experienced ocean racing sailors have said that they would have to be dragged into a life-raft at any time before their yacht actually foundered.

The crew of *Gunslinger* were forced to reconsider their decision to abandon ship when their life-raft was swept away from the yacht when the painter parted and Paul Baldwin was tragically drowned. The water was up to waist-level in the boat, but with a bucket they bailed and provided themselves with the most safe refuge that they could have had until they were picked up.

Nick Ward managed singlehanded to keep *Grimalkin* afloat after he had been left for dead by his shipmates. He had been unconscious and was injured, yet with a considerable will to survive, he coped until a Sea King helicopter took him off.

It is likely, therefore, that there will be much more thought about the possible use of life-rafts in an emergency in future. Those who were aware of the failings of rafts during the Fastnet storm will be much more reluctant to use them and might give greater consideration to trying to keep their main vessel afloat.

Table 2. Use of life-rafts.

	Total	Beau-fort	Avon	RFD surviva	Ange-viniere
BASE	15	5	4	2	2
DID IT INFLATE AS EXPECTED?					
Yes	10 67%	4 80%	4 100%	–	2 100%
No	3 20%	–	–	1 50%	–
No Answer	2 13%	1 20%	–	1 50%	–
WERE THE CREW ABLE TO BOARD WITHOUT ENTERING SEA FIRST?					
Yes	12 80%	4 80%	4 100%	1 50%	2 100%
No	–	–	–	–	–
No Answer	3 20%	1 20%	–	1 50%	–
WAS THERE TIME TO COLLECT SPARE CLOTHING/GEAR BEFORE BOARDING?					
Yes	7 47%	3 60%	2 50%	1 50%	–
No	4 27%	1 20%	1 25%	–	2 100%
No Answer	4 27%	1 20%	1 25%	1 50%	–
WERE YOU ABLE TO STREAM SEA ANCHOR STRAIGHT AWAY?					
Yes	5 33%	2 40%	2 50%	–	1 50%
No	4 27%	1 20%	–	1 50%	1 50%
No Answer	6 40%	2 40%	2 50%	1 50%	–

Table 2 continued

	Total	Beau-fort	Avon	RFD surviva	Ange-viniere
DO YOU FEEL THAT SEA ANCHOR AFFECTED BEHAVIOUR OF THE RAFT?					
Yes	3 / 20%	2 / 40%	1 / 25%	—	—
No	3 / 20%	—	1 / 25%	1 / 50%	1 / 50%
No Answer	9 / 60%	3 / 60%	2 / 50%	1 / 50%	1 / 50%
DID THE RAFT CAPSIZE IN USE?					
Yes	5 / 33%	2 / 40%	1 / 25%	1 / 50%	1 / 50%
No	7 / 47%	2 / 40%	3 / 75%	—	1 / 50%
No Answer	3 / 20%	1 / 20%	—	1 / 50%	—
WAS THE SEA ANCHOR IN USE AT TIME OF CAPSIZE?					
Yes	—	—	—	—	—
No	4 / 27%	1 / 20%	—	1 / 50%	2 / 100%
No Answer	11 / 73%	4 / 80%	4 / 100%	1 / 50%	—
WERE ALL/NEARLY ALL OF CREW SEATED WHEN RAFT CAPSIZED?					
Yes	4 / 27%	2 / 40%	1 / 25%	—	1 / 50%
No	2 / 13%	—	—	1 / 50%	1 / 50%
No Answer	9 / 60%	3 / 60%	3 / 75%	1 / 50%	—
DID YOU FEEL THAT WATER IN THE RAFT WAS ADVERSELY AFFECTING STABILITY?					
Yes	1 / 7%	—	—	—	1 / 50%
No	7 / 47%	2 / 40%	3 / 75%	1 / 50%	—
No Answer	7 / 47%	3 / 60%	1 / 25%	1 / 50%	1 / 50%
DO YOU FEEL THAT REASONABLE DISCIPLINE WAS MAINTAINED DURING BOARDING?					
Yes	10 / 67%	4 / 80%	3 / 75%	—	2 / 100%
No	1 / 7%	—	—	1 / 50%	—
No Answer	4 / 27%	1 / 20%	1 / 25%	1 / 50%	—
WERE YOU ABLE TO TAKE R/T INTO THE RAFT					
Yes	—	—	—	—	—
No	8 / 53%	3 / 60%	3 / 75%	1 / 50%	1 / 50%
No Answer	7 / 47%	2 / 40%	1 / 25%	1 / 50%	1 / 50%
WAS COLD WAS AN IMPORTANT FACTOR?					
Yes	8 / 53%	2 / 40%	3 / 75%	1 / 50%	1 / 50%
No	3 / 20%	2 / 40%	—	—	1 / 50%
No Answer	4 / 27%	1 / 20%	1 / 25%	1 / 50%	—
WERE YOU ABLE TO KEEP ACCESS DOOR CLOSED?					
Yes	3 / 20%	1 / 20%	1 / 25%	—	1 / 50%
No	5 / 33%	1 / 20%	2 / 50%	1 / 50%	1 / 50%
No Answer	7 / 47%	3 / 60%	1 / 25%	1 / 50%	—

153

Most lifejackets appear to have been efficient. A jacket which conformed to BS 3595 was worn by one of those who lost their lives. He was found face down in the water; his head had slipped out of the collar and the lifejacket had moved round to his back. It is not known if he put the jacket on correctly but since the cause of his death was officially given as exposure rather than drowning, it can be surmised that the jacket did work efficiently. There is concern, however, for the British Standard requirements as there is no demand for a retaining strap for the collar. One of the same type of lifejackets worked effectively for a crewman who jumped into the water to be rescued by helicopter but he said that 'the auto-inflation device only semi-inflated the jacket'.

That was perhaps better than the experience of another crewman who also wore a BS 3595 approved jacket — the auto-inflation was accidentally triggered after the jacket had been inflated by mouth and the wearer thought he was going to be strangled before the jacket burst. Of course, after this he had no jacket and rightly considered the death penalty rather a harsh sentence for accidentally contravening the manufacturer's instructions.

The lack of compatibility of lifejackets and safety harnesses is cause for grave concern. Most of those who didn't wear lifejackets during the Fastnet storm were conditioned by the belief that the prime priority is for a safety harness. It is a constantly repeated request of those crews who were in any distress in this storm that there is a need for a really effective lifejacket combined with a safety harness. The general consensus would appear to be that the average inflatable jacket is too flimsy for general wear and there is a marked difference of opinion on the relative merits of the various methods of inflation.

Flares, considering their relatively high costs, did not work as well as might have been expected. One hundred per cent working should not be too much to ask of flares, but on at least twelve yachts there were one or more flares that failed to ignite. Other reports of flares say that they ignited after being in a pool of water on the floor of a life-raft for more than an hour.

The screw-top polythene jar in which one brand of pyrotechnics is supplied is criticised for making it difficult to select the right type of flare. Many crews felt that they didn't have enough flares and there was particular reference to the paucity of red parachute flares in the requirements of the RORC's Special Regulation 11.63.

Human frailty was another factor that was investigated after the

Fastnet Race. Seasickness which might have been considered a major problem does not appear to have been a serious handicap. Twenty-two per cent of the boats had at least one person seriously incapacitated but only 7 per cent had more than one and there was only one boat on which four people were badly afflicted. The figures were higher for those who were 'somewhat incapacitated'. On 53 per cent of the fleet there were crewmen who were seasick. Of those that took seasick pills only 7 per cent found them ineffective in these extreme conditions where the affliction might be expected to have been aggravated by fear.

There was a wide range of experience among the skippers in the race. More than half had done more than three races longer than 500 miles and a third had done more than seven of this length. Considering that the average British ocean race is between 200 and 250 miles, this is a very high level of experience in longer races. Three quarters of those who suffered a B2 knockdown had done a race of 500 miles or more and 30 per cent of them had done more than seven of this length. The figures for abandonment are very similar.

The ability of crewmen to remain efficient depends on their ability to conserve strength. For this reason the watch-keeping system is used. At the height of the storm, it was not always possible to maintain this watch-keeping system and there is no doubt that this had a deleterious effect on some boats. Adequate feeding and the correct amount of sleep are also prime factors for efficiency and many of the competitors reported that extreme cold was a problem. Hypothermia is a known problem and, in general, ocean racing crew make deliberate efforts to guard against it. Only a few reports of it occurring in the Fastnet Race were made.

At the height of the storm many skippers conserved the energy of their crew members by limiting the number on watch to two, in some cases with only the helmsman on deck and a second man waiting in the shelter of the companionway. As fifty-one boats reported that they had had at least one man washed overboard, some on more than one occasion, it would appear that this was a prudent move.

It was obviously desirable to have experienced men on the helm at the height of the storm. A skilful helmsman would be better at avoiding the worst waves and in minimising their effect. There were, however, waves of such shape and size that even the most experienced helmsman would have had no defence against them and these were the waves which did the most damage in rolling yachts or in carrying away gear.

There was a percentage of the fleet which adopted passive tactics to

155

Table 3. Skipper experience.

	Total	Abandoned	B2 Knock-Down Yes	B2 Knock-Down No	Damage Rig Yes	Damage Rig No	Damage Accom. Yes	Damage Accom. No	Damage Steering Yes	Damage Steering No	Damage Hull Yes	Damage Hull No
BASE	235	23	77	136	42	182	31	177	25	196	34	185
100-200 MILES												
None	2 / 1%	–	–	2 / 1%	–	2 / 1%	–	2 / 1%	–	2 / 1%	–	2 / 1%
1-2	7 / 3%	–	2 / 3%	5 / 4%	1 / 2%	6 / 3%	1 / 3%	4 / 2%	–	7 / 4%	–	6 / 3%
3-6	19 / 8%	3 / 13%	8 / 10%	10 / 7%	4 / 10%	15 / 8%	4 / 13%	12 / 7%	–	19 / 10%	3 / 9%	15 / 8%
7 or more	182 / 77%	19 / 83%	63 / 82%	100 / 74%	36 / 86%	137 / 75%	24 / 77%	143 / 81%	24 / 96%	148 / 76%	29 / 85%	145 / 78%
No Answer	25 / 11%	1 / 4%	4 / 5%	19 / 14%	1 / 2%	22 / 12%	2 / 6%	16 / 9%	1 / 4%	20 / 10%	2 / 6%	17 / 9%
200-500 MILES												
None	6 / 3%	1 / 4%	3 / 4%	3 / 2%	–	6 / 3%	–	6 / 3%	–	6 / 3%	1 / 3%	5 / 3%
1-2	28 / 12%	4 / 17%	13 / 17%	24 / 18%	4 / 10%	24 / 13%	7 / 23%	19 / 11%	4 / 16%	24 / 12%	3 / 9%	24 / 13%
3-6	41 / 17%	6 / 26%	14 / 18%	24 / 18%	11 / 26%	28 / 15%	7 / 23%	30 / 17%	1 / 4%	39 / 20%	7 / 21%	31 / 17%
7 or more	132 / 56%	10 / 43%	42 / 55%	75 / 55%	25 / 60%	100 / 55%	16 / 52%	103 / 58%	18 / 72%	105 / 54%	21 / 62%	103 / 56%
No Answer	28 / 12%	2 / 9%	5 / 6%	21 / 15%	2 / 5%	24 / 13%	1 / 3%	22 / 11%	2 / 8%	22 / 11%	2 / 6%	22 / 12%
OVER 500 MILES												
None	29 / 12%	3 / 13%	10 / 13%	17 / 13%	3 / 7%	25 / 14%	4 / 13%	23 / 13%	4 / 16%	24 / 12%	5 / 15%	23 / 12%
1-2	52 / 22%	5 / 22%	20 / 26%	29 / 21%	12 / 29%	39 / 21%	6 / 19%	43 / 24%	8 / 32%	42 / 21%	8 / 24%	42 / 23%
3-6	52 / 22%	6 / 26%	16 / 21%	30 / 22%	10 / 24%	38 / 21%	10 / 32%	36 / 20%	4 / 16%	44 / 22%	10 / 29%	37 / 20%
7 or more	77 / 33%	5 / 22%	23 / 30%	45 / 33%	11 / 26%	61 / 34%	8 / 26%	58 / 33%	7 / 28%	64 / 33%	9 / 26%	62 / 34%
No Answer	26 / 11%	4 / 17%	8 / 10%	16 / 12%	6 / 14%	20 / 11%	3 / 10%	17 / 10%	2 / 8%	23 / 12%	3 / 9%	21 / 11%

Table 4. Comfort below/routine.

	Total	Experience of Skipper-Passages or Races over 500 miles				Fastnet Class					
		None	1-2	3-6	7+	0	I	II	III	IV	V
BASE	235	29	52	52	77	8	40	40	52	46	47
WAS IT POSSIBLE TO MAINTAIN A WATCHKEEPING SCHEDULE?											
Yes	199 85%	20 69%	47 90%	44 85%	68 88%	8 100%	35 88%	33 83%	44 85%	35 76%	42 89%
No	26 11%	7 24%	4 8%	6 12%	6 8%	—	4 10%	6 15%	7 13%	6 13%	3 6%
No Answer	10 4%	2 7%	1 2%	2 4%	3 4%	—	1 3%	1 3%	1 2%	5 11%	2 4%
WAS IT POSSIBLE TO SERVE HOT / ACCEPTABLE FOOD DURING STORM?											
Yes	169 72%	16 55%	37 71%	37 71%	63 82%	8 100%	31 78%	30 75%	37 71%	31 67%	32 68%
No	58 25%	12 41%	14 27%	11 21%	12 16%	—	8 20%	10 25%	13 25%	11 24%	14 30%
No Answer	8 3%	1 3%	1 2%	4 8%	2 3%	—	1 3%	—	2 4%	4 9%	1 2%
DID YOU CARRY FOOD SPECIALLY PREPARED FOR SEVERE CONDITIONS?											
Yes	104 44%	13 45%	25 48%	21 40%	35 45%	1 13%	18 45%	15 38%	25 48%	20 43%	24 51%
No	123 52%	15 52%	27 52%	28 54%	39 51%	7 88%	21 53%	24 60%	26 50%	22 48%	22 47%
No Answer	8 3%	1 3%	—	3 6%	3 4%	—	1 3%	1 3%	1 2%	4 9%	1 2%
DO YOU CONSIDER LACK OF SLEEP / EXHAUSTION WAS A FACTOR IN ACTIONS?											
Yes	43 18%	9 31%	14 27%	7 13%	6 8%	1 13%	3 8%	10 25%	10 19%	10 22%	9 19%
No	178 76%	19 66%	35 67%	41 79%	66 86%	7 88%	35 88%	27 68%	41 79%	29 63%	37 79%
No Answer	14 6%	1 3%	3 6%	4 8%	5 6%	—	2 5%	3 8%	1 2%	7 15%	1 2%

Table 5. Primary and contributory reasons for retirement (primary – then contributory).

	Total	Fastnet Class						Length/Displacement							B2 Knock-down	
		0	I	II	III	IV	V	Less than 120	121–149	150–174	175–199	200–224	225–249	250+	Yes	No
BASE	235	8	40	40	52	46	47	4	15	16	78	50	16	7	77	136
GENERAL CREW FATIQUE																
Yes	13 6%	–	–	2 5%	2 4%	2 4%	7 15%	–	–	1 6%	4 5%	5 10%	1 6%	1 14%	6 8%	7 5%
No	63 27%	1 13%	6 15%	8 20%	15 29%	12 26%	20 43%	1 25%	4 27%	7 44%	22 28%	17 34%	4 25%	–	27 35%	33 24%
No Answer	159 68%	7 88%	34 85%	30 75%	35 67%	32 70%	20 43%	3 75%	11 73%	8 50%	52 67%	28 56%	11 69%	6 86%	44 57%	96 71%
Yes	46 20%	–	3 8%	8 20%	12 23%	10 22%	12 26%	1 25%	4 27%	2 13%	16 21%	12 24%	1 6%	1 14%	17 22%	27 20%
No	44 19%	1 13%	4 10%	5 13%	9 17%	11 24%	13 28%	–	2 13%	5 31%	15 19%	13 26%	3 19%	2 29%	18 23%	23 17%
No Answer	145 62%	7 88%	33 83%	27 68%	31 60%	25 54%	22 47%	3 75%	9 60%	9 56%	47 60%	25 50%	12 75%	4 57%	42 55%	86 63%
SEA-SICKNESS																
Yes	3 1%	–	–	2 5%	1 2%	–	–	–	–	–	1 1%	–	2 13%	–	–	3 2%
No	76 32%	1 13%	6 15%	8 20%	20 38%	12 26%	27 57%	1 25%	6 40%	8 50%	26 33%	20 40%	3 19%	1 14%	35 45%	39 29%
No Answer	156 66%	7 88%	34 85%	30 75%	31 60%	34 74%	20 43%	3 75%	9 60%	8 50%	51 65%	30 60%	11 69%	6 86%	42 55%	94 69%
Yes	22 9%	–	1 3%	3 8%	6 12%	7 15%	5 11%	–	1 7%	1 6%	8 10%	7 14%	1 6%	1 14%	8 10%	13 10%
No	61 26%	1 13%	5 13%	6 15%	11 21%	14 30%	22 47%	1 25%	4 27%	6 38%	21 27%	17 34%	2 13%	2 29%	25 32%	32 24%
No Answer	152 65%	7 88%	34 85%	31 78%	35 67%	25 54%	20 43%	3 75%	10 67%	9 56%	49 63%	26 52%	13 81%	4 57%	44 57%	91 67%
LOW CREW MORALE																
Yes	5 2%	–	–	1 3%	4 8%	–	–	–	–	–	4 5%	–	1 6%	–	2 3%	3 2%
No	80 34%	1 13%	6 15%	11 28%	19 37%	14 30%	27 57%	1 25%	7 47%	9 56%	25 32%	20 40%	4 25%	1 14%	35 45%	42 31%
No Answer	150 64%	7 88%	34 85%	28 70%	29 56%	32 70%	20 43%	3 75%	8 53%	7 44%	49 63%	30 60%	11 69%	6 86%	40 52%	91 67%
Yes	23 10%	–	3 8%	1 3%	6 12%	8 17%	5 11%	–	2 13%	2 13%	9 12%	6 12%	1 6%	2 29%	8 10%	15 11%
No	58 25%	1 13%	4 10%	7 18%	9 17%	14 30%	21 45%	1 25%	3 20%	6 38%	18 23%	18 36%	3 19%	1 14%	24 31%	30 22%
No Answer	154 66%	7 88%	33 83%	32 80%	37 71%	24 62%	21 45%	3 75%	10 67%	8 50%	51 65%	26 52%	12 75%	4 57%	45 58%	91 67%

	Total	Fastnet Class						Length / Displacement							B2 Knockdown	
		0	I	II	III	IV	V	Less than 120	121—149	150—174	175—199	200—224	225—249	250 +	Yes	No
PERSONAL FATIGUE OF SKIPPER																
Yes	3 1%	—	—	—	1 2%	1 2%	1 2%	—	—	1 6%	2 3%	—	—	—	3 4%	—
No	76 32%	1 13%	6 15%	9 23%	19 37%	13 28%	26 55%	1 25%	6 40%	8 50%	25 32%	20 40%	3 19%	1 14%	32 42%	41 30%
No Answer	156 66%	7 88%	34 85%	31 78%	32 62%	32 70%	20 43%	3 75%	9 60%	7 44%	51 65%	30 60%	13 81%	6 86%	42 55%	95 70%
Yes	26 11%	—	1 3%	3 8%	7 13%	6 13%	9 19%	—	3 20%	1 6%	10 13%	7 14%	3 19%	—	9 12%	15 11%
No	60 26%	1 13%	5 13%	8 20%	12 23%	15 33%	17 36%	1 25%	4 27%	5 31%	20 26%	18 36%	2 13%	3 43%	24 31%	33 24%
No Answer	149 63%	7 88%	34 85%	29 73%	33 63%	25 54%	21 45%	3 75%	8 53%	10 63%	48 62%	25 50%	11 69%	4 57%	44 57%	88 65%
ACTUAL DAMAGE TO BOAT																
Yes	45 19%	—	9 23%	4 10%	9 17%	6 13%	16 34%	—	6 40%	7 44%	13 17%	10 20%	1 6%	1 14%	27 35%	18 13%
No	57 24%	1 13%	3 8%	9 23%	16 31%	11 24%	16 34%	1 25%	4 27%	4 25%	21 27%	14 28%	4 25%	1 14%	21 27%	33 24%
No Answer	133 57%	7 88%	28 70%	27 68%	27 52%	29 63%	15 32%	3 75%	5 33%	5 31%	44 56%	26 52%	11 69%	5 71%	29 38%	85 63%
Yes	23 10%	—	1 3%	2 5%	9 17%	3 7%	6 13%	—	5 33%	1 6%	6 8%	2 4%	1 6%	1 14%	15 19%	7 5%
No	54 23%	1 13%	4 10%	7 18%	9 17%	16 35%	17 36%	1 25%	—	3 19%	22 28%	20 40%	2 13%	2 29%	16 21%	34 25%
No Answer	158 67%	7 88%	35 88%	31 78%	34 65%	27 59%	24 51%	3 75%	10 67%	12 75%	50 64%	28 56%	13 81%	4 57%	46 60%	95 70%
INJURY/FATALITY																
Yes	10 4%	—	—	1 3%	2 4%	4 9%	3 6%	—	—	1 6%	4 5%	4 8%	—	—	7 9%	2 1%
No	73 31%	1 13%	6 15%	11 28%	20 38%	10 22%	23 49%	1 25%	6 40%	7 44%	23 29%	18 36%	5 31%	1 14%	27 35%	43 32%
No Answer	152 65%	7 88%	34 85%	28 70%	30 58%	32 70%	21 45%	3 75%	9 60%	8 50%	51 65%	28 56%	11 69%	6 86%	43 56%	91 67%
Yes	13 6%	—	—	—	6 12%	4 9%	3 6%	—	3 20%	—	6 8%	3 6%	—	—	9 12%	3 2%
No	65 28%	1 13%	6 15%	8 20%	13 25%	16 35%	19 40%	1 25%	2 13%	5 31%	24 31%	18 36%	4 25%	3 43%	20 26%	41 30%
No Answer	157 67%	7 88%	34 85%	32 80%	33 63%	26 57%	25 53%	3 75%	10 67%	11 69%	48 62%	29 58%	12 75%	4 57%	48 62%	92 68%

Table 5 continued

RISK OF WORSENING EXISTING SLIGHT DAMAGE

Yes	22 9%	1 13%	–	2 5%	7 13%	4 9%	7 15%	–	5 33%	2 13%	7 9%	3 6%	1 6%	–	13 17%	8 6%
No	63 27%	–	5 13%	10 25%	16 31%	12 26%	18 38%	1 25%	2 13%	6 38%	21 27%	18 36%	5 31%	1 14%	23 30%	38 28%
No Answer	150 64%	7 88%	34 85%	28 70%	29 56%	30 65%	22 47%	3 75%	8 53%	8 50%	50 64%	29 58%	10 63%	6 86%	41 53%	90 66%
Yes	25 11%	–	–	5 13%	6 12%	5 11%	9 19%	–	1 7%	2 13%	12 15%	4 8%	1 6%	–	15 19%	9 7%
No	47 20%	–	6 15%	5 13%	7 13%	14 30%	13 28%	1 25%	–	4 25%	15 19%	16 32%	2 13%	3 43%	11 14%	33 24%
No Answer	163 69%	8 100%	34 85%	30 75%	39 75%	27 59%	25 53%	3 75%	14 93%	10 63%	51 65%	30 60%	13 81%	4 57%	51 66%	94 69%

LACK OF CONFIDENCE IN ABILITY OF YACHT TO CONTINUE

Yes	12 5%	–	–	2 5%	4 8%	2 4%	3 6%	–	1 7%	–	6 8%	2 4%	–	–	9 12%	3 2%
No	68 29%	1 13%	6 15%	10 25%	18 35%	10 22%	22 47%	1 25%	6 40%	9 56%	20 26%	19 38%	5 31%	1 14%	26 34%	40 29%
No Answer	155 66%	7 88%	34 85%	28 70%	30 58%	34 74%	22 47%	3 75%	8 53%	7 44%	52 67%	29 58%	11 69%	6 86%	42 55%	93 68%
Yes	22 9%	–	1 3%	3 8%	5 10%	9 20%	4 9%	1 25%	1 7%	–	8 10%	8 16%	–	–	10 13%	11 8%
No	57 24%	1 13%	5 13%	5 13%	11 21%	13 28%	21 45%	–	3 20%	7 44%	20 26%	16 32%	4 25%	3 43%	20 26%	33 24%
No Answer	156 66%	7 88%	34 85%	32 80%	36 69%	24 52%	22 47%	3 75%	11 73%	9 56%	50 64%	26 52%	12 75%	4 57%	47 61%	92 68%

SEVERE LOSS OF BATTERY CAPACITY

Yes	2 1%	–	–	1 3%	–	–	1 2%	1 25%	–	–	–	1 2%	–	–	–	2 1%
No	81 34%	1 13%	6 15%	11 28%	20 38%	13 28%	28 60%	–	7 47%	9 56%	27 35%	20 40%	5 31%	1 14%	36 47%	43 32%
No Answer	152 65%	7 88%	34 85%	28 70%	32 62%	33 72%	18 38%	3 75%	8 53%	7 44%	51 65%	29 58%	11 69%	6 86%	41 53%	91 67%
Yes	16 7%	–	1 3%	–	7 13%	5 11%	3 6%	–	2 13%	–	3 4%	7 14%	–	–	9 12%	6 4%
No	72 31%	1 13%	6 15%	8 20%	13 25%	18 39%	24 51%	–	3 20%	7 44%	28 36%	20 40%	3 19%	3 43%	27 35%	41 30%
No Answer	148 63%	7 88%	33 83%	32 80%	33 63%	23 50%	20 43%	4 100%	10 67%	9 56%	48 62%	23 46%	12 75%	4 57%	41 53%	90 66%

	Total	Fastnet Class 0	I	II	III	IV	V	Less than 120	121–149	150–174	175–199	200–224	225–249	250 +	B2 Knock-down Yes	No
UNCERTAINTY OF NAVIGATIONAL POSITION																
Yes	5 2%	—	2 5%	3 3%	1 2%	—	1 2%	—	1 7%	—	3 4%	1 2%	—	—	3 4%	2 1%
No	79 34%	1 13%	5 13%	11 28%	20 38%	13 28%	27 57%	1 25%	6 40%	9 56%	25 32%	22 44%	5 31%	1 14%	35 45%	42 31%
No Answer	151 64%	7 88%	33 83%	28 70%	31 60%	33 72%	19 40%	3 75%	8 53%	7 44%	50 64%	27 54%	11 69%	6 86%	39 51%	92 68%
Yes	6 3%	—	—	2 5%	1 2%	2 4%	1 2%	—	1 7%	—	2 3%	—	1 6%	—	3 4%	2 1%
No	76 32%	1 13%	6 15%	8 20%	14 27%	20 43%	25 53%	1 25%	3 20%	7 44%	27 35%	23 46%	3 19%	3 43%	29 38%	43 32%
No Answer	153 66%	7 88%	34 85%	30 75%	37 71%	24 52%	21 45%	3 75%	11 73%	9 56%	49 63%	27 54%	12 75%	4 57%	45 58%	91 67%
SHORTAGE OF FOOD/WATER/FUEL																
Yes	—	—	—	—	—	—	—	—	—	—	—	—	—	—	—	—
No	84 36%	1 13%	6 15%	12 30%	22 42%	13 28%	28 60%	1 25%	7 47%	9 56%	27 35%	22 44%	4 25%	1 14%	36 47%	45 33%
No Answer	151 64%	7 88%	34 85%	28 70%	30 58%	33 72%	19 40%	3 75%	8 53%	7 44%	51 65%	28 56%	12 75%	6 86%	41 53%	91 67%
Yes	1 0%	—	—	—	—	1 2%	—	—	—	—	—	—	1 6%	—	1%	—
No	77 33%	1 13%	6 15%	9 23%	14 27%	20 43%	25 53%	1 25%	4 27%	7 44%	28 36%	23 46%	3 19%	3 43%	30 39%	43 32%
No Answer	157 67%	7 88%	34 85%	31 78%	38 73%	25 54%	22 47%	3 75%	11 73%	9 56%	50 64%	27 54%	12 75%	4 57%	46 60%	93 68%

the storm. On twenty-one boats it was not considered necessary to man the helm when riding out the storm. In general, the pendulum swung in favour of those who adopted active tactics and maintained control of speed and direction.

Retirement from the race was for a multitude of reasons but in 45 per cent of cases the primary reason was of actual damage to the boat and in 22 per cent of cases the prime reason was of the risk of worsening existing slight damage. Many of the yachts which did retire were not significantly damaged but retired because in view of the forecast of more gales they considered it the prudent thing to do. In addition many of the crews were anxious to make port as quickly as possible and allay the fears for their safety.

Twenty-four yachts were abandoned. In seventeen cases the crews abandoned to a ship or a helicopter, six to a life-raft and one to another yacht. Only five have not been recovered and one of these sank under tow. It can be deduced, therefore, that there were those that were abandoned too hastily and this premise is endorsed by the fact that seven lives were lost from life-rafts from three of the yachts which were subsequently recovered. All but two of the abandoned yachts had suffered a B2 knockdown and all had suffered severe damage to their hull, rig or steering.

Only six yachts were abandoned before help was at hand. Of these six yachts, two have not been recovered and may be considered to have been sinking at the time of abandonment. Two had suffered severe structural damage to the superstructure after knockdowns and there was excellent reason to believe that they would not have survived another knockdown. Only two yachts, therefore, were abandoned simply because the skipper believed that the life-raft would provide a safer refuge than the yacht.

Fifteen men died in the storm. Three were lost after the capsize and disintegration of their life-raft, from the yacht *Trophy*. Three were lost from *Ariadne* while attempting to climb the pilot ladder of a coaster from their capsized life-raft. One, from *Gunslinger*, was lost when the life-raft in which he was stowing emergency gear capsized and broke adrift. Two were lost from *Grimalkin* after being trapped in the cockpit of an inverted yacht. Six were washed overboard and lost from the yachts *Ariadne, Cavale, Veronier, Flashlight* and *Festina Tertia*.

The common link between all fifteen deaths was the violence of the sea, an unremitting danger faced by all who sail.

Chapter 11

SOME FURTHER THOUGHTS ON NAVIGATIONAL EQUIPMENT

'All I ask is a tall ship and a star to steer her by'

John Masefield
Sea Fever

The importance of accurate navigation in an ocean race cannot be too highly stressed. Knowing exactly where the yacht is at any one time is of paramount importance. Indeed not knowing where the yacht is puts it in danger. In storm conditions it becomes increasingly difficult to make accurate navigational predictions with the equipment that is allowed by the rules of the races of the RORC. The Club has steadfastly maintained over the years that navigation is one of the prime skills for success in its races and because of this has restricted the amount of electronic aids, preferring navigators to use the basic tools of their trade. The specific prohibitions are listed in general condition 12(n) of the Club's racing rules:

> For the guidance of owners the following are specifically prohibited: Radar; Omni; Loran; Satnav; Decca; Omega; automatic or self-seeking direction finders; pre-arranged radio transmissions for the use of individual competitors including yacht-to-yacht and yacht-to-ship transmissions. . .

The official Inquiry sought to find if the attitudes of competitors had changed towards the use of the more sophisticated navigational instruments. Sixty-four per cent said no. Of these, by far the greater percentages were from those in the three smaller classes, only twenty-seven affirmative replies being received from these classes. The 'anti' feeling from the owners of smaller yachts is generated from a fear of additional expense. In the past, these electronic aids have been expensive and for the owners of smaller yachts the proportion of their cost to the overall cost of the boat has been extremely high. The cost is beginning to diminish. Early in 1980 a satellite navigation system for yachts was introduced to the market at £1,500 and there was every indication that with the reduction in the size of the instruments, and the improvements in electronic engineering, there would be dramatic reductions in cost over the next few years.

The official Inquiry Report states in paragraph 4.23: 'The circumstances of the Fastnet storm were such that accurate navigation was unlikely to be a crucial factor.' This statement has its critics, among them Peter Bowker, probably one of the most experienced yacht racing navigators in the world and navigator of *Tenacious*, the overall winner of the 1979 Fastnet Race. Bowker refutes the statement most strongly. After reading the report he wrote:

I find paragraph 4.23 remarkable in its suggestion that accuracy of navigation was not a crucial factor. It may not have been crucial to those that retired or hove-to but it was certainly of vital importance to the larger boats which were reaching down to a lee shore – the Scillies – in the dark with bad visibility. Such vessels are now usually constructed of aluminium alloy and radio direction finders are at best unreliable. Furthermore it is necessary for the navigator to operate them from a position on deck, a dangerous and hazardous circumstance in the conditions that prevailed during the morning of 14th August.

In retrospect it may be easy for the majority of navigators to state that they were able to keep track of their position within five miles, but it is doubtful if any of us were too certain of our position at the time (how many know how much leeway their vessels make in 60 knots of wind?).

In consequence the leaders were charging blindly down on the Scillies using inadequate and unreliable navigation equipment, whilst carrying so-called sophisticated equipment which would have enabled them to pinpoint their position, but banned from doing so by a short-sighted policy of the RORC. It was particularly frustrating to this observer that in 1978 the RORC saw fit to ban Omni, presumably because before that date they did not know what it was, although I had been using Omni in British races since at least 1969.

There seems to be a marked reluctance of British navigators to speak with aviators and thereby find out what is going on in aviation navigation. I was astounded to read in a recent article in

Yachting World about the possible establishment of VHF marine beacons without any mention of a VHF system that already exists — Omni, or to give it its full title, VHF Omni-directional Range (VOR on aeronautical charts). There are enough Omni stations along the English and French coasts, for example: Land's End, Alderney, Berry Head, Hurn, Beachy Head, etc, to achieve sufficient coverage for the English Channel, although being VHF it is only line-of-sight reception. Land's End is particularly useful when approaching the Scillies as it is actually on a hill at St Just (it was probably freak reception, but in the 1977 Fastnet, I was able to receive Land's End Omni at the Fastnet Rock).

Omni receivers are small, lightweight and, being transistorised, are of negligible drain on ship's batteries. They are also relatively cheap, less than a Brookes & Gatehouse RDF and a lot less than a new sail!

Bowker continues with a criticism of the questioning that led to the high figure against changing the RORC policy towards navigational aids. As stated, sixty-four per cent said no to any change. The question was:

With hindsight, would you support a change of RORC policy to allow the use of hyperbolic fixing equipment and other sophisticated navigational aids (remember that all sophisticated equipment is a drain on yacht's batteries)?

Bowker considers the question biased:

The question would appear to be loaded in that it draws attention to battery drain. In fact, virtually all modern navigational electronics are transistorised and/or printed circuits, and battery drain is minimal and negligible compared with, say, ship's lighting or navigation lights. Even the smallest offshore racing yachts in the USA carry Loran.

The RORC should realise that in banning modern navigational aids in its racing fleet it does a disservice to the yachting fraternity as a whole. It has been the experience in the States that the demand for modern electronics has resulted in them becoming more readily available at lower prices.

The results of the questions clearly indicate that the larger yachts (Classes 0 and I) are in favour of modern aids, the smaller ones are not. In addition to cost and supposed battery drain this is consistent with the fact that the larger boats are usually of alloy construction and the smaller ones of wood or glassfibre.

Table 6.

Question: During the storm, were you able to keep an accurate position plot
    (a) To better than ± 5 miles?
    (b) To better than ± 15 miles?
    (c) Worse than ± 15 miles?

Question: Was uncertainty of position a significant factor in action taken during the storm?

Question: With hindsight, would you support a change of RORC policy to allow the use of hyperbolic fixing equipment and other sophisticated navigational aids, (remember that all sophisticated equipment is a drain on yacht's batteries)?

		Fastnet Class					
	Total	0	I	II	III	IV	V
BASE	235	8	40	40	52	46	47
WERE YOU ABLE TO KEEP POSITION PLOT TO WITHIN 5 MILES?							
Yes	103	5	22	24	25	11	16
	44%	63%	55%	60%	48%	24%	34%
No	53	1	5	6	9	18	12
	23%	13%	13%	15%	17%	39%	26%
No answer	79	2	13	10	18	17	19
	34%	25%	33%	25%	35%	37%	40%
WERE YOU ABLE TO KEEP POSITION PLOT TO WITHIN 15 MILES?							
Yes	109	3	15	14	24	24	28
	46%	38%	38%	35%	46%	52%	60%
No	13	—	1	2	2	4	3
	6%		3%	5%	4%	9%	6%
No answer	113	5	24	24	26	18	16
	48%	63%	60%	60%	50%	39%	34%
WERE YOU ABLE TO KEEP POSITION PLOT WORSE THAN 15 MILES?							
Yes	18	—	1	—	3	7	6
	8%		3%		6%	15%	3%
No	46	2	5	5	8	13	12
	20%	25%	13%	13%	15%	28%	26%
No answer	171	6	34	35	41	26	29
	73%	75%	85%	88%	79%	57%	62%
WAS UNCERTAINTY OF POSITION A FACTOR IN ACTION TAKEN?							
Yes	27	1	7	3	8	4	4
	11%	13%	18%	6%	15%	9%	9%
No	190	4	29	33	43	38	41
	81%	50%	73%	83%	83%	83%	87%
No answer	18	3	4	4	1	4	2
	8%	38%	10%	10%	2%	9%	4%
WOULD YOU SUPPORT CHANGE IN RORC POLICY TOWARDS NAVIGATION AIDS?							
Yes	67	5	19	16	12	9	6
	29%	63%	48%	40%	23%	20%	13%
No	151	1	17	22	39	30	40
	64%	13%	43%	55%	75%	65%	85%
No answer	18	2	5	2	1	7	1
	8%	25%	13%	5%	2%	15%	2%

The latter can rely on RDF bearings and can obtain them from a position below deck — the former can do neither.

Bowker has strong arguments in his favour but yachtsmen are notoriously conservative. Andrew Spedding, who was navigator of the record-breaking *Condor of Bermuda,* says that he feel that these more sophisticated aids will eventually be accepted for all races. Nevertheless he is worried that their introduction might give larger yachts an advantage over smaller ones — not because of the expense but in the logistics of having them on board, particularly in keeping them dry, not the easiest thing to do in the smaller boats. He is scathing, as a former professional navigator, of the racing man's reliance on RDF. This, he says, is only used by the professionals to pinpoint a ship in distress and should only be used in racing boats as a check. He is appalled by the low standards of keeping a dead-reckoning track by most racing navigators. The bad ones, he points out, do not have a high success rate in races.

It may be that there has to be different legislation for different sized yachts. All the maxi raters of Class 0 already have the equipment on board as do many of the Class I yachts. Preventing them from using it when it could make for safer racing does appear to have little value. There have been incidents in other countries where the use of sophisticated navigational instruments has been to advantage and others where the banning has led to accidents.

One ocean race in the United States specifically banned the use of Radar. One yacht, which had Radar fitted but which it was banned from using, hit a freighter in fog. The owner is now suing the race organisers for putting his yacht at risk unnecessarily. From another owner of a racing yacht that has Radar fitted comes the use of it as a tactical instrument. He claims that at night it is still possible to keep track of the major competition; and the knowledge that this is so would stop everyone of them from the dangerous habit that has been prevalent of switching out navigation lights to shake off an opponent.

Undoubtedly if the costs of more sophisticated instruments were to drop and their power requirements were to diminish, there would be a greater demand for their use by British ocean racing sailors.

APPENDIX 1 – STARTERS AND RESULTS FOR 1979 FASTNET RACE

Class Place	Yacht	III or IIIa Age AII. Code	Owner (sailed by)	Elapsed Time	Corrected Time
			Class O – 14 starters		
			(for yachts of 42.1 – 70 feet rating)		
1	TENACIOUS	45.8a E	R.E. Turner	79 52 22	93 44 19
2	CONDOR OF BERMUDA	69.4	R. Bell	71 25 23	97 57 24
3	KIALOA	69.5 C	J.B. Kilroy	71 53 51	98 03 40
4	MISTRESS QUICKLY	64.4a C	W. Whitehouse-Vaux	76 02 00	101 01 59
5	SISKA	66.8	R.L. Tasker	75 55 00	102 46 34
6	GITANA VI	49.4	E. de Rothschild	85 14 43	103 50 45
7	WAR BABY	49.5a Q	W.A. Brown	90 50 23	108 01 17
8	TRAVEL	43.3	R.T. Gustafson	95 41 27	111 09 16
9	G3	50.0	P. Facque & M. Loiseau	91 59 26	112 33 02
10	BOOMERANG	53.6	G.S. Coumantaros	89 49 34	112 38 31
11	WHIRLWIND V	44.3	N.A.V. Lister	96 20 24	112 50 35
12	IL MORO DI VENEZIA	59.7a	R. Gardini	91 09 40	118 43 09
13	ENDEAVOUR	51.8	J. Callow & M. Dunham	130 38 26	160 58 31
	BATTLECRY	44.0	J.O. Prentice	Retired	
			Class I – 56 starters		
			(for yachts of 33–42 feet rating)		
1	RED ROCK IV	34.4	E. Mandelbaum	92 24 11	98 35 05
2	ACADIA	38.8	B. Keenan	88 59 34	99 17 53
3	GREGAL	34.6a A	M. Peche	93 36 21	99 52 39

Class Place	Yacht	III or IIIa Age AII. Code	Owner (sailed by)	Elapsed Time	Corrected Time
4	SLEUTH	41.7a D	S. Colgate	87 53 08	99 53 27
5	VANINA	34.8	V. Mandelli	93 31 38	100 12 52
6	FORMIDABLE	34.5	P.W. Vroon	93 49 44	100 13 07
7	YENA	33.4	S. Doni	95 01 29	100 15 38
8	RAGAMUFFIN	35.2	S. Fischer	93 12 13	100 17 47
9	CARINA	34.7a H	R.S. & R.B. Nye	96 08 06	101 14 58
10	WILLIWAW	35.8	S. Sinett	93 51 32	101 38 23
11	MOONDUSTER	34.8	D.N. Doyle	95 27 24	102 16 55
12	RROSE SELAVY	33.1	R. Bonadeo	97 20 40	102 21 28
13	MATRERO	34.4a F	T. Achaval	97 14 26	102 29 30
14	VANGUARD	34.8	D.T.V. Lieu	95 55 54	102 47 27
15	TOGO VI	33.1	Dr T. Yamada	97 50 46	102 53 07
16	INDIGO	36.0	S. Eotelho	95 09 20	103 15 46
17	UIN-NA-MARA IV	35.0	Mr & Mrs H. Ross	96 27 47	103 34 55
18	APOLLO IV	36.1	J. Barry	95 34 13	103 49 05
19	ARIES	36.4	M. Swerdlow	96 02 17	104 39 10
20	MORNING CLOUD	33.2	Rt Hon Edward Heath	99 25 33	104 39 56
21	TOSCANA	36.0a B	E. Swenson	97 14 00	105 05 23
22	HADAR	34.6	Y.K. Stal (Z. Perlicki)	98 35 23	105 24 44
23	BLIZZARD	39.2	E.G. Juer	94 08 03	105 25 49
24	NORYEMA	37.6	R.W. Amey	95 43 56	105 34 59
25	HAMBURG	34.9a B	Hamburgscher Verein Seefahrt	99 20 48	106 08 31
26	CETUS	34.6	Y.K. Stal (J. Suidy)	99 27 05	106 20 00
27	INCISIF	34.8	A. Loisse	99 22 44	106 29 04
28	DOROTHEA	33.8a B	W.C. Petersen	103 18 29	109 03 44

APPENDIX 1

Class Place	Yacht	III or IIIa Age AII. Code	Owner (sailed by)	Elapsed Time	Corrected Time
29	FESTINA	33.6	N. Mooney	103 22 41	109 19 20
30	MIDNIGHT SUN	39.9	J. Pehrsson	97 01 32	103 23 12
31	ALLIANCE	39.3a C	Naval Academy Sailing Squadron	98 18 10	109 32 20
32	CARAT	35.1	V. Forss	104 14 26	112 03 31
33	NAUTICUS	34.0	Y.K. Kotwica (T. Slewiec)	105 55 47	112 31 07
34	MILENE IV	35.5	A. Mirlesse	109 09 47	117 50 29
35	PARMELIA	36.1	R.J. Williams	112 30 35	122 36 07
36	LUTINE	36.7a G	Lloyds Yacht Club	119 03 05	128 18 06
	ADVENTURE	37.4a E	Ministry of Defence (Navy)	Retired	
	ABACUS	35.9	D.K. Clark	Retired	
	BIG SHADOW	33.1	S. Bjerser	Retired	
	QUAILO	34.6	T.D. Parr	Retired	
	KUKRI	37.6a B	Ministry of Defence (Army)	Retired	
	DASHER	37.5a B	Ministry of Defence (Navy)	Retired	
	TINA	36.0	T. Friese	Retired	
	TYFOON 6	36.3	G. Versluys	Retired	
	JAN POTT	35.2	N. Lorck-Schierning	Retired	
	SCARAMOUCHE	35.4a	H. Blane Bowen	Retired	
	YEOMAN XXI	36.1	R.A. Aisher	Retired	
	SILVER APPLE OF THE MOON	33.2	B. Guttinger & G. Noldin	Retired	
	CASSE TETE V	34.6	D.H. Johnson	Retired	
	MARIONETTE VII	35.9	C.A.F. Dunning	Retired	
	GOLDEN APPLE OF THE SUN	33.1	H. Coveney	Retired	

170

Class Place	Yacht	III or IIIa Age AII. Code	Owner (sailed by)	Elapsed Time	Corrected Time
	SCHUTTEVAER	33.2	Dr J.C.W. Van Dam	Retired	
	SCALDIS	36.9a E	S.T. Nauta	Retired	
	MAGIC ELIZA	35.8	Mr Schuldt-Ahrens	Retired	
	ORYX	36.5a N	E. Adam	Retired	
	CHASTANET	34.5	N.A. Brick	Retired	

Class II — 53 starters
(for yachts of 29 feet — 32.9 feet rating)

Class Place	Yacht	III or IIIa Age AII. Code	Owner (sailed by)	Elapsed Time	Corrected Time
1	ECLIPSE	30.1	J.C. Rogers	95 42 45	97 05 27
2	JUBILE VI	31.5	H. Hamon	94 38 32	97 40 15
3	IMPETUOUS	31.5	G. Lambert & J. Crisp	94 51 25	97 53 33
4	POLICE CAR	31.9	P.R. Cantwell	94 26 46	97 56 26
5	IMP	30.9	D.W. Allen	95 36 36	97 57 09
6	SCHOLLEVAER	30.4	W. Dearns & F. Eekels	96 48 25	98 34 08
7	LA PANTERA III	32.7	C. Ostenfeld & E. de Losala	95 16 38	99 43 36
8	ASSIDUOUS	30.0	N. Beger	99 54 13	101 12 08
9	MARLOO	32.9	Dr N.S. Girdis	97 14 43	102 01 47
10	CAMPSA	32.0	J. Cusi	98 22 35	102 08 04
11	MAGISTRI	32.0 B	C. Bentley	99 12 27	102 34 50
12	KOTERU TERU II	32.0	T. Yamaguchi	99 31 25	103 19 31
13	SUR II	31.6	D.P. Ramos	100 08 42	103 28 47
14	DARLING DEE	32.9	A. Nelis	98 51 23	103 42 37
15	RUBIN	31.6	H-O Schümann	100 28 22	103 49 07
16	LOUJAINE	31.8a F	Sir Maurice Laing	101 51 32	104 13 56
17	DAGGER	31.1a B	J.L. Dolk & Th.E.W. Vinke	103 47 56	106 09 56

Class Place	Yacht	III or IIIa Age AIII. Code	Owner (sailed by)	Elapsed Time	Corrected Time
18	INISHANIER	30.1	G. Bramwell & B. Buchanan	105 02 04	106 32 49
19	PINTA	31.6a B	P. d'Andrimont	114 37 57	117 58 06
20	SARABANDE	31.1a D	J.J. Hozee	120 52 53	123 08 31
21	TORNADO	30.3	W. Singleton	121 35 23	123 38 41
22	CHARLATAN	31.9	R.W. Appelbee	125 00 48	129 38 20
23	QUICKSTEP	30.5a D	S.R. Johnson	138 19 23	139 53 10
	NICK NACK	29.1a	N. Langley-Pope	Retired	
	BELITA VII	28.4a F	J.S. Bouman	Retired	
	SUCA	31.6	W. Kuhrt	Retired	
	FARTHING	29.2	Mr & Mrs E.T. George	Retired	
	AMARANTE	29.7	L. Maisonneuve	Retired	
	FAIR JUDGEMENT	29.2a D	D.C. Dillistone	Retired	
	CAIMAN	31.3a	G. Jeelof	Retired	
	TELEMAQUE II	30.0a C	L. Delacou	Retired	
	GRUNE SEC II	31.5	J. & J. Leguelinel	Retired	
	EVERGREEN	32.5	D. Green	Retired	
	ANIMAL	31.0	F.D. Hogan	Retired	
	GEKKO VI	30.4	S. Namiki	Retired	
	PACHENA	31.5 B	J. Newton	Retired	
	STANDFAST	31.9	J. Hass	Retired	
	DOUBLE O TOO	29.8a C	R.L. Hay	Retired	
	PEPSI	31.5	A. Milton	Retired	
	LA BARBARELLA		M. Hervey	Retired	
	BLAUWE DOLFIJN II	32.0a K	C. Wargnies	Retired	
	SOPHIE B	32.1	B.H. Owen	Retired	

172

Class Place	Yacht	III or IIIa Age AII. Code	Owner (sailed by)	Elapsed Time	Corrected Time
	GOLDEN LEIGH	32.3	L. Kertesz	Retired	
	WILD GOOSE	30.7	J. Ayres	Retired	
	YACHTMAN II	30.7	R. Montagut	Retired	
	REGARDLESS	30.3	K. Rohan	Retired	
	ACCANITO	31.2	S. Poli	Retired	
	IMPROMPTU	31.5	J. Ewart	Retired	
	MAITON IV	30.1a H	K.B. Merron	Retired	
	DUGENOU I	31.6	J. Pajot	Retired	
	LANCER	31.5	G.R. Fuller	Retired	
	GOODWIN	32.1a B	J.N. Van Drongelen	Retired	
	SPICA II	29.1a C	W.L. Riviere	Retired	
	Class III — 64 starters (for yachts of 25.5 — 28.9 feet rating)				
1	REVOLUTION	28.5a E	J-L Fabry	99 21 50	97 42 53
2	BLUE BIRD	24.4a C	A. Gerard	119 11 36	110 48 52
3	CEIL III	26.8a D	W. Turnbull	121 06 30	116 33 18
4	SOLENT OYSTER	27.4	J.A.S. Bassett	119 25 08	116 50 23
5	FLYCATCHER	26.6a D	J.W. Roome	124 05 55	119 05 07
6	XARA	26.8a C	D.C. Barham	145 34 19	140 22 30
	MICKEY MOUSE	26.9	K. Robinson	Retired	
	PORDIN NANCQ	27.2a D	J. Lamouric	Retired	
	NEW BRIG	27.4	Sir Frederick & Lady Coates	Retired	
	INNOVATION	26.8	Sir Peter Johnson Bt	Retired	
	MOONSTONE	26.8	D. Chatterton	Retired	

Class Place	Yacht	III or IIIa Age AII. Code	Owner (sailed by)	Elapsed Time	Corrected Time
	ROCK ON	26.7	P. Farrar	Retired	
	AILISH III	26.0a C	B. Foulger	Retired	
	CROIX DU CYGNE	25.7a F	K. van Exter	Retired	
	DELNIC	26.8a B	L. Rousselin	Retired	
	SILVER APPLE	27.7 B	G. Cryns	Retired	
	CAVALE	27.4	P.L. Dorey	Retired	
	TAI FAT	27.6 E	Hamburger Regatta Gemeinsch (H.R.G. Crew)	Retired	
	GRIFFIN	26.4	R.O.R.C. (N. Graham)	Retired	
	GORM	27.7	S. Brandstedt	Retired	
	CHECKMATE	26.8	R.J.C. Barton	Retired	
	WINDSWEPT	26.8	I. Godfrey	Retired	
	BERNARD II	28.0a B	University of Louvain	Retired	
	VIGILANT	27.3	S.R.G. Jeffery	Retired	
	OYSTER CATCHER	27.5	R.B. Matthews	Retired	
	JOLIE BRISE	27.4	W. Jansen	Retired	
	PEAU D'BOUC	27.0a B	A. Simon	Retired	
	ZEEHAAS	25.2a H	M.J.F. Vroon	Retired	
	VERONIER II	26.8a C	C.J. Vroege	Retired	
	COMBAT II	27.0	D. Gillam & G. Bottomley	Retired	
	SUNDOWNER	27.4	B. O'Donnell	Retired	
	POLYHYMNIA	27.2	O.V. van Tijn	Retired	
	BALLYDONNA	27.2a	R.J. Hodgson	Retired	
	ASTERIE	26.6a C	R. Jeanty	Retired	
	GALLIVANT II	26.7a C	W.R. Binks	Retired	

Class Place	Yacht	III or IIIa Age AII. Code	Owner (sailed by)	Elapsed Time	Corrected Time
	AMANDLA KULU	27.1a	S. Polliack	Retired	
	ALLAMANDA	27.1	M. Campbell	Retired	
	ANDIAMO ROBIN	27.3	J. Harding	Retired	
	SAMURAI III	27.4	R.G. Jordan	Retired	
	ZAP	27.4	W. Stewart-Ross	Retired	
	LIVE WIRE	26.8a A	D.D. O'Brien	Retired	
	POPPY II	27.2a	J.M. Dean	Retired	
	JUGGERNAUT	25.7	A. Cassell	Retired	
	TAM O'SHANTER	26.9a E	J.C. Butler	Retired	
	HOODLUM		C.J. Evans	Retired	
	TIDERACE IV	27.3	D.E.P. Norton	Retired	
	CRAZY HORSE	27.4	C. Goater	Retired	
	GOOD IN TENSION	27.2a A	C.W. Billington	Retired	
	FESTINA TERTIA	26.9a	N. Mooney	Retired	
	PEPSI	26.6a C	J.J. Smith	Retired	
	CARMARGUE	26.8	A.F. Moss	Retired	
	VICTRIDE	26.9a	A. Lanoue	Retired	
	MUTINE	27.4	Cdr E.A. Morrison	Retired	
	FINNDABAR OF HOWTH	27.7a G	J.P. Jameson	Retired	
	TROPHY	27.4	A.W. Bartlett	Retired	
	AUTONOMY	27.2	E. Bourne	Retired	
	CHARIOTEER	27.0	Drs J. Coldrey & J. Lindsay	Retired	
	ASSASSIN	26.8a C	N.G. Watson	Retired	
	STEADY TENSION	26.9a	R.S. Havens & G.W. Havens	Retired	
	PASSING CLOUD	27.7	P.B. Morgan	Retired	

Class Place	Yacht	III or IIIa Age AII. Code	Owner (sailed by)	Elapsed Time	Corrected Time
	ANGUSTURA	26.3	W.W. & A.W. Oliver	Retired	
	PALAMEDES	26.5a B	A.J. Sheldon	Retired	
	FIRANJO	26.7	Gp Capt R. Wardman	Retired	
	HINDUSTAN		Lt Cdr Searle	Retired	
	Class IV — 58 starters (for yachts 23 feet – 25.4 feet rating)				
1	BLACK ARROW	23.8a A	Royal Air Force S.A.	119 37 01	110 35 10
2	SAMSARA	24.5	Madame O. Tran-Van-Dom	118 11 47	110 44 19
2	LORELEI	24.0a B	M. Catherineau		
3	MAHURI	24.0a	G.M. Lowson	131 19 56	122 03 38
4	KALISANA	24.0a H	HMS *Sultan* (Cdr Watson)	137 34 52	125 49 06
5	KARIMATA	24.6	E. Blokzyl	137 48 48	129 19 28
6	TRONADOR	24.1	R.M.H. Edwards	139 53 32	130 13 33
	DAI MOUSE III	24.6a P	D.W.T. Hague	Retired	
	CHALLENGE	24.6	F.M. Murray	Retired	
	BERTHEAUME	23.4	Brest Syndicate	Retired	
	KAMISADO	23.9a A	M.J.W. Green	Retired	
	FRAGOLA	24.5	G.I.C. des Glénans	Retired	
	GOLDEN PRINCESS	24.2a	A. Hagnere	Retired	
	SCATTERED MAGIC	24.0a B	J. Chuter	Retired	
	CHEESECAKE	23.6	D. Hopkins	Retired	
	CONTENTIOUS EAGLE	23.7	Barclays Bank Ltd (B. Roberts)	Retired	
	COSMIC DANCER	24.5	R.G. Warren	Retired	
	MINIPYGE	23.9a	M. Merfabruge	Retired	

Class Place	Yacht	III or IIIa Age AII. Code	Owner (sailed by)	Elapsed Time	Corrected Time
	BARADOZIC	24.2a A	M. Ganachaud	Retired	
	NEPHTHYS II	24.3a B	Y. Bodin	Retired	
	PRAIRIE OYSTER	24.0a	C.F.R. Purchase	Retired	
	GONIOCOQUE	24.0a	P. Barriere	Retired	
	VIRGINIE	24.4	Ecole Navale	Retired	
	DRAKKAR	24.6	R. Morelisse	Retired	
	QUIXOTE	23.8a	E. & I.J. Watts	Retired	
	SIGNALIA	23.7	Major P. Scholfield	Retired	
	ELECTRON II	24.2a D	HMS *Collingwood*	Retired	
	EN PASSANT	24.4	M. Postma	Retired	
	HULLABALOO	24.5	A.J. Otten	Retired	
	CASSIOPEE	24.1a A	R. Hubert	Retired	
	RHAPSODY	23.4a D	J.A Hughes	Retired	
	COTE DE BEAUTE	24.5	M. Amiant	Retired	
	DUMONVEH	24.5	G. Messink	Retired	
	THUNDERFLASH	23.0a B	Royal Naval Engineering College	Retired	
	COPERNICUS	23.8	A. Morton & B. Jackson	Retired	
	IMPETUS	24.7	D.J.C. Longstaffe	Retired	
	CARRONADE	24.5	Mr & Mrs P. Clements	Retired	
	ALVENA	24.0a A	Y. Dreo	Retired	
	SCENARIO	23.9	A. Fitton	Retired	
	MAELSTROM	23.7a A	M.A. Bolson	Retired	
	LIPSTICK	23.9a	C. Clarke & D. Seabrook	Retired	
	SANDETTIE I	23.9a A	J. Krygsman	Retired	
	FIORINDA	24.2a	P.B. Eyre	Retired	

177

Class Place	Yacht	III or IIIa Age AII. Code	Owner (sailed by)	Elapsed Time	Corrected Time
	DETENTE	23.1a B	C.K. Bond-Smith	Retired	
	LOCOMOTION	23.8a A	E.A. & J.A. Clegg	Retired	
	FLASHLIGHT	23.1a C	R.N. Engineering College	Retired	
	HESTRUL II	23.2a	D.A. Lewis	Retired	
	GRINGO	24.5a	A. Morgan	Retired	
	CALLIRHOE III	24.8a M	P. Bouyssou	Retired	
	ARIADNE	24.7	F.H. Ferris	Retired	
	POLAR BEAR	24.1a C	J.C. Clothier	Retired	
	PEGASUS	23.8a	P.J.A. White	Retired	
	OCEAN WAVE	24.0a G	(J. Toler)	Retired	
	CABADAH	23.7	Capt G. Greenfield	Retired	
	ODYSSEA	24.3a A	M. Guichard	Retired	
	MEZZANINE	24.4 A	K. Hancock & L. Chapman	Retired	
	ELESSAR II		W.P.J. Laros	Retired	
	CLARIONET	24.0a N	G. & N. Playfair	Retired	

Class V — 58 starters
(for yachts 21 – 22.9 feet rating)

Class Place	Yacht	III or IIIa Age AII. Code	Owner (sailed by)	Elapsed Time	Corrected Time
1	ASSENT	21.0a E	W. & A. Ker	132 12 45	116 58 55
	FLUTER	21.0a B	Ministry of Defence (Army)	Retired	
	SPREADEAGLE	20.8a A	Barclays Bank Ltd (F. Sanders)	Retired	
	MORNING ROSE	22.4 G	Bank of England	Retired	
	LA NEGRESSE BLONDE	22.0	J. Cruette	Retired	
	TIKOCCO	22.0a K	C. Caillere	Retired	

Class Place	Yacht	III or IIIa Age AII. Code	Owner (sailed by)	Elapsed Time	Corrected Time
	MOSIKA ALMA	22.0a	J. Forrester	Retired	
	PHYNNODDEREE	21.8	Dr J.K. Hinds	Retired	
	SARIE MARAIS	22.0a T	Cdr D. Gay	Retired	
	RAPPEREE	21.1	B. Kelly	Retired	
	FESTINA	21.0a A	G.P. Green	Retired	
	GREEN DRAGON	22.0	Mr & Mrs B. Saffery Cooper	Retired	
	VALROSS	21.1a C	T.H. Bevan	Retired	
	KATE	22.0	Mr & Mrs F. Ellis	Retired	
	SILVER FOAM	21.2a	J.A. Mehigan	Retired	
	BEEP BEEP	21.7	G. Cornier	Retired	
	MORNING MELODY	22.9a H	Y. Prieur	Retired	
	ESPRIT	20.7a F	B. Lesieur	Retired	
	FIRST OF APRIL	21.2a	O. Goguel	Retired	
	THUNDERER	21.3a	Royal Army Ordnance Corps SA	Retired	
	RIGHT ROYAL OF UPNOR	20.9a E	Corps of Royal Engineers	Retired	
	MARINA	20.8a C	Dr J.H. Van der Waals	Retired	
	FLAMINGO	20.5a E	B. Chapman	Retired	
	REDSKIN	20.4a D	P. Van Tongerloo	Retired	
	HURRICANTOO	20.6a D	A.B. & N. Simms	Retired	
	MORDICUS	20.4a D	C. Volters	Retired	
	GUNSLINGER	22.1	National Westminster Bank	Retired	
	TRUMPETER	20.9a E	Ministry of Defence (Army)	Retired	
	OPTION II	21.8	J. Desfeux	Retired	
	GAY GANNET V	22.9a C	General Sir Hugh Beach	Retired	
	TAMASIN II	20.9a D	R.T. Bishop	Retired	

Class Place	Yacht	III or IIIa Age AII. Code	Owner (sailed by)	Elapsed Time	Corrected Time
	CONTESSA CATHERINE	21.1a G	Royal Engineer Yacht Club (Brigadier R. Dowdall)	Retired	
	GOLDEN THISTLE	21.1a A	A.W.F. Russett	Retired	
	SISSYTOO	22.3	R.L. Hill	Retired	
	MALIGAWA III	21.6	G. Foures	Retired	
	ALPHA II	21.2a	H.S. Axton	Retired	
	MORNING GLORY	22.8a G	F.A. Davies	Retired	
	PINBALL WIZARD	22.0	P.T. Lees	Retired	
	BILLY BONES	21.0 B	Ms Boudet & Seuly	Retired	
	SKIDBLADNER III	20.5a E	H.A. Hansell	Retired	
	XAVIERA	22.0	R.A. Woodbridge	Retired	
	KORSAR	22.6a H	R.E. Mollard	Retired	
	OSSIAN	22.1	P. Ratzel	Retired	
	GAN	21.6a D	J. Hercelin	Retired	
	MAGIC	22.7	P.T. Whipp	Retired	
	GRIMALKIN	21.8	D. Sheahan	Retired	
	BONAVENTURE II	22.9a B	Ministry of Defence (Navy)	Retired	
	ARKADINA	21.0	A.J. Boutle	Retired	
	TARANTULA	21.8	P. Le Floch	Retired	
	LITTLE EILA	21.0a F	S.R. Field	Retired	
	CONGREVE	21.2a F	(Major P. Crump)	Retired	
	CORKER	22.8a D	G.T. Davies	Retired	
	EXPLORER OF HORNET	21.0a	Ministry of Defence (Navy)	Retired	
	HUMBUG	21.7	N.R. Palmer	Retired	
	ILLUSION	21.2a	K. Wason	Retired	

Class Place	Yacht	III or IIIa Age AII. Code	Owner (sailed by)	Elapsed Time	Corrected Time
	ENIA V	21.3	M. Touron	Retired	
	KARIBARIO	22.6	J. Legallet	Retired	
	SKAT	(Non-rated)	Dr N. Southwood	Retired	

181

PRIZEWINNERS

Fastnet Challenge Cup & Buckley Memorial Trophy	–	TENACIOUS
Figaro Trophy	–	ECLIPSE
Clarke Cup	–	JUBILE VI
Norlethe Cup	–	TENACIOUS
Clarion Cup	–	ECLIPSE
Quailo Cup	–	TENACIOUS
Founder's Cup	–	RED ROCK IV
Hong Kong Cup	–	SLEUTH
Bloodhound Cup	–	ECLIPSE
Philip Whitehead Cup	–	DAGGER
West Mersea Yacht Club Trophy	–	REVOLUTION
Golden Dragon Cup	–	BLUE BIRD
Foxhound Cup	–	BLACK ARROW
Iolaire Cup	–	BLACK ARROW
Favona Cup	–	ASSENT
Battler Beedle Quaich	–	ASSENT
Elizabeth McCaw Trophy	–	KIALOA
Errol Bruce Cup	–	Not Presented
Erivale Cup	–	CONDOR OF BERMUDA
Jolie Brise Cup	–	KIALOA
Inter-Regimental Cup	–	ALLIANCE
Gesture Cup	–	TENACIOUS
Iolaire Block	–	WAR BABY
Auscrew Trophy	–	TENACIOUS
Seth-Smith Trophy	–	HAMBURG
Swinburne Cup	–	MOONDUSTER
Alf Loomis Trophy	–	Peter Bowker (TENACIOUS)
Whirlwind Trophy	–	TRAVEL

APPENDIX 2 – WOLFSON UNIT REPORT – STABILITY CONDITIONS ON A CONTESSA 32 AND A 1976 HALF TONNER

(This report was compiled by the Wolfson Unit for Marine Technology and Industrial Aerodynamics at the University of Southampton and is reproduced by kind permission of the RORC/RYA.)

INTRODUCTION

The following report describes an investigation into the statical stability of a Contessa 32 and a Half Tonner designed in 1976. (The designer feels that the Half Tonner is representative of yachts of her size and type designed at that time.)

A programme of work was set out in a proposal issued by the Wolfson Unit on 18th October 1979 and was agreed by Cdr W. Anderson, co-ordinator of the Fastnet Race Inquiry, in his letter of 26th October 1979.

Hydrostatic and statical stability data were computed for the two yachts and were used in conjunction with data on the respective IOR rating certificates to assess and compare the stability of the two yachts.

THE YACHTS CONCERNED

The yachts selected for the investigation were a Half Tonner, and a Contessa 32. Both yachts took part in the 1979 Fastnet Race.

PREPARATION OF HYDROSTATIC AND STATICAL STABILITY DATA

Lines plans of the two yachts, together with drawings of their deck coachroof and cockpit arrangements were supplied by their respective designers and builders. Suitable data were lifted from these drawings adequately to define the vessels for the Department of Trade approved computer programmes used to carry out the calculations. Figures 1 and 2 illustrate the data used in each case.

Hydrostatic calculations were performed to obtain values for displacement, LCB, VCB and BM for each yacht floating at its measured waterline. A value for the righting moment at one degree of heel was supplied on the rating certificate in each case, and with this a value of GM was calculated using the equation:

$$\text{RIGHTING MOMENT} = \text{DISPLACEMENT} \times \text{GM Sin } \theta$$

A value for the centre of gravity height was then yielded by the equation:

$$\text{VCG} = \text{BM} + \text{VCB} - \text{GM}$$

A summary of the results of these calculations is presented in Table 1.

Free trimming stability (GZ) curves were then calculated for the yachts, for both intact and flooded conditions. The intact GZ curves are compared in Figure 3. GZ curves for the yachts experiencing two stages of flooding are compared in figures 4 and 5 with their intact curves.

DISCUSSION OF RESULTS

Examination of the GZ curves for the yachts in their intact state (Figure 3) reveals the following main points.

1. The initial stability of the yachts is similar, i.e. the slopes of their GZ curves at zero heel angle are similar. In fact the Contessa 32 is initially slightly more stable with a GM of 3.1ft compared to the Half Tonner's GM of 2.78ft.

2. The Contessa 32 has a greater maximum GZ value. This is largely due to the Contessa's low centre of gravity location and large coachroof. The latter is the cause of the hump in the GZ curve which appears after 70^0 heel.

3. The Contessa 32 has a greater range of positive stability. The point of vanishing stability occurs at 156^0 compared with 117^0 for the Half Tonner. When a vessel heels past its point of vanishing stability it will become stable in the inverted position. Its stability whilst up-

side down will depend upon the slope of the GZ curve at 180^0. The Contessa 32 would be less likely to remain upside down after a capsize since the slope of its GZ curve at 180^0 is low, and it need only be rolled through 24^0 in order to regain its upright stability.

4. The energy absorbed by a yacht from a sudden gust of wind is represented by the area under its GZ curve multiplied by its displacement. The Contessa 32, with a greater displacement, and a greater area under its GZ curve at any given angle, can absorb more energy than the Half Tonner. It cannot be assumed, however, that the Contessa would survive a gust capable of capsizing the Half Tonner, since the work done by the wind on the yacht is dependent on the sail plan and hull windage. As we have confined ourselves to an examination of the hulls, we can draw no conclusions on this point. The effect of flooding on the two yachts is very similar (see Figures 4 and 5) in that the angle of vanishing stability of the flooded boat is increased in both cases examined, which implies it will be less likely to remain inverted should a capsize occur.

It is likely that a capsized yacht will experience flooding, and as sinkage continues it will become increasingly easy for a wave or gust of wind to roll the boat back into a stable, upright position, since the area under the negative part of the GZ curve is decreasing.

In interpreting these data it must be remembered that the results are dependent on the following assumptions:

A. The VCG derived from the rating certificate represents an accurate assessment of the vessel's centre of gravity.

B. When flooding, the flood water uniformly permeates the underwater space by 95%.

C. The aluminium mast is free flooding.

D. The displacement calculated using data contained in the rating certificate correctly represents the sailing trim of the vessel, e.g. no crew were aboard.

CONCLUSIONS

The Half Tonner has an initial GM of 2.78ft, a maximum GZ value of 1.61ft at a heel angle of 53^0, and a heel angle of vanishing stability of 117^0. The Contessa 32 has an initial GM of 3.1ft, a maximum GZ value of 2.3ft at a heel angle of 78^0, and a heel angle of vanishing stability of 157^0. For both yachts the addition of flood water increases the range of positive stability.

NOMENCLATURE

LCB – Longitudinal position of the centre of buoyancy
VCB – Vertical position of the centre of buoyancy
VCG – Vertical position of the centre of gravity
BM   – Vertical distance of the transverse metacentre (M) above VCB
GM – Vertical distance of the transverse metacentre (M) above VCG
GZ   – Horizontal length of the righting lever

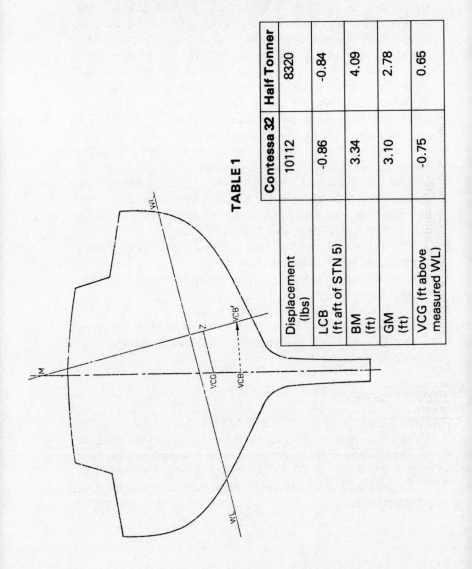

TABLE 1

	Contessa 32	Half Tonner
Displacement (lbs)	10112	8320
LCB (ft aft of STN 5)	-0.86	-0.84
BM (ft)	3.34	4.09
GM (ft)	3.10	2.78
VCG (ft above measured WL)	-0.75	0.65

FIGURE 1

Hull Data lifted for Computer Calculations
— Contessa 32 —

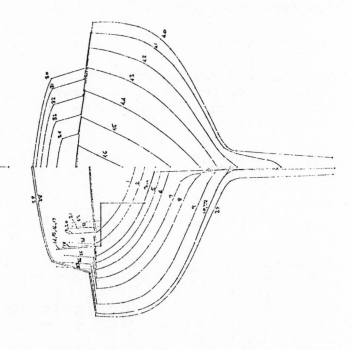

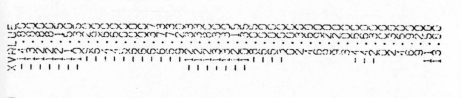

FIGURE 2

Hull Data lifted for Computer Calculations
— Half Tonner —

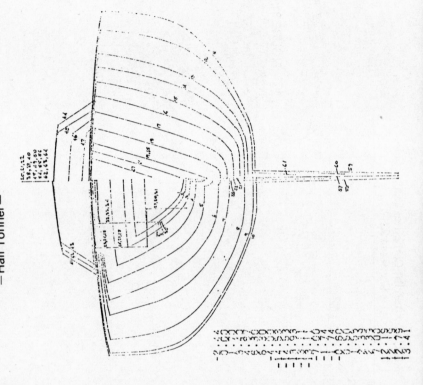

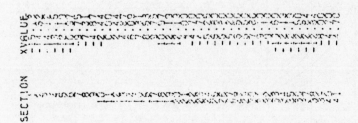

188

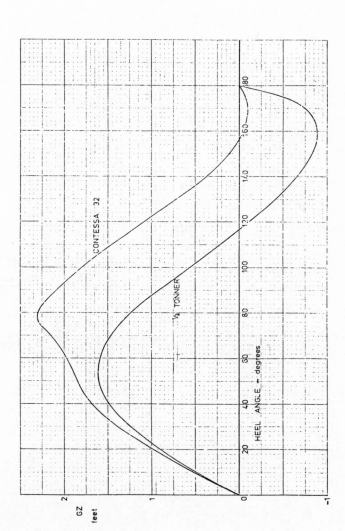

FIGURE 3

Intact GZ Curves for Contessa 32
and Half Tonner

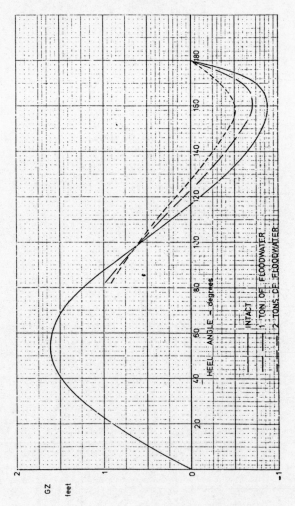

FIGURE 4

Effect of Flooding on
Stability of Half Tonner

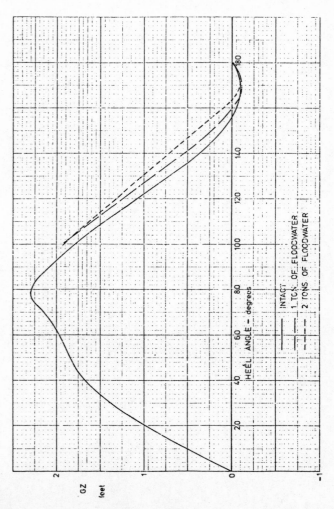

FIGURE 5

Effect of Flooding on
Stability of Contessa 32